SPANNING THE WORLD ▶▶

LEN

SPANNING THE

BERMAN

WORLD ▶▶

The Crazy Universe of Big-Time Sports, All-Star Egos, and Hall of Fame Bloopers

wm

WILLIAM MORROW
An Imprint of HarperCollins *Publishers*

HarperCollins books may be purchased for educational, business, or sales promotional use. For information please write: Special Markets Department, HarperCollins Publishers, 10 East 53rd Street, New York, NY 10022.

FIRST EDITION

Designed by Jeffrey Pennington

Printed on acid-free paper

Library of Congress Cataloging-in-Publication Data

Berman, Len.
    Spanning the world: the crazy universe of big-time sports, all-star egos, and hall of fame bloopers / Len Berman.
        p. cm.
    ISBN 0-06-075752-3 (alk. paper)
    1. Sports—Miscellanea. 2. Athletes—Miscellanea. I. Title.

GV707.B47 2005
796—dc22
                                                                    2004065633

05 06 07 08 09 WBC/RRD 10 9 8 7 6 5 4 3 2 1

To the incomparable Jillie B.

CONTENTS

CONTENTS

WHO IS THIS GUY?

If you're a New Yorker, or if you've spent a good bit of time in New York, you probably know me from my nineteen years as the lead sportscaster on Channel 4, the local NBC affiliate. You may also know me from some of my national sports broadcasts, including the Olympics, college basketball games, and heavyweight prizefights. Or you may know me from the hundreds of pre- and postgame shows I've done for the Super Bowl, the World Series, and other major sporting events over the years. But if you're like most of the viewers who recognize me, it's because of "Spanning the World," my sports bloopers program that has aired in New York since 1987 and has garnered me invitations to appear on the late-night shows of David Letterman and Conan O'Brien as well as a monthly spot on NBC's morning program, the *Today* show.

People come up to me all the time and ask, "Hey, aren't you the guy who does the goofy highlights?" Some résumé, huh?

LEN BERMAN
New York, NY

JOB DESCRIPTION: Guy who does the goofy highlights.

References available upon request.

I don't mind the recognition, but I wonder if airing footage of an outfielder running smack through the center-field fence is really going to be my legacy. I mean, I actually have done a couple of other things in my forty years of broadcasting. In addition to working Super Bowls, the World Series, and the Olympics for NBC, I've called TV play-by-play for the Boston Celtics, the Big East Conference, HBO Sports, and for three heavyweight championship fights, including the 1991 bout between George Foreman and Evander Holyfield. I also created *Sports Fantasy,* a television program that gave viewers the chance to compete against Michael Jordan, Arnold Palmer, Chris Evert, Wayne Gretzky, and other all-time greats. And I've done a ton of newscasts and broadcasts from most of the major sporting events. All this has given me entrée to just about anybody who's anybody in the world of sports—including Willie Mays Aikens.

You may not remember Aikens, but in the early 1980s he

was one of baseball's most feared sluggers. A cocaine addiction was his downfall. He was out of baseball in 1985 (although he continued to play down in Mexico, hitting .454 with 46 home runs and 154 RBIs one season). I interviewed him in 1983 for the NBC baseball *Game of the Week* at a prison in Texas. He had the distinction of being the first active major-league baseball player to be sent to jail. He was sent to the slammer for ninety days after pleading guilty to attempting to buy cocaine. (In 1994, he was sentenced to over twenty years for selling drugs to an undercover officer.) It was quite a comedown for the first player to have two multihomer games in a single World Series, a feat he accomplished with Kansas City in 1980. Aikens agreed to speak to me from prison and to discuss his personal demons. He admitted to me that he once played a major-league game while high on coke. It wasn't the kind of interview that would be recycled in one of those "Baseball Fever" or "I Love This Game" commercials. So what's the point of this digression? Well, *USA Today* used to ask athletes to list their five favorites in various categories: their five favorite movies or fast-food items, for instance. In 1984, the paper asked Willie Mays Aikens to name his five favorite sportscasters. I came in fifth. So perhaps that will be my epitaph. "Len Berman: Willie Mays Aikens's fifth-favorite sportscaster."

A s a nightly sportscaster, at times I think I'm doing sports for the sports impaired. News executives say that the overall percentage of viewers who are sports fans is small. And let's face it: more and more of those fans are getting their scores and highlights from the Internet and ESPN or some other cable sports channel. Luckily my wife, Jill, is here to remind me who's out there watching. She has told me—her loving husband who has made a life out of sports—that football is dumb. Why? Because "all they do is jump on each other and then measure." It's a good line actually, and pretty accurate, too.

The weather forecasters have it made. Everyone wants to hear what *they* have to say, and no one ever blames them when they're wrong. And these guys are often wrong. The long-range forecast? All the Doppler technology in the world, and you still may be better off playing with your Ouija board. I once had a six A.M. tee time. The eleven o'clock news had started after midnight due to a late NBA game. The weatherman had said it would be sunny in the morning and instead it was raining. The five-day forecast? He couldn't even get the five-hour forecast right!

The television execs also tell me that when 11:25 comes along, those who forget to change the channel after the weather are probably just biding their time until Jay Leno comes on. Before everyone had a remote control, the local NBC stations had a huge late-news advantage. People didn't want to have to get out of bed to change the channel, so if they wanted to watch Johnny Carson, they set their TV to NBC earlier in the evening.

This affects the way I handle my sportscast. My goal is to report sports for those who care about the games, and to make sports understandable and enjoyable for those who are just waiting for Leno. I'm not sure that either category of viewer realizes that I might say, "Jason Giambi was placed on the disabled list," rather than "Jason Giambi was placed on the DL." I don't like to use sports shorthand because I realize that plenty of viewers out there don't know a DL from a DH (designated hitter—the position Giambi is best suited for). It's a delicate balancing act. That's also why you see water-skiing squirrels and boxing monkeys on the sports news—although I try to confine such highbrow fare to the monthly edition of "Spanning the World."

◆　　◆　　◆

It wasn't too many years ago that some news directors were predicting the death of sports on local newscasts. Now, you have to understand that many news directors hate sports to begin with. Maybe hate is too strong a word, but they either don't really care for it, or they don't know much about it. Or both. I once had a producer on the six P.M. news in New York who would often say to me, "Great sportscast." Were my highlights terrific? Was my commentary insightful? No. It's just that I had wrapped up my segment right on time. To her, that made a perfect sportscast.

The typical news director will say to his or her sportscaster something like, "Millions of people jog. How come you don't do jogging stories?" It doesn't dawn on these news titans that there is no such thing as the National Jogging League and that a viewer might enjoy jogging but have absolutely no interest in watching others do it. I once had a news director suggest that I do a special report during a ratings sweep period. He had noticed—clever guy that he was—that most hockey players were white and that most basketball players were black. "There has to be a story here," he said. He wanted to call the special report: WHITE HOCKEY, BLACK BASKETBALL. I wanted to call it: NUT-JOB NEWS DIRECTOR. (Perhaps I may have saved his job by passing on his story idea.) Years later, when Scott Gomez entered the National Hockey League, I can only imagine what that news director might have dreamed up. Gomez, a center for the New Jersey Devils, is Mexican American and grew up in Alaska. His story might have made for a five-part series!

Anyway, some of these same news directors thought that ESPN would render local sportscasts obsolete, particularly on the West Coast where by eleven P.M. many results are hours old. The news directors missed a couple of important points. First, fans watching a local sportscast in Los Angeles want Lakers and Dodgers highlights. Even viewers who aren't sports fans want to know what's going on with their local teams. When their coworkers are huddled around the watercooler talking about Eric Gagne's record-breaking consecutive save, they at least want to know what the hell a Gagne is. Also, ESPN's *SportsCenter* runs for hours at a time. A local sportscast is on at a specific time. The Dodgers fan knows that around 11:22 P.M. he will get his Dodgers fix. He doesn't have to sit through highlights from the Tigers–Devil Rays game (if there are any) while waiting for the news from Dodgerland. On top of all that, viewers are familiar with their local sportscasters and, if the sportscasters are any good, they want to hear their take on the local issues.

It's not the same when the analysis comes from some ESPN comedian wannabe in Bristol, Connecticut. Actually, ESPN has changed my way of sportscasting in at least one way—for the better, I think. I like to be funny at times, and I used to think that if I didn't have some hilarious highlight in every sportscast, then it wasn't a good show. Too much ESPN has made me rethink that. Today, if I just do a solid job of reporting what's going on in the sports world and don't let shtick get in the way of facts, I'm pleased with the show. Imagine that: sports news in a sportscast!

So despite the dire forecasts of the television execs and news directors, I know there are men and women out there watching who are just like me—fanatics who connect life's dots the way I do. Mention a year, and I think of who won the World Series: 1957, Milwaukee Braves; 1972, Oakland A's. It works the other way, too. Princess Diana's death? Jets at Seahawks . . . opening day . . . August 31, 1997. Elvis's death? World Team Tennis match . . . Boston University . . . Boston Lobsters . . . a chubby, young Martina Navratilova . . . August 16, 1977. I remember once reading a newspaper headline that stated that a right-winger had taken over Bolivia. And I thought, *Gordie Howe?*

But there are also viewers like Jill. In 2001, I tortured her by taking her to the Super Bowl. This was the game where the Giants were trounced by the Baltimore Ravens. The final score was 34–7. At one point, she looked at me and plaintively asked, "Did the Ravens score again?" Well, the fans in Tampa were going nuts and big galoots in white jerseys were dancing in the end zone. So, uh, yeah. In 2004, when the Yankees signed Alex Rodriguez, the highest-paid (and, many thought at the time, best) player in baseball, she asked me why everyone was making such "a big fuss over this A-Rap guy." The truth is that I'm thankful she's not a sports fan. Not only does she keep me grounded, but after being immersed in sports all day long, the last thing I want to hear when I come home for dinner is "Honey, when are the Rangers going to fix that lousy power play?"

A s with my sportscasts, I have written this book with both audiences in mind: the fanatics and the Jills of the world. So interspersed throughout these pages among many of my favorite "goofy highlights," you'll find my impressions of some of the sports figures whom I've come in contact with—from my hero Mickey Mantle, to O. J. Simpson, Evel Knievel, and Pete Rose—some stories from the press box and TV studio, and some of my thoughts about big-time sports. I've mixed in some analysis, some complaints, and hopefully a couple of laughs.

I guess I could say something pseudointellectual to tie it all together, something like: "The sports world is just one big blooper." But that would be an oversimplification. At the same time, though, I don't view sports as life and death. It's not the "real world," but it is one heck of a great diversion from it. And without a lot of the people I've come in contact with over the years, that sports world would be a much duller place.

By the way, every so often I get letters from viewers admonishing me for having the earth spin backward at the end of my "Spanning the World" segments. Somehow, I get the feeling they've missed the point!

2

IN THE BEGINNING

JUNE 2000, EDISON FIELD, ANAHEIM. Giants first-base coach Robby Thompson tossed a ball to a young boy in the first row. The ball missed the kid's glove and hit him in the face. The kid was in tears. So Thompson signed a "note of apology" on another baseball. This time he tossed it to the boy's dad.

When I was about nine or ten years old, I would play a baseball board game where you spun an arrow to determine what the player did. It was sort of an ancient sports version of "Wheel of Fortune." Each ballplayer had his own card to fit over the spinner. If the arrow landed on "1," it was a home run. If it landed on "10," it was a strikeout. Babe Ruth had the largest number 1 range. Mickey Mantle's 1 was also big, but then so was his 10. My friends and I would play this game for hours. It was nothing like today's noisy, glitzy video games. In fact, there was no video, no crowd noise, no announcers. All we had was an arrow and our imaginations.

One day I was playing the game by myself, and while I was spinning I announced the game out loud: "Here's the pitch. Mickey swings . . . and it's a long drive to center field. It's going, going, gone." (I don't think he ever struck out when I was doing my imaginary announcing.) "You'll never be a sportscaster," called out my older brother, Arnie, from the next room. "Your voice is too high!" Me, a sportscaster? I had never even thought about it. And, truthfully, for years to come I didn't think it was possible. I thought to be on the air you had to be the son of the tycoon who owned the radio or TV station or a former jock. After all, the guys reading the sports on the TV newscasts in New York when I was a kid were former football Giants: Frank Gifford, Kyle Rote, Pat Summerall. My dad was far from a tycoon. He published a mom-and-pop magazine for songwriters. He would write most of the articles himself, fold the magazines into paper wrappers, and take them to the post office for mailing around the world. As for being an athlete, I had a fine jump shot (but I couldn't play defense worth a lick) and I was decent at stickball. I knew I'd never be a former jock. I was hardly a present one.

The first time I ever thought about using my voice professionally was in high school. I went to Stuyvesant High in New York City. It's a public school, but supposedly one for only bright kids. An English teacher of mine named Sterling Jensen was rather theatrical. He would tell colorful stories to make his point, even if the stories had nothing to do with the subject matter at hand. He told me, "You should work on getting that deep voice of yours up out of your stomach and into your mouth." PROJECT! he said. He thought I should be an ACTOR! An actor? I had once acted in the fourth-grade play. That was about it, and it was such a memorable experience that I can't even tell you what the play was or what role I had. Mr. Jensen was alone in his assessment. I had taken a battery of aptitude tests in high school and the testing service determined that I had an introverted personality and a knack for math and science.

So I applied to Syracuse, Cornell, and Penn to be an engineer. Syracuse accepted me. The first day on campus, in September 1964—even before I registered for my first engineering class—I went to the college radio station, WAER. I have no idea why. It wasn't even open yet. But I returned a few days later and announced that I wanted to try out to be a disc jockey. I was told to "join the club." Everyone wants to do that. How about reading the sports, though? The station had an opening for somebody to read scores on Saturday nights. I was flabbergasted. I was a big Yankees fan as a kid and kind of followed all the other sports, but I really didn't think I could make it on the air as a sports guy.

I certainly didn't go to Syracuse to become a sportscaster as so many others, before and after me, have. Beginning with the great Marty Glickman, the Syracuse roster of sportscasters is pretty impressive. Marv Albert, Bob Costas, Dick Stockton, Sean McDonough, Andy Musser, Hank Greenwald, Ian Eagle, Mike Tirico, and many others call Syracuse their alma mater. I remember being on a panel at an alumni function several years ago. Someone in the audience asked me, "Why is it that so many famous sportscasters went to Syracuse?" I rubbed my chin in a professorial way and responded, "Because none of us could get into Cornell." There was some truth to that. The schoolwork at Syracuse wasn't exactly rocket science, so we had plenty of time to goof off at the radio station. And also, so as not to offend my good friends at the prestigious Newhouse School of Communications, I'll throw in the fact that they've got a great program up there. But the truth is, you don't learn sportscasting in the classroom. You learn by doing it—by spinning the arrow and announcing a board game or by turning down the sound on the TV and pretending to call the action. That's how you become a sportscaster. You don't read it in a book.

I learned it in part by reading the scores on Saturday nights in the WAER studio. Every Saturday in the fall, about a trillion college football scores would come across the wires. I had to choose which ones to read. One time, I just reported every tenth score; it made no difference to me whether the game had any relevance to listeners in upstate New York. Nonetheless, at the conclusion of my freshman year, I was picked by the senior staff to be WAER's sports director. I kept the job for three years. As sports director I wasn't paid, but I did get to assign myself all the good stuff. At Syracuse, that meant I announced basketball.

Dave Bing was the star, and Jim Boeheim, who would later coach the Orangemen, was also on the team. Boeheim was quite a player—he didn't look smooth, but he sure hustled and got the job done. When Syracuse made the NCAA tournament in 1966, the Orangemen had to play the Duke Blue Devils. As good as Bing was, it was Boeheim who starred that night. Duke still won the game by ten points, but if it weren't for Boeheim, the game would have been a rout.

When I'd broadcast a road game, I was a one-man traveling band. I'd take a bus or sometimes fly in a small plane. The announcer for a commercial radio station in Syracuse, which also broadcast the road games, was a pilot. So he'd get one of those twin-engine planes and invite me along. I was nuts for accepting his invitation. One winter night we flew back from the University of Massachusetts. It was freezing and the plane started to drop. Thankfully he righted it in time, but it scared the hell out of me. Anyway, when I would arrive at a road game, I'd plug my equipment into a telephone line, and that was it. Broadcasting a game on radio was like making a two-hour phone call, except the phone company supposedly gave you a higher quality line.

One time I went to announce a Syracuse–St. John's game at Alumni Hall in Queens. My uncle Joe came along and sat next to me. The entire game, he was asking me, "How do you know the game is actually going on the air?" I give him an exasperated look and said, "If there was a problem, they would have called." The next day, I took a flight back to Syracuse. At the radio station, I was asked if everything went well at the game before the "transmitter blew" in Syracuse. When exactly did the transmitter blow? Right before the opening tip-off. I had announced the entire game to myself! Actually it was one of my better calls. Did anyone hear any mistakes? Don't answer that, Uncle Joe.

There was another game, at the University of Pittsburgh, where I arrived late for the tip-off. I had miscalculated how long the drive from Syracuse would take. A quick-thinking technician back at WAER piped in the Pittsburgh college station's broadcast, so when I got there I just joined my counterpart on the broadcast, which was now being heard in two cities. The Pittsburgh announcer was a little over the top, but I joined right in. I called one of the Syracuse players, a center by the name of Val Reid, "uncoordinated." That's a description we used all the time on the playground. I thought nothing of it. Six-foot ten-inch Valentine Reid thought differently. One of his friends told him about my comment, and when I got back to Syracuse, Reid was waiting at the station to have a little chat with me. Sitting in my little sports director's office, Reid looked anything but uncoordinated. Actually, he looked like he was going to methodically re-coordinate me and my office! I don't know exactly what I said—probably some "taken out of context" mumbo jumbo—but I somehow calmed him down. He seemed satisfied and left—in a very coordinated way, I might add. I had learned a valuable lesson from that encounter. People out there are actually listening!

For me, the highlight of announcing Syracuse games was the 1967 National Invitational Tournament (NIT). In 1967, the NIT was still a big deal. Not every team made the NCAA tournament, and playing in New York City was something special. Tournament games were played at the old Madison Square Garden—the very place where, as a kid, I saw countless Knicks and Rangers games, not to mention college basketball and Harlem Globetrotters games. What a thrill! I was just nineteen years old, and I entered through the press gate, where I had never walked before. Standing off to the side was Muhammad Ali! Just standing there, no entourage or anything. That's the way it was at the old Garden.

Syracuse played New Mexico in a first-round game. I was so nervous about calling the game that I memorized the starting five of the New Mexico Lobos and kept saying it over and over in my head. "Hoover, Nelson, Morgan, Monroe, and Daniels." Daniels was Mel Daniels, who went on to star in the ABA. I engrained that starting five in my head so deeply that to this day, nearly forty years later, it's still there. New Mexico won the game by one point, and there was a controversial foul call at the end that went against Syracuse. The details are a little fuzzy. What is clear is the Lobos' starting five. I wish I could remember what I did yesterday as well as I can recall "Hoover, Nelson, Morgan, Monroe, and Daniels."

At the end of my sophomore year at Syracuse, all the kids who worked at the college station got together for a year-end party. Big time: Coca-Cola and chips. For a goof, my roommate, Dug Gillis, and I decided to fill the sportscast with the most ridiculous clichés we could think of. I remember we were reading minor-league baseball scores. As I recall, the Toronto Maple Leafs had lost to the Syracuse Chiefs so we said something like "Syracuse shook the Leafs 6–4." The Louisville Colonels got "outsaluted 4–2." I know this sounds pretty tame today—in the ESPN era where the sportscasters make up all kinds of off-the-wall phrases—but back in 1965, my roommate and I couldn't stop laughing. When we finished our little spoofcast, the program director called us over and said he thought it was the best show we had ever done! That guy probably went on to become some high-ranking ESPN executive.

During my sophomore year, I also developed the idea of hosting the "First Annual College Sportscasting Conference." I invited kids from East Coast colleges to attend. Marty Glickman and Marv Albert, then a young New York sportscaster, both agreed to speak, for only the price of a plane ticket. Glickman gave the keynote address. It was the winter of 1966, and yet I still remember his speech. He said, "When you're announcing, speak English, not jock talk." He said that you never hear a football player tell a teammate, "Here I am toting my pigskin." The football player is carrying the ball. Keep it simple! And Glickman said, "Do your homework." It sounded kind of odd. After all, sports is supposed to be fun. But he said you have to prepare thoroughly for your broadcasts. Learn the players, learn their hometowns. And learn how to pronounce their names properly. He told of how he once went to announce a game at North Carolina State. When he was given the roster, he asked how to pronounce a certain name. The first name was Bernie and the last name was Yurin. It was pronounced just as you would guess, and just as he feared: urine. Glickman said his radio technician was rolling in the aisles during the broadcast as Glickman uttered such broadcast pearls as, "Yurin is dribbling down the court," "Yurin shoots," and "Yurin is really hot tonight!"

On Saturdays during my senior year, I would do the hourly newscasts on the AM rock station in Syracuse. The big news was generally about fires and car accidents. In 1968, though, after Martin Luther King was assassinated, the news was much more than that. There were riots going on around the country. To me, that was real news. So I canned the local car accident stories and read wire copy about the riots that were taking place. The program director called me on the phone and told me to "cut it out." I'll never forget what he said next: "Do some stories about Haile Selassie of Ethiopia. Anything. You don't want to make the natives restless." His exact words. I thought that was abject censorship of the news, not to mention racism. I was rattled, but I certainly didn't want to be the cause of riots in the city of Syracuse. I did what I was told; no martyr was I. And I certainly didn't want to jeopardize my $2.75 an hour, or whatever the station was paying me to be a big-time radio newscaster.

Incidentally, also during my senior year, I would work one hour a night—from 10:30 to 11:30—for the local ABC television station. I ran the audio board for the late news. The station didn't have a full-time audio man, if you can believe it. My job was to turn the anchorman's microphone on and off. Tough job. In those days, TV stations weren't on all night. After the news, this station would run a late movie, play the national anthem, and sign off. That meant the technician on duty could go home when the movie ended. One night, I stayed late after my "exhausting" audio shift—on, off, on, off—and I peeked into the control room. A movie projector in the control room played the film, just like in the movie theater, so during the commercials the projector would stop. The technician would unthread the movie and tug on the film so that it would go directly from the top reel to the bottom. Then, before the commercial was over, he would rethread the movie and start showing it again. During every commercial break, he would spool off several minutes of the film. In so doing, he would substantially advance his quittin' time. No one ever called the station. There were stories at this station of famous movies being played with the reels out of order. And still nobody called. That's television.

AND NOBODY GOT HURT

MARCH 2002, HI CORBETT FIELD, TUCSON, ARIZONA. In a spring training game, Colorado's Mark Little was beaned by a pitch. He went down for a moment. When he got up, he ran to third. Give that man a road map!

A kid from my dormitory at Syracuse once asked me, "Do you actually listen to what you're saying?" "What do you mean?" I asked. He explained, "You make no sense!" That did wonders for my confidence. But undaunted, during the spring of my senior year, I sent out 150 letters and résumés to the three network television stations in the top fifty markets. One hundred forty-seven stations ignored me. An NBC affiliate in New Orleans asked for a tape. I sent it in and never heard from them again. WCBS-TV in New York City actually called me in for an interview—that was big time—but then they told me I should go get a job in Minneapolis or somewhere and get back to them. Minneapolis turned out to be Dayton, Ohio, and, as it turned out, I got back to WCBS nine years later. I had struck out looking for a sports job, so I took a job at WLWD-TV in Dayton as a newsman.

I had interned at WLWD during the summer following my senior year at Syracuse, and the station offered me a full-time job after I completed a master's program in communications at

Syracuse in the winter of 1970. (In the midst of going for my master's, I served four months in the Army Reserves.) I was hired as a news anchor and reporter for the hefty salary of $170 per week. I was thrilled! I was getting married to Jill, and this was a great opportunity. We married about six months after I started in Dayton. The station's program director told me that when I returned from my honeymoon we'd discuss a contract. Wow. They wanted to lock me in, and I'd be rich. I had delusions of grandeur. I fancied myself breaking the $10,000-a-year barrier. Maybe I'd hit $10.5K! A couple of weeks after returning from Bermuda, I asked the program director if he was ready to talk contract. He said, "No," that it was just something he had told me so that I wouldn't go looking for a new job during my honeymoon. As if I was planning to go door to door on the island looking for "on-air" work. *Welcome to broadcasting,* I thought.

I stayed in Dayton for three and a half years. At one point, the station named me coanchor of the eleven o'clock news. I was teamed with a smooth, veteran newsman named Dick Bay, and the station promoted the newscast on billboards throughout the city as the *Bay-Berman Report.* At the time, the afternoon talk show at the station was *The Phil Donahue Show.* It was then just a local show that a couple of other affiliates in Ohio had started to pick up. Phil used to walk through our newsroom to look at the pictures that came over the wires, so one day I told him that I had a terrific idea for one of his shows. Me: the youngest eleven P.M. anchorman within miles! Phil said that would be "great," terrific even, for the first three minutes of his show. But "what would I do for the other fifty-seven?" I just skulked away, never getting even my three minutes on *Donahue.*

At one point during our run, Dick Bay asked me if I wanted to fill out a ratings book. Turns out one of the ratings services, either Nielsen or Arbitron, had sent him a diary to fill out to help determine the broadcast ratings. Dick had explained to the rating company that he worked at a TV station, but they didn't care. They just wanted as many diaries completed as possible. Dick had gotten tired of filling his out, so I did it one week. I marked down that my household watched WLWD-TV News every night at six and eleven. In the comments area I wrote, "That Len Berman guy is really great." Didn't help; the newscasts' ratings were worse than ever. The *Bay-Berman Report* lasted just thirteen weeks.

I never loved working in news. In those days, almost nothing was "live." Moonwalks and political conventions were carried live, but that was about it. I found sports to be a lot more exciting. So, during my years in Dayton, I kept applying for sports jobs in other cities. Somehow I became a finalist for a sports job at WBZ-TV in Boston, an NBC affiliate. Boston! Big city. Big-time sports. And I read in the *Boston Globe* that the salary was $37,500. At the time, my wife and I thought that was all the money in the world. Turns out, it wasn't—and that's why the job was still open. Frank Deford, the great *Sports Illustrated* writer, among others, had rejected the job because it didn't pay enough. So it all came down to a second audition between me and a kid from Peoria. The kid from Peoria won. But . . . his wife was pregnant, they didn't want to leave Peoria, et cetera, et cetera. And that's how I got the job. Timing, dumb luck, and, I hope, a bit of skill. Of course, the job didn't pay the advertised $37,500. The station started me on the weekends for a few months and paid me around $22,000. I was still ecstatic.

When I was just starting out in Boston, the Sunday *Globe*

greeted me one October morning with the headline: CHANNEL 4'S BERMAN OFF TO A SLOW START. Really? It was news to me. I thought I was doing okay. My bosses seemed satisfied. I wasn't getting too much hate mail written in crayon. I thought my job was to please my audience and the people who hired me. Now there was something new in the equation. TV sports critics. (More on them later!) The article was written by Jack Craig, the longtime TV sports critic of the *Globe*. It wasn't a cheap-shot article. In fact, Craig treaded in very controversial waters. He made the point that I was an outsider. True. I was a New Yorker who had worked in Ohio. I wasn't a native New Englander who had lived and died—make that died and died—with the fortunes of the Red Sox. (When I first joined the station, Craig asked me if I knew Red Sox history from the 1940s and 1950s. I lied and said, "Sure." What was the point, really? If Rico Petrocelli hits a homer for the 1973 Sox, does it really matter what happened in 1942? To Boston fans, apparently so. I played along.) But Craig brought up another interesting point in his column. He said because so much of the Boston audience is Catholic, it is possible that the viewers are unwilling to accept a Jewish sportscaster. I thought that was a great issue to raise. But it upset a lot of individuals and more than a few Jewish groups. I think it's a legitimate question, though. Craig made the point that you can't look inside the viewers' hearts to determine the answer.

In truth, it took me nearly three years on the air to be accepted by the Boston audience. I probably owe my biggest thanks to the 1975 Red Sox. That year, the team made it to the World Series. All of their games were broadcast on my TV station. Fans like winners and, by extension, the people who broadcast winners.

It was during my years in Boston that live shots came to pass. I have the distinction of doing the very first "live shot" with a Minicam in the history of WBZ-TV. It was June 7, 1976, and the Celtics had just won the NBA title. The team was returning from Phoenix, and there I was for WBZ's virgin live shot at Logan Airport. One minor problem. There was a union dispute going on at the station and the TV technicians were out on strike. They were not a happy bunch, and one of the union guys tipped over the mast on the TV truck. That's the tall antenna that relays the video to the television station. Good-bye live shot! Fortunately (or not), live shots were here to stay. After that, if the mayor blew his nose: live shot! And to this day when somebody is on remote, his or her station puts the word *LIVE* on the screen the entire time. It's as if they fear that were they to drop the LIVE for a split second, some guy at home would say to his wife: "My goodness, Mabel, Berman *was* live, but now it doesn't say it. So he must be dead!"

After five years in Boston, I was "dead." The station fired me—well, actually, they didn't pick up my option. One guy who wasn't unhappy to see me go was the great Bobby Orr. Orr is unquestionably one of the greatest hockey players ever, and he is New England royalty. Take a look at that classic still photograph of Orr scoring the winning goal during overtime against St. Louis in the 1970 Stanley Cup Finals. He is flying through the air as he shoots the puck. The camera catches him in midair, parallel to the ice. It is a moment frozen in time for all of New England to cherish. Fans talk of another great Bobby Orr moment that wasn't caught on film. In a hockey game against the California Golden Seals, Orr lost his glove at center ice and later started a rush from behind his own goal line. He headed up the ice eluding Golden Seal after Golden Seal. As he approached center ice, he reached down and scooped up his glove while skating in full stride. And he kept going: a length of the ice rush to take a shot on goal! The fairy-tale ending has Orr scoring. He didn't, but the story nonetheless captures the beauty of Orr. He was a defenseman who controlled the game offensively.

I admired him, but it wasn't mutual. Here's what happened. In 1973, the Mets played the Reds in the National League play-offs. During Game Three, things got ugly at Shea Stadium. Pete Rose slid hard into second base, taking out shortstop Buddy Harrelson's legs. Harrelson and Rose tangled, and then all hell broke loose. When Rose headed out to left field in the bottom of the inning, a fan threw a whiskey bottle at him from the upper deck at Shea. I went on the air in Boston and criticized "those New York fans." A New Yorker was upset by my commentary and wrote me a nasty note saying I was wrong to blame the fans. Blame the players, he said. Monkey see, monkey do. I filed that thought away. Now fast-forward to a Bruins game at Boston Garden the following January. Bobby Orr was playing on fragile knees and got nailed with what all of Boston thought was an illegal check. No penalty was called. Orr, generally a mild-mannered player, went nuts. As he skated off the ice, he whacked his stick into the boards breaking it in pieces. Then, a fan from the upper deck of Boston Garden chucked a folding chair onto the ice. On the eleven o'clock news that night, I declared that "if Bobby Orr doesn't smash his stick, he doesn't incite the crowd" and that Orr should be given some blame for the mayhem that ensued. Talk about blasphemy. Orr was incensed.

I requested an interview with Orr the next day and he told the Bruins PR man to "Tell Berman to go fuck himself." Wow. He wasn't the only one. Bep Guidolin, the Bruins coach, wouldn't talk to me. Eventually, Guidolin said something like, "How could you say such a thing? Bobby Orr is Jesus Christ." He really said that. Right on camera. Now I haven't spent all that much time curled up with the New Testament, but I'm fairly certain when the big guy walked on water way back when, he wasn't wearing skates. But that's how they felt about Orr in Boston—and they didn't need some know-it-all sportscaster criticizing him. Over the years, Bobby and I have smoothed things over. We've joked about the incident, and he has even invited me to his home in the Boston area. He's as classy an athlete as they come. In retrospect, there might even have been a modicum of truth to my assertion. But I'm blaming the whole episode on that New York sports fan. If he'd have kept his opinion to himself, I wouldn't have been able to steal it.

I don't think the Orr incident had much to do with it, but in any case in June 1978 I was off the air in Boston. Talk about a wake-up call! Here's how I found out. First, I became suspicious when they stopped airing my promo. As most stations do, WBZ had these cute little ads promoting its news talent. A friend at the station told me they took mine out of the rotation. That was a tip-off, only a bit more subtle than returning from vacation and finding someone else sitting at your desk. A few weeks later, one of my wife's friends called from Miami. She had read in the paper that a sportscaster down there had accepted a job at WBZ in Boston. I figured he wouldn't be sitting in my lap at the news desk, so I knew my time was short. People will tell you, "It's not what they did, it's how they did it." I hate that line. Of course it's *what* they did. They could have dropped me from the top of the Green Monster at Fenway Park and it wouldn't have changed a thing. I was fired. *How* they did it? Who cares. Dead is dead.

A fter about year of freelancing for HBO Sports, I once again applied for a job at WCBS-TV in New York. I figured that I had done my stint in "Minneapolis." They were looking for a six P.M. weekday sportscaster. The auditions again came down to two people: veteran New York sportscaster Sal Marciano and me. Marciano wasn't living in Illinois, his wife wasn't pregnant, and he got the job. The station gave me the booby prize: weekends.

I started sportscasting in New York City in 1979. That year, the Seattle Supersonics won the NBA championship. In the twenty-five years since, Seattle's baseball, football, and basketball teams have yet to win another title. (In 2004, the Seattle Storm, of the WNBA, won the championship.) In other major cities, such as Cleveland, the drought has lasted far longer. Meanwhile, New York area teams have won fifteen championships in the four major sports: that's four each for the Yankees and Islanders, three for the Devils, two for the Giants, and one each for the Mets and Rangers. I guess we're a bit spoiled in the New York City area.

"Spanning the World" was born in the summer of 1981. There was a wire-service item about a harness race somewhere in the Midwest. As the horses neared the finish line, the lead horse turned and bit the horse running next to him in the neck. Now, when you're working TV sports, this is one of those "I've gotta see that highlight!" stories. So my producer, Cliff Gelb, tracked down the footage. We were flabbergasted. Now admittedly we weren't the biggest horse racing fans on earth, but, my god, this was unique. The track announcer yelled into his microphone, "This is the damndest thing I've ever seen!" A horse racing fan later told me that this behavior wasn't so unique—in the trade, it's known as "savaging"—but to a couple of city kids raised on stickball and hoops, this was a big deal.

So Cliff and I were sitting there dumbfounded by this footage and we decided that we couldn't just treat it as a normal, run-of-the-mill nightly news highlight: "The Mets won, the Yankees lost, and a horse bit the crap out of the nag in second place." So we decided to "package" the highlight. In TV news, it's all about the packaging. Whatever it is, it might be commonplace, but if you label it as *something* it becomes special. It's "Exclusive!" Or it's "The result of a six-month investigation." Whatever. We wondered what we should call our "one-of-a-kind" find. We decided that since ABC Sports "Spans the Globe" in *Wide World of Sports,* we should span something else. So we chose the world. I guess we could have spanned the galaxy, but if aliens were running into walls chasing fly balls on the planet Ork, I couldn't be sure we would get the footage.

We found some old Movietone music and some goofy black-and-white footage and put together a nice, neat package. The introductory footage featured a fight between two cats wearing boxing gloves and film of some guy taking a cannonball shot to his stomach. You know, real classy stuff. And voilà! "Spanning the World" was born. We had just one highlight in the first spanning: an overly aggressive, famished horse.

When I moved over to WNBC-TV in 1986, I knew I wanted to do a monthly edition of "Spanning the World." Two outfielders colliding in baseball was old hat. But a guy trying to pick up a ball in left field and instead picking up a hot dog wrapper—now that had potential. An out-of-control skier tumbling down a mountain? Mildly funny. An ambulance comes to get him? Not funny. So I had one basic rule: NOBODY GOT HURT! I must admit though, if a guy skis off a cliff in Liechtenstein, I don't always know his physical condition. So I do the journalistically prudent thing. I lie! Just kidding. (Okay, not entirely.)

My producers and I created a new opening to "Spanning the World." We used some goofy color footage and added the incomparable voice of NBC's longtime announcer Don Pardo (*Saturday Night Live, The Price Is Right, Jeopardy!*). At the end of the package, Don intones: "Join us next time for 'Spanning the World' . . . if there *is* a next time!" I honestly didn't know if there would be. That was March of 1987. "Spanning" has aired every month since on WNBC. In August of 1989, it began airing monthly on NBC's *Today* show. Along the way I've appeared on Dick Clark's blooper shows, David Letterman, and Conan O'Brien. And all because a racehorse got hungry!

During my first appearance on the *Today* show, Bryant Gumbel called over to Jane Pauley. "Watch this poor slob run full speed *into* the vault in gymnastics instead of *over* it!" said Gumbel. The gymnast was Brian Meeker, of the University of Minnesota. He was a two-time Big Ten all-around champion. Quite a gymnast, really. But as he was competing at the National Sports Festival in Syracuse in 1981, he had a slight mishap. The idea is to run really fast, put your hands on the vault, and flip over it. This time, though, Meeker ran smack into it. Thud! He wasn't hurt, but he was slightly embarrassed. He is better known for that mishap than for all of his accomplishments. Several years later, I gave Meeker a second-chance vault. He easily cleared the exercise. I showed the new footage on "Spanning the World." As Meeker flew through the air in slow motion, we played the "Hallelujah Chorus." Meeker's flub was in "Spanning's" original color opening.

It has since been replaced by footage of a baseball player running full speed right through the wooden fence in the outfield. In May 1991, at Civic Stadium in Portland, Oregon, the minor-league Beavers were hosting Vancouver. Chip Hale hit a long fly ball to right. Vancouver outfielder Rodney McCray went back for it and ran full bore through the plywood outfield fence—right through the wall! He didn't make the grab. What makes the clip so terrific is the audio. You hear a hollow thud. McCray became an instant celebrity. He later made it to the major leagues, playing sixty-seven games with the White Sox and Mets, but all anybody wanted to talk to him about was his running through the wall. The day that it happened, there were wire reports claiming McCray had lost a tooth, but I interviewed him the following day via satellite and he denied the reports. He was in one piece. Halfway through our television interview, though, the satellite went down and the screen turned to "snow." Somehow, I thought that was fitting. We've used this clip of McCray in the opening of "Spanning the World" for years. It's a step up from a couple of cats fighting, and it still brings a laugh—no matter how many times you see it.

There was one clip that I never used on "Spanning the World." I didn't think it was appropriate to show on an evening newscast or on a morning show such as *Today*. But I did air it one night on *Late Night with Conan O'Brien*. Conan's show airs after the *Tonight Show,* at a time when a little PG-13 humor wouldn't be inappropriate. In a mid-1990s soccer match between two European teams, the players lined up for a free kick. Bunched in front of the goal mouth, a player from one team reached back and tickled a player from the opposing team. Let me put it this way: it was a particularly sensitive area and the assaulted player was not at all happy. He threw up his arms in a beseeching manner, as if to ask the referee and anyone else who happened to notice, "What in the world is this jerk doing?" On Conan's show, we played the clip at regular speed. We played it in slow-motion replay. We drew a circle around the offended area, just in case the viewer wasn't focused on it. After playing the footage several times, I said that I could understand why the player was upset. "Because in soccer," I explained matter-of-factly, "you're not supposed to use your hands." Now, every time I've used that line at a party or at a speaking engagement, people laugh. When I said it on Conan's show, though, you could have heard a pin drop. When NBC replayed that show several months later, anchorwoman Sue Simmons, my partner in crime on the New York news, was only too happy to point out that "Nobody laughed the second time, either!"

4

SPANNING THE WORLD
OF BASEBALL

APRIL 2004, VICTORY FIELD, INDIANAPOLIS. Indianapolis Indians first baseman Jeff Liefer went to the bathroom in the clubhouse between innings. He couldn't get out. He was locked inside the bathroom and the game was delayed for twenty minutes. After he was rescued, Liefer said, "I don't want to be remembered as the guy who got stuck in the bathroom." I don't think he has a choice in the matter. In fact, I think his place in baseball history is secure. I've dubbed him the Sultan of Squat.

JUNE 1996, SHEA STADIUM, NEW YORK. Edgar Renteria, of the Florida Marlins, hit a comebacker to the mound. Mets pitcher Pete Harnisch stuck out his rear end and "butted" the ball over to third baseman Jeff Kent who threw to first for the out. Now that's what I'd call a major-league ass-ist!

JULY 2000, COORS FIELD, DENVER. Dodger Todd Hollandsworth's bat shattered as he hit the ball. The ball went to second base and half the bat went toward first. Rockies second baseman Todd Walker came up with the ball, but his off-balance throw was in the dirt. It bounced off the broken portion of the bat and rolled away. Hollandsworth was safe at first. The official scorer gave him a hit; some thought he should have been awarded two.

OCTOBER 1992, ANAHEIM STADIUM. Texas Ranger David Hulse fouled off a ball. It went zooming into the Angels' dugout. He fouled off a second ball. Same spot. And then a third ball. At this point, the Angels players moved down to the other side of the dugout, huddling together for safety. Some of them waved white towels as if to say "We surrender." The next pitch, would you believe it? Hulse fouled it off again, directly into the area of the dugout the Angels had vacated. Too bad Hulse didn't have the same accuracy when it came to hitting fair balls. Eventually, he grounded out to the shortstop.

MAY 2004, DODGER STADIUM, LOS ANGELES. The count was 2-2. Dodger Alex Cora was standing in against Cubs pitcher Matt Clement. The count remained 2-2 for eleven minutes and thirty seconds as Cora fouled off pitch after pitch after pitch after . . . Finally, on the eighteenth pitch—thirteen minutes and fifteen seconds after the at bat began—Cora hit the ball into fair territory. It was a two-run homer. He was just waiting for his pitch.

SPANNING THE WORLD OF BASEBALL

AUGUST 1993, OLYMPIC STADIUM, MONTREAL. The Houston Astros weren't thrilled with Expos pitcher Dennis Martinez. So when Martinez came to the plate, Astros pitcher Todd Jones tried to hit him. First, Jones pitched inside and missed. And then, with a three-ball count, he tried again. Martinez knew what was coming and backed off the plate. He took first on the walk, and Jones was ejected. Doug Jones was brought in to finish the job. The Astros first baseman did not hold Martinez on—in fact he was playing nowhere near the bag. Nonetheless, Jones attempted to pick off Martinez. He aimed a fastball at Martinez! It also missed. But if at first you don't succeed . . .

OCTOBER 1992, SKYDOME, TORONTO. On Fan Appreciation Day in Toronto, lucky Blue Jays fans took home prizes. One of the gifts was a green SUV. It was driven onto the field with Blue Jays Joe Carter and Dave Winfield inside. Outfielder Derek Bell watched this from the dugout with particular interest. It was his SUV. Bell looked dumbstruck as the "lucky winner" was called to claim his prize. It was all an elaborate practical joke on Bell. With teamwork like this, it was no surprise when the Blue Jays won the World Series later that month.

MAY 1993, WORLD WAR MEMORIAL STADIUM, GREENSBORO, NORTH CAROLINA. After the umpires made a controversial call that went against the home team Hornets, audio man Jerry Burkot played the theme from the *Twilight Zone.* The umpires were not amused; they threw him out of the game. What's worse: Burkot was led out of the stadium in handcuffs. Perhaps they feared that with free hands he'd play "I Fought the Law (And the Law Won)" on his way home.

AUGUST 2001, WRIGLEY FIELD, CHICAGO. A close call at the plate went against the home team Cubs. Former Chicago Bear and current professional wrestler Steve McMichael was scheduled to sing "Take Me Out to the Ball Game" during the seventh-inning stretch. Before beginning the song he said to the crowd, "Don't worry. I'll have some speaks with that home plate umpire after the game." Home plate umpire Angel Hernandez was not happy. He ejected McMichael.

AUGUST 1987, WILLIAMSPORT, PENNSYLVANIA. Williamsport hosted Reading in a minor-league baseball game. Reading had a runner on third base, but Williamsport catcher Dave Bresnahan had a clever idea. He had hidden a potato in his catcher's mitt. After a pitch, he took the potato and threw it wildly toward third base. The runner on third, thinking it was the baseball, trotted home. But, surprise! Bresnahan was still holding the baseball and tagged the runner out. The umpire didn't find this at all amusing—he called the runner safe. The ump wasn't alone. The next day, Bresnahan was fired!

MY HERO!

FEBRUARY 2002, KEY ARENA, SEATTLE. In the third quarter of a Supersonics-Celtics game, Seattle's Rashard Lewis swore at a referee and was ejected. The promotion that night? It was Rashard Lewis bobblehead doll night. At least Lewis's fans had something to remember their hero by.

We all have heroes. Mine was Mickey Mantle. How original. I must have been the only kid in America attracted to a guy who played in the World Series every year, could bat from either side of the plate, run like the wind, and hit tape-measure home runs. I might have been better off had I put some real thought into it and come up with somebody more deserving, someone with a real effect on my life, like my dad, the most honest and hardworking person in history. Or a teacher, such as my ninth-grade French teacher, Miss Sharon, who refused to believe all the "bad behavior" reports she had read about me and drew her own conclusions. Those are real heroes. Not the baseball players I idolized who hit a bunch of homers when they weren't getting drunk or philandering. But that's the way it goes, and once you latch onto someone, he's your hero for life.

When I was a kid, my schedule revolved around The Mick. I'd wake up and before even saying good morning to my mom I'd ask, "Did Mickey hit one last night?" (I can't remember how mornings began during the off-season, or when Mantle was on the disabled list.) When it was time to go to a relative's house on the weekend or to run any kind of errand, invariably it was: "Can we wait a few minutes? The Mick is coming up to bat the next inning."

Mantle wore number 7. He *was* number 7. But when he first came up with the Yankees, he actually wore number 6 before being sent down to the minors. When he came back up later that summer, number 7 had become available, so he took it. Thousands of people my age chose seven as their lucky number because of him. When we played Little League baseball, we would fight over who got to wear the number 7 jersey. (Even players in other sports, guys including hockey stars Phil Esposito and Rod Gilbert, wore number 7 because of Mantle.) Since then I've remained obsessed with the number. It's even part of my e-mail address. I add up the numbers of a date. Take June 14, 1994, the day the New York Rangers won their first Stanley Cup championship in fifty-four years: 6-14-1994. Add up all the digits, 6 plus 1, plus 4, et cetera. They add up to 34. And, of course, since 3 plus 4 equals 7, it's a "7 day." Every ninth day is a "7 day"—and something good always seems to happen on those days. You're probably reading this and thinking, "This guy is nuts!" And you're right, but it all comes down to the number 7 and, of course, to Mickey Mantle.

It wasn't just the home runs. It was how Mantle hit them. In 1953, he bashed one in Washington off Senators pitcher Chuck Stobbs. Yankees executive Red Patterson tracked down the ball in the backyard of a home across the street from Griffith Stadium. To figure out how far the ball had traveled, Patterson took out a measuring tape, thus giving birth to the term "tape-measure home run." That homer, Patterson claimed, was a 565-foot shot. Mantle also came the closest to hitting a fair ball out of Yankee Stadium. No one has ever done that—at least not in a game. (Bernie Williams supposedly did it during batting practice a couple of years ago.) It was May 30, 1956, and Camilo Pascual was pitching the second game of a doubleheader for the Senators. Witnesses say the ball was still rising when it crashed into the right-field façade. They say it might have traveled six hundred feet if it hadn't been stopped from leaving the stadium.

Mantle would sometimes be out for weeks, having come up lame when racing to first base, and in his first game back, in his very first at bat—as I remember it, it was always in Cleveland—he'd belt a homer. I guess the injuries had something to do with my fascination as well. I'd hear stories about how he was taped up from head to toe, that he was always playing hurt. He would run around the bases with a kind of limp, and as kids we would imitate that running style. That's the way we would run out home runs—hobbling around, instead of running smoothly.

Of course what we didn't hear back then were all the stories about his boozing and his womanizing. None of that stuff was mentioned in those days. And truthfully, it wouldn't have mattered anyway. (I've interviewed Mantle's widow, Merlyn, and we've discussed these issues. She's a wonderful woman who raised four sons, basically by herself. Every time I speak with her I get goose bumps. Just the thought of speaking to my hero's wife gets to me.) I mean we all know about Babe Ruth's excesses, but does any of that diminish the fact that he was the most significant sports figure of the twentieth century?

M antle wasn't always adored in New York. In fact, he was consistently booed by Yankees fans during his first few seasons. He struck out too much, some would complain. But the real complaint was simple: *He's no Joe DiMaggio!* It was, of course, an unfair standard. Joe D. was baseball royalty. Over thirteen seasons with the Yankees, from 1936 to 1951, DiMaggio hit 361 homers, averaged 118 RBIs, and compiled a .325 lifetime batting mark. In 1941, he hit in a record fifty-six consecutive games. You would only have to catch a glimpse of him to know that DiMaggio was someone special.

One of my biggest thrills was introducing my father to DiMaggio in the Yankees' clubhouse on an Old Timer's Day. My dad was a lifelong Yankees fan, and I'm pretty sure that's why I got interested in sports. We would watch the games together on TV, and he would tell me stories about having seen Babe Ruth play. He would say, "Babe had this huge bat in his hands, and it looked like a toothpick." My dad was a very shy man, so I got a kick out of the fact that he met another quiet, reserved guy like Joe D. (I'm not a big trivia nut, but here's one of those oddball coincidences courtesy of collector Barry Halper. The only public fit of anger that Joe ever showed was during Game Six of the 1947 World Series. Dodger Al Gionfriddo made a circus catch in left field, robbing DiMaggio of a home run. Joe shook his head and kicked at the dirt between first and second base. That was it, Joe's big emotional outburst. Here's the trivia part: DiMaggio died in 1999 on March 8. Gionfriddo's birthday.)

I always heard two things about DiMaggio. First, no one ever mentioned Marilyn Monroe—his wife for nine months in 1954—in his presence. And, second, at any function, he always wanted to be introduced last and always as "the greatest living ballplayer." It was true that even people who knew him well never mentioned Marilyn. Barry Halper and his wife, Sharon, traveled through Europe with Joe. They called him "Uncle Joe," and they wouldn't even dare mention her name.

Until a few years ago, when he auctioned off most of his collection at Sotheby's for nearly $22 million, Barry Halper had the most amazing collection of memorabilia in his basement. What I liked most about Halper's stash were the oddball artifacts, quirky stuff including Babe Ruth's smoking jacket and Ty Cobb's dentures. One time, DiMaggio was wandering around Barry's basement. Joe looked wistfully at a collection of artifacts, including the premiere issue of *Playboy* magazine, with Marilyn Monroe on the cover. Sharon softly said, "Marilyn?" and DiMaggio just nodded with that faraway look. Another time, Joe saw that magazine on Barry's desk and asked, "What's this?" He thumbed through the magazine and then wrote, "Best wishes, Joe DiMaggio" on the cover. When Halper auctioned off much of his collection at Sotheby's in 1999, that magazine went for $40,230. When Barry drove Joe to Cooperstown for the annual Baseball Hall of Fame induction ceremony one year, Joe grew weary of talking about baseball and finally asked, "Did you see that movie on TV last night?" Coincidentally, there had been a movie about Marilyn. Joe wanted to know what Barry thought of the guy who played him. DiMaggio just stared out the window and said, "I really loved that woman." Halper knew DiMaggio for nearly a quarter of a century. That was the first and last time Joe talked about Marilyn.

As for how he wanted to be introduced, toward the end of his life, I had the honor of doing just that. I was emceeing a dinner for which Joe was the featured guest. I walked over to his table and asked him how he wanted to be introduced? He said, "Len, however you want. I don't care." None of this greatest living ballplayer stuff. Then I asked him if he wanted to say a few words. He said, "No way. Last year I talked and they thought I did a lousy job." Talk about pride. Joe could have gotten up there and recited, "Mary had a little lamb" and the crowd would have loved it. When I introduced DiMaggio, there was an instant standing ovation. Imagine going through life like that.

Kind of a tough act to follow.

🏐   ⚾   🏀

The first time I met Mantle was also at an Old Timer's Game at Yankee Stadium. It was 1979. I walked right up to him, introduced myself, and said, "You were my hero." (He must have heard that millions of times. But he never forgot it. I always had the feeling that he went out of his way to be nice to me because I had said that to him. In fact, on my wall unit in my office at home, I have a baseball that he signed, "To Len, Thanks a Lot, Mickey Mantle." I never asked him what he was thanking me for. I just assumed it was for caring.) I told him that I once wrote to him when I was a kid. I still remember what I wrote:

> *Dear Mickey:*
>
>   *I hope you're having a nice off-season. Please find enclosed a self-addressed, stamped envelope and a card to sign with your autograph.*
>

Sincerely,
Lenny Berman

I sent my request to Yankee Stadium, never imagining that Mantle probably received a zillion of them. Though he didn't tell me about his off-season, he did sign my index card. I put it into my Mickey Mantle scrapbook, which also included a couple of his baseball cards. Of course, as all mothers seem to have done, my mom threw out the scrapbook. We didn't know until years later that those collections had real value. I always heard stories that Mantle only opened envelopes that looked like they were written in a woman's handwriting. When I mentioned this to Mantle during our first meeting, he said, "Well, you must have written like a girl."

❧   ●   ⚫

W here there are heroes, there must be villains. When I was growing up, everyone's favorite sports question was, "Who is the best center fielder in New York City?" Mickey Mantle, Willie Mays, or Duke Snider? There were three *good* answers, but depending on your team allegiance, there was only one *right* answer. Truthfully, though, as much as I idolized Mantle and loved his Yankees, I thought Mays might have been the better all-around player. (Even as a kid, I exercised a touch of journalistic objectivity.) But Duke Snider? No way. I couldn't even look at him on television. For me, Mantle and the Yankees were the be-all and end-all. It followed, then, that Snider and his Brooklyn Dodgers were the hated enemy.

Here's how bad my hatred was: I wouldn't even step into Ebbets Field, where the Dodgers played. What's worse, I refused to even enter the borough of Brooklyn! Pretty sick, huh? (With the perspective of maturity, I now wish I would have gone to Ebbets Field. In 1970, I saw a game at Crosley Field in Cincinnati and thought the ballpark was great. I feel the same way about Wrigley in Chicago and Fenway in Boston. The old ballparks have a special charm, and I mourn their loss, as I do for basketball shrines such as the old Madison Square and Boston Gardens.) Long after the Dodgers had moved to Los Angeles, I visited the site of Ebbets Field, where apartment buildings now stand. I was doing one of those anniversary pieces about the Dodgers and "good old Ebbets Field." Waxing poetic—and lying through my teeth.

Years later, I told Snider about my strong dislike of the

Dodgers, though I left out the part about not being able to look at his face. In response to my confession, he said simply, "Everyone can't be perfect!"

To Duke, though, I owe a debt of thanks. When I was in grade school, David Nussbaum, a neighborhood kid, and I bet on the winner of the 1955 World Series. No odds, just a straight-up bet. He picked the Dodgers and—no dummy—I took the Yanks. The Yankees always beat Brooklyn in the World Series. Except, of course, that year. Snider batted .320 and hit four home runs in the series, including two in Game Five. The Dodgers won the decisive seventh game. Our wager? Thirteen cents. All the money I had. I cried—more over the money than the Yankees' defeat. I learned my lesson. So thanks to David Nussbaum, Duke Snider, and the "awful" 1955 Yankees, I have almost never bet on a sporting event since.

◆　　●　　●

Several years later, I ran a series of luncheons in the Rainbow Room in New York City. I would pay athletes to come and speak to businessmen who belonged to the old Rainbow Room Club. The club members were some of the most successful entrepreneurs in the world. I've often suspected that many would come not so much to listen to the athletes but to get their autographs. I, of course, invited Mickey Mantle to speak at a luncheon. When I called up his girlfriend/agent, she told me I couldn't afford him. She was right. But I asked her to please ask Mantle if he would do me a favor—not that he owed me one, but maybe it counted for something that he was my hero. Mantle agreed to participate.

About a week before the luncheon, I called him to go over some of the details. He was concerned that he would have to make a speech. I told him that that wasn't the case, that he could just answer questions. He enjoyed doing that. He could spin his tales about Billy Martin shooting some guy's cow on a farm or talk about how he once testified before Congress alongside Casey Stengel. It was at an antitrust hearing involving Major League Baseball. The Ol' Perfessor mumbled some unintelligible gobbledygook, somehow covering the national highway system, night ball, and Greta Garbo in a single thought. And then it was Mantle's turn. Senator Kefauver asked him if he had "any observations with reference to the applicability of the antitrust laws to baseball." Mantle volunteered, "My views are just about the same as Casey's."

So, anyway, there I was discussing the luncheon with Mantle when my daughter, Rachel, walked into the family room. She was nine years old then and I had told her hundreds of stories about The Mick. As she approached me, I mouthed to her, "I'm on the phone with Mickey Mantle." It truly was one of the highlights of my life.

Mantle was great at the luncheon. I remember that one of the Radio City Hall honchos had brought along his nine- or ten-year-old son. The executive said hello to me as Mantle and I entered the Rainbow Room, and I introduced the executive to Mantle. At lunch, Mick asked me why I hadn't introduced him to the kid. I felt like an idiot. So during the luncheon, I made a big deal about the kid in the audience. I called him up to meet The Mick and to get his autograph. I think, to the end, Mantle was trying to make up for his slights of the past. He had always regretted treating people poorly when he wasn't in a good mood or sober.

Somewhere, I must have a canceled check from this luncheon, endorsed with Mantle's signature. It has to be worth something, but I would never sell it. Today, people will sell anything—and why not, when there is a guy out there willing to pay $3 million for Mark McGwire's seventieth home run ball? It has gotten out of hand, though, and Mantle knew it. In his final days, as he was resting in a hospital, he took a soiled rubber glove that had been used to examine him, autographed it, and sent it to Barry Halper. He did it as a joke—the famous Mantle sense of humor.

Barry Halper once showed me a piece of paper. It was a letter addressed to Mickey Mantle, dated December 14, 1972. It was from Bob Fishel, the longtime Yankees public relations director. Fishel was asking Mantle, as well as many of his former teammates, to help the Yankees celebrate the fiftieth anniversary of Yankee Stadium in 1973. In his letter, he asked the former Yankees to name their most outstanding moment at Yankee Stadium. Now, The Mick had more than a few outstanding moments in the House That Ruth Built. He could have written about any number of home runs or the incredible catch in which he robbed Gil Hodges of an extra-base hit, helping to preserve Don Larsen's perfect game in the 1956 World Series. He could have written about all those championship teams for which he starred or even about something that wasn't as positive, such as injuring his knee as a rookie in the 1951 World Series.

So what great moment did Mantle select? The heading was "I consider the following my outstanding experience at Yankee Stadium." Mantle wrote: "I got [oral sex] under the right-field bleachers by the Yankee bullpen." The questionnaire continued: "This event occurred on or about (give as much detail as you can)." The Mick's response: "It was about the third or fourth inning, I had a pulled groin and couldn't fuck at the time." Mantle continued, giving as much detail as he could, but I'll spare you the rest. At the end of this letter, Mantle signed his name. And under his signature he wrote: "The All-American Boy."

My hero!

6

GOING, GOING . . .

MAY 1993, MUNICIPAL STA-DIUM, CLEVELAND. Carlos Martinez, the Indians' reserve infielder, lofted a fly ball to the warning track in right. José Canseco was playing right field for the Texas Rangers. He raised his glove and the ball hit him squarely on top of his head. Then it bounced over the wall. Martinez rounded the bases with a home run, and sportscasters everywhere took pleasure in noting that this was the first time they'd seen Canseco use his head.

Ruth, Maris, McGwire, Bonds. Home runs are the best. That's what people want to see. I remember the first home run I ever saw in person. It was at Yankee Stadium, and though I don't recall who hit it, I do remember it being majestic. Ask the average sports fan who holds the record for the most touchdowns or the most hockey goals in a season. He won't know. Or if he does, he almost certainly won't know the number. (FYI: It's Marshall Faulk's twenty-six TDs and Wayne Gretzky's ninety-two goals.) But everyone knows sixty—Babe Ruth's record number of homers in 1927. And sixty-one—Roger Maris's total from 1961. Seventy—Mark McGwire's 1998 tally—and seventy-three, the current record set by Barry Bonds in 2001.

Really, though, I think sports fans are more comfortable with sixty as the magic number. It's a "natural" number—in more ways than one. First, there's its roundness: a nice, round number hit by a nice, round man. But more than that, sixty doesn't come with any asterisks attached.

Ruth's sixty homers in 1927 bested the record of fifty-nine he had set in 1921, which bested the old record of fifty-four (Ruth again, in 1920), which had bested the record set in 1919 (twenty-nine: yup, Ruth). Ruth was huge, in every way. Sixty was a mythic number, and only somebody like Ruth, who was larger than life, might actually attain it. When he finally did it, it was thought that it was one of those records that would never be broken. There are lots of those. A couple actually never will be broken, but Ruth's sixty was truly a "magic number" in the eyes of baseball fans. Wouldn't you love to know all the inside dirt of his life? I heard the following story thirdhand—from Babe, to a former teammate, to a sportscaster. After the Yankees won the World Series in 1927, the Yankees had a team party at the Waldorf Hotel. Ruth supposedly got up and announced to the crowd, "Any woman here who doesn't want to fuck: get out!" I have no idea if this story is true, but it sounds good, though.

Chasing the Babe was nearly impossible for all who tried. His sixty home run total was a legendary landmark, and it survived for thirty-four years. Then came 1961 and Mickey Mantle and Roger Maris. The purists like to pooh-pooh it. (Actually, they like to pooh-pooh everything.) That's why asterisks were born. The season was eight games longer than when Ruth played, and 1961 was the year of expansion in the American League, the year the Los Angeles Angels and the Washington Senators were born. So, the argument goes, you had lots of pitchers who otherwise would have been toiling in the minors, facing off against the mighty Yankees hitters who, in a longer season, had the opportunity for more at bats. If you want to discount every record ever set, it's an easy thing to give the old expansion-watered-it-down argument.

I was at summer camp and the home run race was the buzz of the summer. Every day we heard the reports. "Roger hit one." "The Mick hit two today." It was no secret who I was rooting for. I wasn't alone. The same fans who had booed Mantle during his first several seasons had started booing Maris. In the end, most Yankees fans were disappointed that it was Maris who wound up breaking Ruth's record. Mantle was sidelined in September with an injury and ended up with fifty-four homers. I was home from camp and watching on TV the night the Yanks played their 154th game of the season. Ford Frick, the commissioner of baseball, had declared that if Maris didn't break Ruth's record in 154 games, then he would place an asterisk next to the new record. That night, against the Baltimore Orioles, Maris hit his fifty-ninth. When he came to the plate his final time, looking for number sixty, he reportedly said to the Orioles' catcher, Gus Triandos, "Boy, is my ass tight." He didn't homer. He hit number sixty-one in the Yankees' 162nd game. By that point, though, Commissioner Frick had taken much of the joy out of it. Only twenty-three thousand fans showed up for the game.

There were stories of how Maris lost his hair and became irritable during that campaign. It's understandable: I mean how many times could he face the question, "Rog, do you think you can do it?" Almost all I ever heard about Roger was how surly he was. So the first time I approached him at an Old Timer's Game, I timidly asked if he would be willing to tape an interview. He said, "Sure, where do you want to do it?" I would have been willing to do it in the john if that's what he wanted, but he suggested the Yankees' dugout. You have to understand the significance of that. When Maris hit his sixty-first, he literally had to be pushed out of the dugout to take a curtain call. Maris enjoyed joking about that. He would say, "Nowadays a guy hits a sacrifice fly and he's out there waving to the crowd."

Maris was always a terrific interview, and I found him to be a great guy. Of course, I wasn't one of those reporters in 1961 making his life miserable. Many years later I ran into Johnny Blanchard, who was one of Maris's teammates on the 1961 Yankees. I told him that I thought Maris was a good guy. Blanchard then told me about his own son who had met Roger Maris in the clubhouse one day. Blanchard said his son was not a very talkative kid, that he grunted his answers to people. But he noticed that Roger and his son were having a prolonged conversation; the two were really connecting. Obviously Maris made an impression on Blanchard's son. When the young Blanchard had a son of his own, he named him Maris. How's that for a tribute? Johnny Blanchard's grandson is named Maris Blanchard.

In my book, there is no asterisk next to Roger Maris's name. I always thought the asterisk was an absurdity. In fact, in 1991, baseball commissioner Fay Vincent officially removed the asterisk from the record books. But when you think about it, all of the record-setting home run hitters could have asterisks next to their names. Lengths of seasons vary, ballparks change, there's expansion. Fine. Why not blame global warming and its effect on the flight of the ball? And what are records anyway? Just numbers written down in history books. The best, the first, the most? Ruth was special. Maris was special. McGwire and Bonds, too—each in his own way. The fact that Maris hit sixty-one doesn't diminish the Babe in my mind, nor does the fact that Bonds blasted seventy-three lessen Maris's accomplishment. They're just numbers.

Of course, try telling that to the millions of Americans who went gaga over Mark McGwire and Sammy Sosa in the summer of 1998. For a younger generation, 1998 was their 1961. And it was special. Baseball had shot itself in the foot when the players went on strike in 1994 and there was no World Series for the first time since 1903. Doomsayers predicted that baseball would wither away, that the game was too slow for the MTV generation. Then McGwire and Sosa came along and lit up the summer. Sports being sports, though, you can always take potshots at the stars going for the glory. For Maris, it was expansion and the longer season. When McGwire was making his assault on the record, a bottle of androstenedione was found in his locker. Andro boosts testosterone levels. In 1998, it was perfectly legal, but today it's not. Major League Baseball banned the substance in April 2004, on the same day that the Food and Drug Administration told companies to quit selling the over-the-counter supplement. Andro acts like a steroid, so even though it was permitted at the time, McGwire was effectively using steroids during the 1998 season. Does it take away from his record? To me, it does—at least a little.

Five seasons later, Sammy Sosa was batting at Wrigley Field in an interleague game against the Tampa Bay Devil Rays. He broke his bat on a pitch from Jeremi Gonzalez, and out popped cork. Sosa claimed he only used the corked bat during batting practice, "to put on a show for the fans," and that he picked it up by accident for the actual game. A corked bat is lighter than a regular bat—cork replaces ash wood in the core—so players have a quicker swing. No one but Sosa knows if he had used a corked bat before in a game or, if so, whether he might have used one during the 1998 season. But there will always be a fan or two who figure that if he cheated once, he must have cheated other times. Andro for McGwire, cork for Sosa. And who knows what for Barry Bonds. Is anything on the level?

When Bonds broke in with Pittsburgh in 1986, he looked like a ninety-eight-pound weakling. In recent years, as the star of the Giants, he has looked like the Incredible Bulk. He broke McGwire's total in 2001. In 2004, he joined one of the most exclusive clubs on earth: The 700 Club. Hank Aaron and Babe Ruth are the only other members. As Bonds has continued his ascent through the record book, though, he hasn't exactly been greeted by ticker-tape parades at each intersection. His personality doesn't help his cause. When the Giants came to Shea Stadium during the 2004 season, one of my producers approached Bonds for a quick interview. Said Bonds: "If you put that camera in my face, I'll slit your throat." Lovely.

Suspicions trail his every move: the change in his body; his connection to the Bay Area Laboratory Cooperative (BALCO), the nutritional supplement lab at the center of a steroids scandal in sports; and the indictment of his personal trainer, Greg Anderson, for distributing illegal drugs. Of the steroids accusations, Andy Van Slyke, a teammate of Bonds's for six seasons in Pittsburgh, said what many thought: "Unequivocally, [Bonds has] taken them. . . . I can say that with utmost certainty. Now, I never saw him put it into his body. But, look, Barry went to the bank with the robber, he drove the car, he got money in his pocket from the bag that came out of the bank. Come to your own conclusion. Did he spend the money? You decide. I think he did." I know the rule is innocent until proven guilty—and I'm sure Van Slyke does as well—but I also know what the average fan thinks: where there's smoke, there's fire.

Bonds's remarkable 2004 season, though, quieted some of the skeptics for a while. In just 373 at bats—he was walked 232 times; won't *anyone* pitch to this guy?—he hit 45 homers, knocked in 101 runs, and batted a cool .362. He was awarded his seventh MVP award. Why does this matter? He played the entire season under the bright light of an interrogation lamp, knowing that in addition to the media circus and catcalls from the fans of opposing teams, he also faced a random drug test. That test finally came in September, and though Major League Baseball does not publicize results, all indications are that Bonds was clean. I was reminded of Bobby Valentine's great line when asked about Bonds and steroids. Valentine, a former big-league manager who now leads a team in Japan, said, in reference to the fact that Bonds never swings at a pitch outside the strike zone, "Does he shoot them [steroids] in his eyes?" Actually no. He rubbed it on his body and placed it under his tongue. That according to the *San Francisco Chronicle*. The paper got ahold of his secret grand jury testimony. Bonds's defense? He didn't know the stuff he was using was illegal. Oh.

Whatever the truth is about Bonds, I think you could be drinking liquid titanium and it wouldn't mean you're going to hit a home run. It takes remarkable skill to turn around a ninety-five-mile-an-hour fastball, not to mention a slider or a split-fingered fastball. But experts will tell you steroids can make the ball go farther once you hit it. Dr. Gary Wadler, a member of the World Anti-Doping Agency's medical research committee, told me that steroids won't increase your skill, but they will increase the production of that skill. In hits, runs, and errors terms, he explained, the juice won't take a .240 hitter and turn him into a Hall of Famer, but it may cause a fly ball that was hit to the warning track to carry out for a home run. (Wadler also explained that steroids help athletes heal faster. Who would steroids help the most, then? Pitchers: they're the ones trying to recover faster between starts. People seldom talk about that.)

I'll say it one more time: I think it is often unfair to compare accomplishments across the eras in the baseball. Today, the ballparks are smaller and pitching is said to be more watered down than it was in the days of Ruth. But here's something that is rarely mentioned. Ruth didn't compete against everyone; the game was lily-white when he played. There were no Pedro Martinezes or Bob Gibsons in baseball. In addition, Babe played mostly day games and traveled shorter distances and by train. Today, most games are at night and ballplayers fly all over the country. What this means is that a home run in

1927 is not the same as a home run in 2004. Heck, the ball it-self is probably different. You've heard the line: the players, the ball, and the stadiums—they're all juiced up! If you want, you can diminish anybody's record, in any era. You could give everyone his own asterisk.

* * *

Bonds will probably break Henry Aaron's record of 755 ca-reer homers and, outside of San Francisco, sports fans will yawn. They'll just figure the record was artificially induced. But Hank was truly special, and he becomes even more special as time passes. In addition to his home run record, Aaron also amassed more extra-base hits, total bases, and runs batted in than any other player in history. But he didn't get respect.

I remember the night well. It was April 8, 1974. *Monday Night Baseball* on NBC. Curt Gowdy at the microphone. In his first at bat, Aaron hit number 715. Just like that, he passed the Babe. As he rounded the bases, a couple of yahoos ran onto the field in Atlanta and started running beside him. Aaron didn't look happy. He had endured so much in his journey, and he wasn't about to share it with a couple of wiseass kids. Aaron looked like he wanted to elbow the interlopers out of the way, but he later told me he wasn't trying to shoo them off. Who could blame him if he was, though?

Many Americans were outraged that this black guy from Mobile, Alabama, had the nerve to challenge the great Babe Ruth. They sent Aaron hate mail by the boxload. He saved all the letters. For so many years, he was bitter and angry about all the abuse that he took. Maybe it was a numbers thing. Since Babe Ruth started his career as a pitcher, he really spent only six-teen full-time seasons as a slugger. Aaron played twenty-three seasons and had four thousand more career at bats than the

Babe. Some fans played the numbers game to knock Aaron. And for a long while, he received very little credit. His accomplishment was discounted. (How ironic that when you pick up the *Baseball Encyclopedia*—a book thicker than most metropolitan phone books—Aaron, who received so little respect, is the very first hitter listed. Of course, the book lists players alphabetically. Much was made of pitcher David Aardsma's alphabetical superiority. Aardsma was called up by the Giants in 2004. Although he moved ahead of Aaron in the overall alphabetical listing of major-league baseball players, the *Encyclopedia* lists hitters and pitchers separately, so Aaron remains first among batsmen.) There were, of course, some people who gave Aaron the credit he deserved. Tigers announcer Ernie Harwell was one. He wrote the song, "Move Over Babe" in Aaron's honor: "Move over Babe, here comes Henry, and he's swinging mean. Move over Babe, here comes Henry. He'll reach that 714."

After breaking the record with Atlanta, Aaron played his final two seasons for the Milwaukee Brewers, then an American League team. The Brewers' first series in 1975 was at Fenway Park, and television reporters mobbed him. He referred to them as "vultures." Before the second game of the series, I took a fan with me to Fenway. He had a ball autographed by Babe Ruth and he wanted Aaron to add his signature to it. Pretty cool. As the Brewers were warming up along the third-base line, I called over to Aaron and explained about the Babe Ruth ball. Without departing from his routine, Aaron barked: "Fuck Babe Ruth!" I thought right then and there, thirty years ago, that if I ever wrote a book, that would be my title. *Fuck Babe Ruth!*—a little catchier than *Spanning the World,* don't you think? It was not the first time I heard the line. A sportscaster in Ohio once told me that during the 1961 World Series, when the Yankees were pummeling the Reds, reporters asked Reds third baseman Gene Freese about their latest loss. Supposedly

Freese responded, "Fuck you, fuck the Yankees, and fuck Babe Ruth!" I guess the Babe had that kind of effect on people. Anyway, as Aaron was walking off the field, I approached him again. He couldn't have been more gracious or charming. He signed the fan's ball and chatted with him. Everyone lived happily ever after.

Since his playing days ended, whenever I've met or interviewed Aaron, he has seemed like a much happier person. I think as time went by he finally started to get the respect he deserved from sports fans. The fans realized that he was the real deal. Ho hint of steroids here. No trash talking. No stopping to admire his homers. No hotdogging at all. He was just a damned great baseball player. Fans appreciate that, and they've told him so. He, in kind, has returned the favor. Once an uptight player chasing a ghost, Aaron has become a relaxed elder statesman. I like that.

P eople like to make up a list of the most dramatic home runs in baseball history. To my way of thinking, there should be only one home run atop that list. October 3, 1951: Bobby Thomson wins the pennant for the New York Giants against the Brooklyn Dodgers. Those two teams defined rivalry. The players didn't like each other, their fans were passionate, and—unlike today's great rivals, the Yankees and the Red Sox—they shared the same city. In 1951, with one swing of the bat, one team won the pennant and the other lost. Everyone has heard Giants announcer Russ Hodges screeching, "The Giants win the pennant. The Giants win the pennant!" Still today, though, walk down a quiet street in Brooklyn, and you can almost hear the echo of an entire borough moaning, "The Dodgers lose the pennant."

GOING, GOING . . .

In 2002, MasterCard and Major League Baseball hosted a promotion in which fans were asked to vote for the most memorable moments in baseball history. Bobby Thomson's Shot Heard 'Round the World? Didn't crack the top ten. Number one was the game in which Cal Ripken broke Lou Gehrig's consecutive games played streak. Of course that "moment" was made up of thousands of moments, and it had none of the drama of Bobby Thomson's ninth-inning blast. All this promotion proved is that most of those voting weren't alive when Thomson hit his shot. They probably didn't even know the Giants once played in Manhattan. Although I'm too young to remember 1951, I do have a sense of baseball history. I've also had the privilege of meeting both Thomson and Ralph Branca, the poor soul who had the misfortune of giving up the homer. I've seen how he's lived with that moment his entire life, and how he's overcome the immediate trauma to handle everything with good grace and humor.

So, Bobby Thomson's homer has to rank number one. Period. But, for the sport of it, I'll suggest three more that have come since. They all occurred within my lifetime, so I can't help but give them more weight than, let's say, Babe Ruth hitting number sixty, or Babe Ruth hitting the first home run in Yankee Stadium history, or Babe Ruth hitting a homer in the first All-Star Game. In any case, to me the homer must have been hit late in the baseball calendar to make it onto the all-time dramatic category. Numbers two through four have the dates October 13, October 2, and October 21.

OCTOBER 13, 1960, FORBES FIELD, PITTSBURGH

I was at Joey Kramer's house. He lived in the neighboring apartment complex in Queens. We were watching TV in the afternoon on a small black-and-white television. Of course in

1960, all World Series games were played in the daylight, and, unless you had the good fortune to be at the stadium, they were all "played" in black and white. It was the bottom of the ninth inning of Game Seven. Bill Mazeroski, a little "good field–no hit" second baseman, hit the home run to win the Series for the Pittsburgh Pirates. This was a major upset; after all, the Pirates beat the Yankees. I was devastated. The Yankees, led by Mantle, had outscored the Pirates in the seven games 55–27.

Here is the setup. The Pirates had scored five runs in the eighth inning and led the game 9–7. But the Yankees came back to tie in the top of the ninth, thanks in large part to the slick baserunning of Mantle. The Mick was on first when Yogi Berra hit a ground ball to first baseman Rocky Nelson. Nelson stepped on first, thus removing the force play at second. When Nelson threw down to second, Mantle did a U-turn and dove back safely into first. While he was doing that, Gil McDougald scored the tying run. I had never seen a move like that before, and frankly I'm not sure I've seen it since. So with the score tied 9–9 in the bottom of the ninth, Mazeroski lofted a Ralph Terry pitch over Yogi Berra's head in left. Ball game. The hit made quite an impression on me, and clearly I wasn't alone. Maz was voted into the Hall of Fame in 2001. Sure, he won eight Gold Glove Awards, but he only hit .260 for his career. If he doesn't hit that home run, he doesn't get within a million miles of Cooperstown. Then again, if Hal Smith, a career .267 hitter, doesn't blast a three-run homer in the eighth inning for the Pirates, Mazeroski doesn't get anywhere close to becoming a hero.

OCTOBER 2, 1978, FENWAY PARK, BOSTON

Picture the perfect fall Monday in New England. Over the course of a 162-game season, the Boston Red Sox and the New

York Yankees have each won 99 games. A one-game playoff will determine the champion of the American League East. My contract with WBZ-TV had expired in June, but I was still living in the Boston area while I tried my hand at freelancing. I decided to go to the game. I didn't have a ticket or a press credential, but the ushers knew me. I walked right in. Some security, huh? Three years later, I was on the field at Yankee Stadium before Game Three of the 1981 World Series. A security guard approached me and said, "Hi, Len, did you enjoy the first two games in L.A.?" I told him I did, and then he said, "Can I see your credential?" But that's Yankee Stadium. This was Fenway Park. As I was walking beneath the stands, John Havlicek called out to me. He had retired the previous April after sixteen seasons as a Boston Celtic, the winner of eight NBA championships. Havlicek asked me where I was sitting and when I told him "nowhere," he said he had an extra seat and invited me to sit with him. That alone would have made for a memorable game.

But this game was to be more than memorable; it was unforgettable. I don't have anything close to a photographic memory, but I can recall half a dozen plays from that game as though the game had been played yesterday. Most of all, of course, I remember Bucky Dent's home run. He came to bat in the seventh inning with two men on and with the Yankees trailing 2–0. Dent, the Yankees' shortstop, was a career .247 hitter; he hit five homers in 1978. Mike Torrez was pitching, and Dent lofted a little fly ball to left. It cleared the Green Monster. This was about as cheap a homer as you'll ever see, an out in every other major-league ballpark and probably most minor-league parks as well. But not in Fenway. The most memorable part for me? The ballpark was dead quiet as Dent rounded the bases. Nothing. The air was let out of the balloon. Go to a Sox-Yankees game at Fenway today and you'll find many Yankees fans, but I don't recall many Yankees fans in the ballpark that day.

Dent's homer wasn't the winning hit. The Yankees wound up scoring four runs in the seventh, and then Reggie Jackson added a solo home run in the eighth inning to make the score 5–2. In the bottom of the eighth, though, the Red Sox scored twice on RBI singles from Carl Yastrzemski and Jim Rice. But it wasn't enough, and the Yankees won 5–4. No one seems to remember Jackson's homer, but Reggie's was really the game winner. If the Red Sox had won, Dent would have been but a footnote. As it is, though, he is remembered by Sox fans by the name Don Zimmer, then the Boston manager, called him: Bucky *Fucking* Dent.

OCTOBER 21 AND 22, 1975, FENWAY PARK, BOSTON

To me, the 1975 World Series was the best ever played. The Cincinnati Reds led the series three games to two. It was a Tuesday night in Boston, and in the bottom of the first inning, Red Sox center fielder Fred Lynn hit a three-run homer. With the Red Sox up three nothing, I left Fenway. That may be a World Series record: earliest departure from a possible clincher. But, as you'll see later, I'm pretty good at setting records of this sort. I had to return to the studio to prepare that night's sportscast. The news was to air after the game on NBC. This game, though, technically didn't end that night. It ended at 12:33 A.M. on Wednesday.

Carlton Fisk hit the game winner off the left-field foul pole in the bottom of the twelfth inning. I'm told that truck drivers on highways throughout New England were honking their horns and flashing their lights. I was in the videotape room at WBZ-TV, selecting highlights for my late sportscast. There were a ton of highlights, and of course Fisk's homer would be one of them. As I was leaving the tape room, I saw the network's replay out of the corner of my eye. If you're a baseball fan, you've since seen this replay a million times: Fisk jumping and waving and willing the ball to go fair. I went on the air and called this the greatest replay in television history. Perhaps I was a bit hyperbolic, but it was probably true at the time. What I love about this shot is that it was captured by mistake. A complete fluke. An NBC cameraman was positioned in Fenway's old manual scoreboard. He was supposed to follow the flight of the ball, but just at that moment he was scared by a huge rat crawling around in the decrepit scoreboard. His camera remained focused on Fisk.

When I went on the air, I was hoarse. It wasn't Fisk's homer that had done me in, though. It was Bernie Carbo's. With four outs to go and the Red Sox trailing 6–3, Carbo, a career .264 hitter, was made to look ridiculous as he fouled off a pitch from Rawly Eastwick. The next pitch: redemption. A three-run bomb to center field. I remember Joe Garagiola's perfect call. All he said was, "We're tied."

So there you go. Three dramatic home runs, all of them in classic one-run games. And all three were made possible by eighth-inning homers by somebody else. If Reggie Jackson, Hal Smith, and Bernie Carbo hadn't hit their blasts, then Mazeroski, Dent, and Fisk would hardly be as famous. The next time somebody speaks of a hero, ask who it was that pushed him onto center stage. Maybe add an asterisk.

It's obvious why fans love the home run. But the truth is that sportscasters love it every bit as much—in no small part because it gives them an opportunity to shine, or so they think. It seems the guys at ESPN are always trying to one-up each other with their distinctive calls: "Back. Back. Back"; "Boo-Yah!"; "Busting out the whuppin' stick!" During the 2004 postseason, Budweiser aired a tongue-in-cheek commercial starring Joe Buck, the son of the Hall of Fame announcer Jack Buck and a fine play-by-play man in his own right. In the commercial, Joe's agent encourages him to coin a catchphrase. Why? So they could license it. Joe rebuffs him initially, but at the end of the spot you see Joe calling a homer and hitting a cowbell. He wears a silly hat and T-shirt upon which is written his new home run call: Slam-a-lam-a-DING-DONG! It's an amusing commercial, but it makes an important point. The guys I respect found a call that worked for them, and they stuck with it. Like the number sixty, they were natural.

Mel Allen's signature home run call—"Going . . . going, gone!"—is the best I've ever heard. Sportscasters have since tried to come up with a better one, but there is nothing better. The ball is going, it's still going, it's gone. You can't improve on this call's simplicity or its accuracy. I'm not a big fan of clichés. In fact, I abhor them. So when a player "goes yard," I cringe. He doesn't go yard; he hits a home run. (Just ask Marty Glickman.) I for one would prefer that the sportscaster not mess with the simplicity of a beautiful event with a cluttered, affected call.

7

NO CHEERING IN THE PRESS BOX

APRIL 1992, MCCOY STADIUM, PAWTUCKET, RHODE ISLAND. Sportscaster Joe Rocco, of WJAR-TV in Providence, was doing his six P.M. sportscast live from the ballpark before the Pawtucket Red Sox's home opener. The um-pires were ready to start the game. Standing in foul territory, he told the umps that he'd be fin-ished in thirty seconds. They said, "No. Now!" And then they turned off the lights on the camera and kicked Rocco out of the game.

When I was growing up as a sports fan, I had three sportscasting idols: Mel Allen, Curt Gowdy, and Howard Cosell. The Yankees were my team and Allen was the "Voice of the Yankees." In addition to his signature "Going . . . going, gone" home run call, he punctuated dramatic plays (generally when they favored the Yankees) with the exclamation, "How about that!" To this day, I can't hear that phrase without thinking of Allen. "How about that!" It seems so natural and says so much.

Later on, I realized that if you weren't a Yankees fan, you probably disliked Mel Allen. "Dislike" may actually be too mild a word. If "Yankee-hater" is an accepted denomination of fan zealotry, then Allen was probably the number one target. Of course, I never thought of him that way. He was announcing my team and my team was winning all the time. That's all I cared about. I never really knew what objectivity meant until I started taking sportscasting seriously. Allen was not an objective announcer. When the Yankees were getting blown out, he would say something like, "My mother told me there'd be days like this." He certainly wasn't describing the feelings of the team crushing the Yankees. For them, the game probably felt like Christmas Eve, and Allen's "woe is me" attitude would have hardly been appropriate. But for a kid rooting for Mantle and the Yankees, none of that mattered. Mel Allen was just-fine-thank-you.

From 1939 to 1964, when the Yankees were in their heyday, Mel Allen was their lead announcer. For a good portion of that stretch, he was joined by Red Barber. During the course of a game, Yankees announcers would rotate between radio and television broadcasting. Barber was an icon. He had been the voice of the Brooklyn Dodgers and was lauded for the simplicity of his calls. I never *got* him. I was a Mel Allen fan, and nobody else would do. Where Allen was passionate, Barber seemed distant. But then I was partisan and Barber wasn't a Yankees fan. So in my house, we would set the radio right on top of the television. When Allen was announcing the game on the radio, we'd turn down the volume on the television and turn up the radio. It was the best of both worlds. Years later, on my *Sports Fantasy* program, I gave a viewer the opportunity to announce a game alongside Allen. To tell you the truth, I was jealous. I would have loved to announce a Yankees game next to Mel Allen. When the guest announcer finished his stint in the broadcast booth, I had him boom, "How about that!" The perfect exclamation.

Curt Gowdy was the voice of all the big events on NBC: the World Series, Super Bowl, and NCAA basketball championship. I thought of him as having an elastic voice. With his intonation, he would make even the most banal sentence sound interesting. I could envision his announcing, "The chalk is moving effortlessly across the blackboard." And, with that voice, you'd pay attention. He announced Red Sox games forever. Few remember, though, that Gowdy was a Yankees announcer alongside Allen for the 1949 season, before the Red Sox hired him away.

In 1972, when I was working in Dayton, Gowdy came to town with the NBC crew for an NCAA basketball tournament doubleheader. The day before the games, the four teams practiced in the arena. Gowdy took a folding chair, plopped it at half-court, and took notes. Players and coaches would come by to chat with him and, while talking, he'd keep writing. That made an impression on me: being a great sportscaster required more than a great voice. Preparation didn't hurt.

When I was just starting out in Boston, Gowdy leaned over to me in the press room at Fenway Park and, without even having been introduced, said, "Kid, you're doing a good job." I was floating. A couple of years later, he was calling a game at Foxboro Stadium for NBC. This was a rarity because at the time the Patriots were never the primary broadcast. But the Pats were improving, and NBC had sent its "A" broadcast team. I walked into the broadcast booth before the game to talk with Gowdy. I said something insightful like, "How great is this? Fifty-yard line, Patriots at home. Wow, what fun!" And to my surprise he said it was fun. But then he went on to say, "Sportscasting would be the greatest job in the world, if only they *let* you broadcast." I didn't ask him what he meant, but I believe he was referring to all the outside pressures: the commercials, the promos, the ratings, management tinkering, personal appearances, sportswriters just waiting to pounce on every mistake. The list goes on and on. At some point, you have to step back and say to yourself, "What about the game?"

When NBC took Gowdy off its baseball broadcasts and replaced him with Joe Garagiola in 1976, it was a big story. I was stunned. The rumor was that Chrysler, the broadcast's big advertiser, wanted Garagiola because he was one of their pitchmen. I remember walking into Boston Garden and running into sportscaster Dick Stockton. I told him that I felt bad for Gowdy. Stockton was more of a grizzled pro than I was. He said, "Weep not for Curt Gowdy." Gowdy owned radio stations and had other business interests. Stockton insisted Gowdy wasn't hurting for cash. But I thought back to Gowdy's "if only they *let* you broadcast" comment, and I was certain that for all the fame and fortune he had amassed, he would still rather be calling the Baseball Game of the Week.

One of my biggest kicks was hiring Curt to host a Super Bowl special for the CBS-owned TV stations. It was 1981 and I was the producer of the show. I couldn't believe a broadcast legend was working for me. The game was at the Silverdome in Pontiac, Michigan, and a few weeks before, on the day of the taping, we went out for dinner at a seafood restaurant in the Detroit area. Our table was not ready when we arrived, and we were told that it would be a long wait. So Curt just ambled over to the seafood display and started chatting with one of the cooks. As the host of *The American Sportsman,* the long-running outdoor series on ABC, Gowdy was beloved by every fisherman and hunter on earth. The cook recognized Gowdy, and we had our table immediately.

A t the end of my freshman year at Syracuse, after I was named sports director at WAER, I decided to try to get an interview with Howard Cosell. I simply called ABC and asked for him. This was 1965, and Cosell wasn't quite the COSELL he would later become. This was the pre-*Monday Night Foot-*

ball Cosell. He was basically a New York guy on WABC radio and television. I thought he was great, though. In fact, I set my alarm clock radio to wake me with his show. The program aired at 7:25 A.M. and at 8:25 A.M., always beginning with his signature music and then his staccato voice. "This . . . is . . . Howid . . . Co-sell . . . speaking of . . . sports!" I had my alarm clock timed perfectly. The radio would come on and, *presto,* his music would begin.

Cosell was the first sportscaster who really said something. I didn't know if he was right or wrong—but he had opinions, and I liked that. It is said that he would do his radio show without any notes. I'm not sure whether that was true, but supposedly when the former Reds manager Fred Hutchinson died, Cosell went on the air and delivered a five-minute eulogy, totally off the top of his head. It was articulate, captivating. In a million years, I couldn't do that. Cosell loved to say, "Isn't it absolutely amazing what wondrous verbiage flows from my mouth." And it was. I often wondered if he spoke a little too slowly because he was funneling those College Board vocabulary words from his brain down to his mouth.

I used to place an old tape recorder up against my radio when big sporting events were broadcast. No event seemed bigger than the Cassius Clay–Sonny Liston fight on the night of February 25, 1964. Twenty-two-year-old Clay was the prohibitive underdog to heavyweight champion Liston. I still have the tape from that broadcast. Cosell did the blow-by-blow call. Before the fight, he interviewed boxing writer after boxing writer. Excepting one, every writer picked Liston to win. I think some were simply rooting against the cocky young wise guy. Come the seventh round, Liston didn't answer the bell. I remember Cosell screaming, "He's not coming out. . . . Sonny Liston is not coming out." It was bedlam. Cassius Clay was the new heavyweight champ of the world.

The next day, Clay converted to Islam and changed his name to Muhammad Ali. No sports figure in the universe was bigger. All he had to do was walk down the street in Manhattan and a crowd gathered to follow him as if he were the Pied Piper. I first interviewed him in Boston in the early 1970s. The way he would throw around perfect sound bites and poems, he was amazing. "Float like a butterfly, sting like a bee" was just one of hundreds of little rhymes and ditties Ali would toss out—all at a rapid-fire pace. Today, he seems to loom even larger. When he lit the Olympic flame in Atlanta in 1996, his hand shaking from Parkinson's, it was a majestic moment. Greatness had descended from the mountain to ignite the torch. I saw him again in Sydney at the 2000 Games. We were staying at the same hotel. People would stop and silently watch him as he shuffled through the lobby. It was as though he was a religious figure. It is the stuff of tragedy that the man who turned up the volume in modern sports is now barely heard over a whisper.

It was only natural that Cosell and Ali would become foils. The sports world wasn't quite big enough for two big mouths. They verbally sparred, feeding off each other. Each made the other more famous. In 1974, Cosell stated that he doubted Ali could beat George Foreman in their "Rumble in the Jungle" fight in Zaire. Ali responded: "You say I'm not the man I was ten years ago! Your wife said you're not the same man you were two years ago!" Then Ali spun this little rhyme: "That thing you got on your head is a phony/And it came from a pony!" Cosell's hair may or may not have been the real deal (it wasn't), but Ali still was. He knocked out Foreman in the eighth round.

Cosell called *Monday Night Football* games for fourteen years, but he may wind up being remembered most for his coverage of boxing. His most memorable call has nothing to do with his over-the-top linguistic gymnastics. In 1973, George Foreman squared off against the heavyweight champ, Joe Frazier, and Foreman dropped the champ in the second round. Cosell's call was classic: "Down goes Frazier, down goes Frazier, down goes Frazier." He didn't get up. In announcing, as in many things, less is often more.

Anyway, I called WABC and was put through to Cosell. I stammered, "Mr. Cosell, I'd like to come and interview you." He bellowed into the phone: "How old are you, son? Where do you go to school? What high school did you attend? Where do you live?" He immediately put me on the defensive. But that was his way. Cosell always had to have the upper hand, in any situation. He'd be walking into Yankee Stadium and he'd spot pitcher Tommy John with his pregnant wife, Sally. Cosell would call out for everyone to hear, "Sally, tell Tommy I'm really the father of that child." Typical Howard.

He granted my interview request. When I arrived at his office at ABC, frightened as could be, his secretary was hanging a poster promoting an upcoming TV show that Cosell was hosting. He snapped at me, "Hey, help her." So there I was, Mr. Big-Time College Radio Announcer, helping Howard Cosell's secretary hang a poster. Man, did I feel special! For the duration of the interview, pretty much all Cosell did was tell me how important he was. I kind of agreed—after all, of all the sportscasters working in New York City, he was the only one I had called. He went on and on about all the mail he had in his desk from people telling him how great he was, how, despite all the criticism, he was "number one."

At the time, I really didn't know what criticism he was talking about. Years later, after he had pranced onto the national stage, it was clear that people either loved Cosell or hated him. Some of his defenders accused his critics of anti-Semitism. I never really accepted the anti-Semitism theory, though. Cosell could be loud, abrasive, overbearing, opinionated, and boorish. Sure, he was Jewish, too, but if he had been Catholic, Hindu, or Muslim, he would still have been loud, abrasive, overbearing, opinionated, and boorish. During our interview, though, I was stunned that he was going on and on about how great he was. I thought to myself, *This is one weird guy*. I later figured out it was called "insecurity." Despite his accomplishments, Howard Cosell was incredibly insecure. Insecurity really explains everything: why he was so loud, why he flaunted his intelligence, why he always had to be the center of attention, why he was on the air to begin with.

During the interview, I asked him if he thought the Yankees would win the pennant again. They had won the previous four. "I couldn't care less," he bellowed. "I don't care if they win 162 games or lose 162 games. I'm a *journalist*. I DON'T CARE IF THEY WIN OR LOSE!" I was really taken aback. But you know what, it wasn't a bad answer. It's just how he handled it. I also remember him telling me not to go into broadcasting. He thought it was a lousy business. (Maybe he and Gowdy had talked.) I, of course, figured that the real reason he wanted to discourage me from entering the field was that he didn't want the competition. I really thought that. How ridiculous was I at the age of eighteen? When I got home to replay our hour-long interview, I found that my tape was blank. I had plugged the wire into the wrong hole and had recorded nothing for sixty minutes. I was devastated. I've often thought about how much I would like to listen to that interview again.

The next time I met Cosell in person was about fifteen years later at the West Hampton Tennis Club. I was taping an episode for *Sports Fantasy*. Tennis great Arthur Ashe was my guest. He had recently had a heart attack. Cosell walked over to say hello to Ashe. I shook Cosell's hand and introduced myself: "Hi. Len Berman." Cosell looked right through me; he didn't say a word. Nothing. Just turned around and walked away. Well, he had told me not to go into broadcasting! Maybe if I had listened, I wouldn't have been so humiliated by the Great Cosell treating me like dirt. (There's only one other time something like that happened to me. I was at a wedding reception and I spotted Barbara Walters. I introduced myself. She looked at me, didn't say a word, turned around, and walked away. I would think that this must be an ABC-cultivated attitude, except I once had a nice conversation with Ted Koppel, in a men's room of all places. When we finished talking, Koppel said, "Bye, Marv." He thought I was Marv Albert, but I wasn't offended. At least he spoke to me!)

SPANNING THE WORLD
OF BASEBALL FANS

MAY 1998, FENWAY PARK, BOSTON. A fan dangled his girlfriend over the right-field wall to fetch a baseball on the field. Red Sox right fielder Darren Bragg walked over, picked up the ball, and flipped it into the stands. The fan let go of his girlfriend, dropping her to the field, so that he could catch the ball. Priorities!

JULY 31, 1990, COUNTY STADIUM, MILWAUKEE. Nolan Ryan defeated the Brewers 11–3 for his three hundredth career victory. While Ryan was pitching in Milwaukee, thousands of his fans gathered in empty Arlington Stadium in Texas to watch the game on the video scoreboard and cheer him on. Many fans brought their gloves. It would have had to be one hell of a foul ball.

AUGUST 1992, TIGERS STADIUM, DETROIT. A foul ball was hit to the left side, landing in the front row. It was caught by a nun in full habit. She was sitting amid a group of nuns. Moral of the story: when you pray for a foul ball, it always helps to "have connections."

AUGUST 2003, JOSEPH P. RILEY, JR. PARK, CHARLESTON, SOUTH CAROLINA. The minor-league RiverDogs hosted a "Silent Night" promotion at the ballpark. The stands were full, but no one cheered. When a run scored, all you would hear were teammates clapping in the dugout. Charleston broke the record for the "quietest baseball game" set in 1909! (Don't ask me the circumstances of the earlier game.) Silent Night was staged the season after the RiverDogs set the record for smallest attendance: zero. After the game was official in the fifth inning, they had their cherished record, and fans were allowed to go into the stadium. Guess who was the mastermind behind these wacky promotions? It was Mike Veeck, the president of the RiverDogs. His father was Bill Veeck, the original P. T. Barnum of baseball. It was Bill Veeck who had a three-foot seven-inch midget by the name of Eddie Gaedel bat for the St. Louis Browns in a game in 1951. Before the at bat, Veeck reportedly told Gaedel that he had a man in the stands with a high-powered rifle who would shoot if Gaedel swung the bat. Gaedel walked on four pitches.

JUNE 1995, DURHAM BULLS ATHLETIC PARK, DURHAM, NORTH CAROLINA. A brawl erupted during a minor-league game between the Durham Bulls and Winston-Salem. Ten players were ejected. It was "Strike Out Domestic Violence Night" at the ballpark.

JUNE 2001, YANKEE STADIUM, NEW YORK. Yankee Derek Jeter hit a home run. The ball rolled down a runway in the right-field stands. Moments later, cameras showed a fan emerging with the ball. As he waved his arms, holding the ball in triumph, his shirt creeped up, revealing a pistol in a holster on his belt. The fan was packing heat. No one dared try to get that ball away from him!

MAY 2003, CINERGY FIELD, CINCINNATI. Between innings at Reds games, there is a "Kiss-Cam." Camera operators show couples on the scoreboard and they're supposed to kiss. On this night, David Horton kissed his girlfriend on the cheek. Well, it just so happens David's parole officer was at the game and he had been looking for Horton for a parole violation. Police led Romeo away in handcuffs. He was nailed by the Kiss-Cam.

SPRING HAS SPRUNG

MARCH 1997, JACK RUSSELL STADIUM, CLEARWATER, FLORIDA. During a spring training game, the Phillies had a Hooters Girl working as a ballgirl. She was dressed in hot pants and a tight T-shirt promoting the restaurant chain. One of the Phillies hit the ball down the left-field line. The ballgirl picked up the ball and tossed it into the crowd. Small problem: the ball was in play. I'm pretty sure the team has since rethought the idea of using Hooters Girls in official baseball capacities.

In 1979, HBO flew me down to Florida to host a preseason baseball special. Every producer who ever works at spring training thinks he's reinventing the wheel. In truth, it's all the same. The pitcher pretends to cover first on a ground ball to the right side. The shortstop pretends to practice his bunting. And before they can work up a sweat, they hit the buffet table and then the links. For their part, the writers and producers wax poetic about how the game reflects a "simpler time" or "the meaning of life." C'mon already. There's ninety feet between the bases, three outs per inning. That's about it. All the romanticism is basically hooey.

So there I was in 1979 doing what my producer told me. For the opening of the TV special, he had me walking among the Dodgers players as they stretched on the grass at their spring training complex in Vero Beach. I actually said something on camera like, "The rites of spring are like a tonic to this northerner. . . . Blah blah blah." I wanted to gag. A tonic? Yeah, sure, it was better walking around Vero Beach than Jones Beach in the snow. But I'd rather have an egg cream.

◆　　◆　　◆

I've reported from spring training for roughly thirty years. In 1975, I headed down to the Red Sox camp in Winter Haven, Florida. Winter Haven is located in no-man's-land in central Florida, halfway between Tampa and Orlando. In the era before live shots, we were stuck with the old film-shuttle system. We'd shoot our material on film, drive it to the airport, get it on a plane, fly it to Boston, have it driven to the TV station, process it, edit it, and then play it on the air. It sounds like this would take several days, but we were actually able to shoot some material early in the morning and have it ready for the six P.M. news that night.

The first day was always the same. Here's what we'd do. We'd fly from Boston to Tampa and land around midday. We'd then find the palm tree nearest to the terminal, stand in front of it, and do a "stand-up." What scintillating television that turned out to be: "Here we are at spring training. It's like a tonic to this northerner." Then we'd walk back into the terminal and send the film back to Boston where WBZ would proudly air our first wonderful report on television. I once confided in Dick Stockton what we did. He had preceded me at the Boston station. He said he used to do the exact same thing. And I thought I was so original.

Spring training is really just one long "one-joke movie" where the reporter from up north takes advantage of every chance he gets to rave about the beautiful weather in Florida or Arizona while the windchill hovers around minus gazillion back home. One year, while covering the Mets in St. Petersburg, I did a "lie-down" rather than a stand-up. I went to the nearest yacht club, lay down in a hammock on a boat, and spoke about the long hours I was putting in. It was really lame. Stand-ups can be silly, but they are a necessary part of news reporting. They are where the reporters inject them-selves into the story. Why must reporters inject themselves into the story? Largely to prove to the boss and anyone else who cares that the reporter was really on the scene. (The worst stand-up I can remember involved a medical reporter. He was playing a doubles match in tennis. During play, he ran over to the camera and in hushed tones said, "I'm playing tennis with a lady who has cancer." Then he ran back onto the court and continued the game. I was hoping his partner would then run over to the camera and say in an equally somber mood, "I'm playing tennis with an asshole who thinks he's a medical reporter.")

Anyway, in Winter Haven, the Red Sox headquarters was the Holiday Inn. In addition to the media, some of the players stayed there. I always got a kick out of watching reporters' chil-dren playing out back with Carl Yastrzemski's kids. You'd never see that today. The coolest moments in Winter Haven, though, were when Ted Williams would show up. Talk about some-body being bigger than life. Talk about charisma. Williams was captivating. Everyone—the players and the media—would just gather around him and listen to him spin tales of hitting. He'd turn to a rookie and say, "Two-and-one count, runner on first: what are you thinking?" Great stuff. His famous line was "The hardest thing in the world is to hit a round ball with a round bat square." Williams did it better than anybody. I remember him telling one player that if you're expecting a certain pitch, you get it, and you still strike out, then "you have to tip your cap to the pitcher." He used those exact words. Listening to him say this, my mind wandered to the stories about how Williams didn't get along with the media and the fans, about how he would never, ever tip his cap. Finally, at the 1999 All-Star Game at Fenway Park, Williams tipped his cap. He threw out the ceremonial first pitch and then acknowledged his adoring fans—which included a number of current All-Stars. It was a welcome gesture, albeit forty years too late.

W hen the superstars return to spring training, it's like royalty coming on the scene. Once a year, Dodgers great Sandy Koufax visits the Mets in Port St. Lucie. That's the name of the town in south-central Florida. Pitcher Ron Darling used to call it "Port St. Lonesome" because there ain't much there. Rickey Henderson once called it "St. Port Lucie." It's surprising Henderson got that much of the name right. The story about Henderson was that he was always playing cards. Somebody once asked him if he knew whom he was playing with. He said, "Sure, him, him, and him." That was Rickey. He didn't know anyone's name except his own, which he always used in the third person. "Rickey is happy to be here in St. Port Lucie." You need subtitles when he speaks.

With Koufax, though, subtitles are wholly unnecessary. He so rarely speaks with the media. That's his way: shy, quiet, doesn't want to draw attention to himself. I would almost feel honored when he would walk over to me, shake my hand, and just say hello. He doesn't do that with everyone. A couple of years ago, he was watching Mets pitchers on one of the practice fields when the fans got wind of his presence. They descended on him like locusts. Rock stars don't get this kind of treatment. He was sitting in a golf cart with his boyhood buddy Fred Wilpon, who owns the Mets. They gave up trying to move. More than thirty years after he retired, Koufax was engulfed by his fans.

The active players and managers aren't nearly as interesting during spring training. The only time I saw an active player treated like royalty was in Jupiter, Florida, in February 1999. It seemed like every camera in the world showed up to watch Mark McGwire take batting practice for the Cardinals. The previous season he had shattered Roger Maris's home run record. I never claimed to have any originality, so I showed up as well. McGwire held one of the biggest spring training news conferences that I've ever seen. Everyone jammed in to hear what he had to say moments before stepping into the batting cage. McGwire said he had never seen a spring training like this, ever. I couldn't have agreed more. He also said that he would be willing to talk about the previous year's home run record until the end of spring training, and then no more. The statute of limitations on discussing his seventy homers ran short. When he started hitting, I remember counting the number of balls that went over the fence, as if it were a predictor of the upcoming season.

Ten years earlier, on Mets Picture Day in Port St. Lucie, all hell broke loose. That day in 1989, it was more like "Port St. Lunacy." The Mets were a rowdy bunch of superstars. They had won the World Series three years earlier and they might have won it again in 1988 if they hadn't flamed out against the Dodgers in the playoffs. When they were posing for the picture, Darryl Strawberry said to Keith Hernandez something like, "I've been tired of your crap for years." There recently had been some anonymous quotes critical of Strawberry in newspaper articles, and Strawberry assumed that Hernandez was "Mr. Anonymous." Let the fun begin. Fists started flying. Strawberry punched Hernandez, and the two were restrained by teammates before any serious damage was done. This was Picture Day, for goodness' sake, when the teammates were supposed to smile and pose and pretend they might actually care for one another. All hell broke loose in our newsroom at WNBC that day as well. We didn't have a camera crew in Port St. Lucie so we had to scramble for footage of the fight. We finally tracked it down with just minutes to spare from a local Florida station. We averted a television disaster. You can't go on the air with some sort of pompous "Isn't this a shame" commentary, if you don't have the goods to prove it.

In 2003, I thought there might be blows once again in Port St. Lucie. My cameraman and I were taping Jeromy Burnitz in the batting cage when he swung and missed three straight pitches. Burnitz was a guy who struck out a lot, but no one whiffs during batting practice. Batting practice pitchers groove their pitches so that players have no trouble making contact. I thought I'd have some fun and ask Burnitz about his strikeout. Burnitz didn't think it was funny at all, and he stalked off right in the middle of our interview. It made for some slightly riveting television back in New York. (Truthfully, it was better than Mets manager Art Howe saying, "Yup, we're much improved this year," which of course the Mets really were not.) I later went over to Burnitz and explained that I was just trying to have some fun, pulling out my best Valentine Reid soft-shoe business to save my ass. Burnitz seemed satisfied.

In 1989, at Yankee camp in Fort Lauderdale, my producer suggested that I interview a young kid who wanted to play both baseball and football. I begrudgingly sat down next to this skinny guy named Deion Sanders. I went right for the jugular. I asked him which sport he liked better, baseball or football.

He said that he thought baseball was "metal." At least that's what I thought he said. So I asked him to repeat it, and he said, "Baseball is more metal." I didn't have a clue what he meant. I actually wondered if he was talking about metal bats, which aren't allowed in the majors. It wasn't until I got back to New York and replayed the tape that I figured out he was saying, "Baseball is more mellow." Who would have possibly guessed that this soft-spoken kid who was mumbling in the dugout would turn out to be a television personality?

Fast-forward to Yankee spring training in 2004. The Yanks had long since moved to Tampa, and Alex Rodriguez had just signed with the team. It was a marriage made in baseball heaven. Rodriguez, the most expensive player in sports history, had signed with the sport's biggest spenders. Before spring training began, the Yankees allowed each television station a few minutes of one-on-one with A-Rod. I went right for the jugular again. The HBO show *Sex and the City* had just wrapped and much was being made about the characters' fashion accessories. So I asked A-Rod how many pairs of Manolo Blahnik shoes his wife had. He had no idea what I was talking about. He is a smooth, well-rehearsed interview subject. I think this may have been the only time he was ever stumped by an interviewer. I had gotten him. Aha! It was a regular *60 Minutes* moment! It also shows you how seriously I take spring training.

Occasionally, though, all the spring training blather becomes serious. The day all the players were scheduled to arrive in 2004, Jason Giambi, the Yankee slugger, walked into the locker room. He was immediately surrounded by newspaper reporters. (Cameras aren't permitted in the Yankees' clubhouse.) Giambi shook hands with all the newspaper guys. It seemed like a peace offering, because everyone knew the questions were about to get nasty. During the off-season, Giambi had testified before a grand jury in the BALCO case. BALCO is the San Franciso–area company that was indicted for the distribution of steroids. Giambi had admitted to having contact with BALCO. He said he was interested in "vitamins, supplements, stuff like that." For one thing, he looked noticeably thinner. The bulk was gone. Was it because he was now off the juice? He said no. He said he had only lost a couple of pounds by not eating as much junk food. Joel Sherman of the *New York Post* asked Giambi directly, "Have you taken performance-enhancing drugs?" Giambi paused, then answered, "You mean steroids?" Sherman said, "Yes." "No," Giambi said. I thought it was a telling exchange. Did Giambi take other illegal stuff? If it wasn't steroids, was it human growth hormone? Was he interested in discussing this further? No.

An hour later, in the Yankees' dugout, Giambi was surrounded by television cameras. You could tell he was uncomfortable. When the questions were about baseball, about a big home run that he hit, Giambi could be quite animated and expansive. Ask him about steroids, though, which I did repeatedly during this interview, and he clammed up. Giambi's response stuck with me. I thought about it often, particularly as he suffered through a season full of injuries and ailments. He had a parasite. He had a benign tumor. Were they somehow the result of something he had illegally taken? I wondered. I wasn't alone. The questions dogged him throughout the season. And each time they were posed, he dismissed them as ridiculous. But were they? I thought then, *Welcome to the 2004 baseball season, where every home run will lead fans to ask, "Do you think he's on something? . . . Was he ever on anything? . . . When did he quit?"* It was going to be a season of whispers. And during the off-season, the chorus became deafening. The *San Francisco Chronicle* reported his grand jury testimony as well. Despite what Giambi told Joel Sherman and the rest of us, he reportedly told the grand jury that he took all sorts of steroids and human growth hormone. I have him saying on camera that he didn't take anything. Apparently he was lying. Who will ever be able to hear the name Jason Giambi again and not think *Cheater!*

Giambi was hardly the only elite athlete implicated in the BALCO scandal. Barry Bonds, Gary Sheffield, and track star Marion Jones, among others, were also linked to the company. Bonds had another superb season, and Sheffield came up big in his first season with the Yankees. But for Giambi and Jones, who finished fifth in the Olympic long jump and botched a handoff in the 400-meter relay, 2004 was a lost year. Sheffield (according to *Sports Illustrated*) actually admitted to having used an illegal steroid cream on his surgically repaired knee in 2002, but he said that he didn't know the cream was illegal at the time. Major League Baseball essentially said, "No harm, no foul," the action was outside the "statute of limitations." Sheffield later disavowed the *Sports Illustrated* story. Same holds true for Giambi. None of what he did could be punished by Major League Baseball retroactively. Bonds, too, but of course *he didn't know that what he was taking was illegal.*

Between Giambi's leaked testimony and a tell-all steroids book written by former Giambi teammate José Canseco, 2005 threatened to dwarf 2004 on the fans skepticism-meter. Perhaps a new, tougher steroid policy that players and owners agree to would be a step in the right direction to help clean up this mess.

Like most kids, I had gotten interested in sports because of the joy of the game. But as a professional I have found myself spending more time reporting on drugs, lockouts, and court proceedings. Oh, how it makes me yearn for the simpler days, days spent meandering around the green grass of a spring training field in sun-drenched Florida. It would be like a tonic to this northerner, blah blah blah blah blah.

10

YAN-KEES SUCK!

APRIL 2004, BROWN STA- DIUM, BATTLE CREEK, MICHI- GAN. The Battle Creek Yankees weren't exactly setting attendance records. So, for a game against Fort Wayne, every fan was admitted for free and given a dollar at the gate. Attendance zoomed! Six hundred sixty fans showed up—an increase of 145 from the night before! Of course, it was a team named the Yankees that was throwing around money.

In 2002, the New England Patriots pulled off a major Super Bowl upset. They defeated the defending champion St. Louis Rams 20–17 on Adam Vinatieri's forty-eight-yard field goal as time ran out. The game was played in New Orleans. The next day, after returning home to Boston, the Pats staged a victory celebration for their fans. So what did these diehard football fans cheer? In unison, they chanted, "Yan-kees suck!"

I liked that. As ridiculous as it seemed at a football rally, this cheer wasn't at all out of place. Boston is a wonderful sports town and has had more than its share of sporting success: sixteen Celtics championships; a couple of Bruins Stanley Cup championships in the 1970s; the Patriots, once the laughingstock of football, winning two Super Bowls, then setting a record for consecutive victories, and topping it off with a third Super Bowl victory in four years. But it's the Red Sox–Yankees rivalry that really gets Bostonians going. Actually not just Bostonians. The Red Sox are a six-state team; baseball fans from Maine, Massachusetts, New Hampshire,

Rhode Island, Vermont, and part of Connecticut live and die with the fortunes of their beloved Red Sox. A lot more dying, as I've already mentioned.

Although I grew up a Yankees fan, working in the media has forced me to stop rooting for teams. I know a lot of hometown sportscasters would disagree, but I really believe that the only way I can do my job well is to be objective. Many sports fans will never understand this. They think, once you're a fan, you're a fan for life. But I ceased being a fan of any uniform long ago. Sure, I was a Mickey Mantle fan, but that doesn't necessarily qualify me as a Mickey Rivers fan. Individual athletes have earned my adoration, but not teams. For example, I'm a Don Mattingly fan. I loved the way he carried himself on and off the field. You never heard of a single negative incident involving Mattingly. Class all the way, and I root for a guy like that. Another one? Celtics star John Havlicek. Knicks fans would accuse me of rooting for the enemy. But the day Havlicek retired from his remarkable NBA career in 1978, he gave out gifts to those around him. He gave *me* a pocketwatch! It has engraved on the inside, "Time for a Friend." Enough said.

That I don't root for teams doesn't mean I don't root for stories—and for as long as I've worked in broadcasting, the Yankees–Red Sox rivalry has been one of my favorites. It is a glorious rivalry and ridiculously one-sided. Having worked as a sportscaster in both Boston in the mid and late 1970s and in New York through the 1990s and into this century, I've come to appreciate it from both sides. For many people, the story begins with Red Sox owner Harry Frazee. The Sox won the World Series in 1918. The star of the team was Babe Ruth. A year later, though, Frazee sold Ruth to the Yankees. Since then the Red Sox have played in five World Series. They lost four of them in the seventh game, before sweeping the Cardinals for the 2004 title. They were also in two one-game playoffs in 1948 and 1978 and lost both of those. The official scorecard since 1918 reads:

Red Sox   1 World Championship
Yankees   26 World Championships

A bit one-sided, no? For me, though, the story really begins with another owner: Yankees boss George Steinbrenner. Managers, players, announcers—they've all come and gone. But since I started working in Boston, Steinbrenner has been the one constant.

⦿ ⚈ ⚾

Sometimes it seems that everything the Yankees do is determined in relation to the Red Sox. And since 1973 pretty much everything the Yankees have done—off the field—has been determined by Steinbrenner. When Boston was ready to snare center fielder Bernie Williams as a free agent in 1999, Steinbrenner couldn't and wouldn't let it happen. When José Canseco was placed on waivers in 2000, the Yankees signed him. Manager Joe Torre was mystified; the team certainly didn't need Canseco—not his bat or his sideshow. The best explanation was that Steinbrenner didn't want Boston to get him. When the Yankees signed Cuban pitcher José Contreras on Christmas Eve, 2002, they dramatically overpaid. Why? Boston was after him. That's when Red Sox president Larry Lucchino coined the phrase "evil empire" to describe the Yankees. The Red Sox may be cursed, but at least they are not evil.

I don't love everything about Steinbrenner, but I can't quibble with his success as owner of the Yankees. The first time I walked into his office, his desk was basically clear except for a small sign that read: LEAD, FOLLOW OR GET THE HELL OUT OF THE WAY. I like that. Steinbrenner was an unknown shipbuilder in 1973 when he cobbled together a group of investors to plunk down $10 million for the hallowed New York Yankees franchise. Steinbrenner now says the real number was about $8.8 million. In 2004, when $8.8 million wouldn't even buy a first-tier shortstop, *Forbes* magazine estimated that the Yankees were worth $832 million. Not a bad return. What's more, George didn't even put down the whole $8.8 million. He may have put down a hundred thousand dollars of his own money. He had a group of limited partners who invested the rest. It's said, however, that nothing is as limited as being a limited partner to George Steinbrenner. Steinbrenner is simply The Boss.

Donald Trump has tried to patent the phrase "You're fired." Well, Steinbrenner invented it. He's been known to fire and rehire employees in the blink of an eye—and not just Billy Martin, who managed the Yankees five different times. The Martin stuff was just wacky. He and Reggie Jackson nearly came to blows on national TV during a 1977 Yankees–Red Sox game. Martin didn't think Jackson had hustled after a fly ball, so he pulled him out of the game—right in the middle of the inning. One time Martin said of Jackson and Steinbrenner, "One's a born liar, the other's convicted." He was referring to Steinbrenner's 1974 conviction for illegal campaign contributions. Not a good way to butter up your boss. That accounted for one of Martin's firings. Another time, Martin punched out a marshmallow salesman. You can't make this stuff up.

Steinbrenner's office in Tampa, where the Yankees play during spring training, overlooks the field. Word has it that he will almost fully close the window drapes, squat on his knees, and peer down at his players through the opening with binoculars. There have been coaches in the clubhouse who have been thought to be "George's guys," people who let him know what's really going on down there. Don Zimmer was not one of them. "Popeye" served as the Yankees' bench coach in 1983 and 1986 and from 1996 through 2003. Eventually, the carping and criticism from Steinbrenner got to be too much. Like the real Popeye, Zimmer finally said, "That's all I can stand, I can't stands no more." It's a shame. Zimmer is a *great* baseball man, and the Yankees are poorer for not having Popeye in their dugout. You won't find a more honest person in baseball. Zim tells it like it is and damn everyone else. I remember talking with him about a former Red Sox owner who fired him. Zimmer let loose such a torrent of expletives, and he didn't care if he was quoted or not. So when he says he'll never return to the Yankees under George Steinbrenner, that's exactly what he means.

I recently asked Zimmer what he would do if Steinbrenner called him and offered him a job. Zimmer said, "I'd hang up."

Steinbrenner's employees keep an equally close eye on him. I remember standing outside Steinbrenner's office a few years ago in the Bronx. When George headed toward the elevator, the woman sitting at the desk outside his office picked up her phone, hastily dialed someone, and whispered, "He's on his way." I'm convinced Yankees employees keep track of Steinbrenner more closely than the Secret Service watches the president. In Tampa, George exits the stadium down the left-field line and heads toward his car. After he drives away, count to twenty. The coast is clear and it's quittin' time. The employees come scurrying out of the stadium. No one dares to leave before The Boss.

The truth is, when you cover the Yankees as a member of the media, you also have to know where Steinbrenner is at all times. If a competitor gets a juicy quote or if Steinbrenner rips a player and you don't have the video, you're in big trouble back at the station. So everywhere anyone walks in Yankee-land, George's presence is felt. One time, hours before a game, I was sitting in the box seats behind the dugout. Nobody else was there. A Yankees employee came and told me I wasn't allowed to sit there. There were no fans in the stadium, and I was behaving myself. Yet, I was evicted. I didn't have to ask why. The Boss didn't like it.

The thing about Steinbrenner is that the man just can't stand to lose. During Game Seven of the American League Championship Series against Boston in 2003, he was sitting in the owner's box at the start of the game. When Boston took a 4–1 lead in the fourth inning, though, he disappeared. No one knows where Steinbrenner goes when the Yankees are losing. I don't think anybody wants to know. But when the Yanks came back and eventually won the game, George was in his box leading the cheers.

For better or worse, Steinbrenner appeared to have mellowed in 2004. During the Yankees' Game Seven calamity against Boston, he stayed in his seat the entire time. Actor Billy Crystal and newsman Mike Wallace were among his guests. When the game ended, and Boston had won 10–3, George was on the verge of tears. He said, "I'll be damned! I can't believe it happened." But surprisingly enough, his first response wasn't to fire anybody, not even General Manager Brian Cashman. Cashman "can't hit or pitch," Steinbrenner allowed. One thing that Steinbrenner might have regretted, though, was not trading for Arizona's Randy Johnson in late July when he had the chance. During the previous off-season, Boston had traded for Johnson's teammate Curt Schilling. According to insiders, the Yanks could have acquired Johnson for catcher Jorge Posada and left-handed pitcher Brad Halsey, but the word was that Steinbrenner wouldn't part with Posada. After watching Posada drive in just two runs in the seven-game series, though,

Steinbrenner would probably trade him in a heartbeat if he could do it all over again. If he had Randy Johnson starting Game Seven, rather than Kevin Brown, who knows, he might not have been in tears when it was over. Three months later the Yankees acquired Johnson. It was three months too late.

I don't think I've criticized another sports figure on the air more than I've criticized Steinbrenner. He used to bellyache about what a rotten place the South Bronx was. About how nobody would come to Yankees games. About how he needed a new stadium—one in a nicer neighborhood, with more luxury boxes and better parking. Then his Yanks won a few World Series and set attendance records. Suddenly the South Bronx wasn't such a bad place. I did an on-air commentary when the Yankees didn't try very hard to sign pitcher Andy Pettitte after the 2003 season. Pettitte, who had won twenty-one games for the Yanks in 2003 and was a clutch postseason pitcher, left to play for Houston. I spoke about how everyone loves to talk about Pinstripe pride and tradition, but the only tradition the Yankees have is raising ticket prices, which they had just done, and frittering away a great pitcher like Pettitte. Pettitte was a homegrown Yankee, a big-time winner and class act. He was a true Yankee, through and through, and I felt the Boss had let Yankees fans down by not aggressively trying to keep him.

Steinbrenner's frequent press releases also make him an easy target. The releases often refer to generals such as Douglas MacArthur and use motivational clichés such as "Winners never quit." Before the 2004 playoffs, he issued the following enlightening statement: "I'm just hopeful—hopeful that the pitching is okay and that we are playing championship baseball.

I am hopeful for New York and I want to give New York a championship." That was a lot of hopeful for a two-sentence press release. I read the statement on the air and remarked that Steinbrenner had set a record (three hopefuls). At times, he acts like a caricature of himself.

To his credit, though, through all the years, Steinbrenner has never said a word to me about my critiques. He hinted at it, just once. During a rambling give-and-take interview with reporters in Tampa before the 2004 season, he was boasting about all the people he knew. So I asked, "Who don't you know?" To my surprise, he said, "You—sometimes." I know he's watching what I say about him. In his Tampa home, he's rumored to have several television sets wired so that he can watch the local New York stations. He also has people cut out every newspaper article mentioning the Yankees—from any paper, anywhere. He knows exactly what is said about him.

I can't imagine what it will be like some day to walk into Yankee Stadium after Steinbrenner is no longer running the team. There will come a day when he isn't master and commander, but he's not ready to abandon ship just yet. During spring training a couple of years ago, he said to me, "People ask for my autograph, waiting for me to die." Then he laughed. You may not want to follow Steinbrenner. But you definitely want to get the hell out of his way.

In the early 1990s, the Hayden Planetarium in New York City was producing a video show. The premise was a solar-aided wind race through the universe. I was asked to announce the race as though it were occurring in the year 2050. They put makeup on me to make me look old and then we went to work. I ad-libbed my first line: "Welcome to the year 2050. The Red Sox and Cubs still haven't won the World Series!" To my surprise, the Planetarium liked the line enough and kept it in the video.

They could finally burn that tape in 2004. Of course, the Planetarium might have also had the matches and gasoline out in 2003. Both the Cubs and Red Sox were five outs away from the World Series that October, and each had three-run leads in the seventh inning of the deciding game. You know the rest. Neither wound up in the Fall Classic. Through 2003, luck had been so sorry for these two teams that there were those who firmly believed that if the Cubs and Red Sox would ever meet in a World Series, neither team would win!

I worked in Boston long enough to really understand the pain some Red Sox fans felt prior to the team's 2004 triumph. I was crouching in the stands at Fenway Park during the ninth inning of Game Seven of the 1975 World Series. Both the Reds–Red Sox series and Game Seven were tied at three. I was waiting to jump out onto the field to conduct celebratory interviews should the Red Sox win it. They were on the verge of their first World Series championship since 1918. My stomach was churning, and I've rarely had that feeling in sports. I could only imagine what born-and-bred New Englanders were feeling. Of course what happened is history. Red Sox manager Darrell Johnson brought in rookie Jim Burton to pitch to Joe Morgan. Morgan got a hit, scoring Ken Griffey, and the Sox couldn't come back in the bottom half of the inning. The final score of the game and World Series was Reds four, Red Sox three. As for Burton, he pitched in exactly one more major-league game in his career. Those are the twists and turns that destroy Red Sox players and fans.

After the game, I went into the Red Sox clubhouse for post-mortem interviews. I'll never forget Carl Yastrzemski saying, with tears in his eyes, "I can't wait for spring training to start." That World Series was as close as the Red Sox got to the promised land while I was working in Boston. (By the way, no one referred to the Curse of the Bambino at that time. That moniker didn't come along until years later when Dan Shaughnessy, the fine *Boston Globe* sportswriter, wrote a book with that title.) My last broadcast was Friday, June 16, 1978. After the late news, I would tape a minisportscast that would run during the *Tonight Show.* I remember that Tom Seaver pitched a no-hitter that night for the Reds in Cincinnati. I also remember my very last words to air on local Boston television: "I've left you with a seven-game lead [over the Yankees]. Don't blow it!" Of course they did. In a one-game playoff. Bucky *Fucking* Dent!

The pain for Red Sox fans just kept on coming. During the 2003 ALCS playoffs, the Red Sox again lost in Game Seven. This time it was the Yankees' Aaron Boone who finished them off with a home run. This series was downright wacky. In Game Three, the seventy-two-year-old Zim rushed out of the Yankees' dugout to fight Red Sox ace Pedro Martinez. Zim didn't fare so well. There was also a fight in the Red Sox's bullpen involving a couple of Yankees, Jeff Nelson and Karim Garcia, and a part-time groundskeeper. It was nuts. But this is a story about Red Sox pain—and neither Zimmer nor the tag team of Nelson and Garcia inflicted much of that. I guess it's fitting that they're the *Red* Sox. This sort of pain runs through the generations, coursing though the blood of New Englanders.

My press seat for Game Four was located in fair territory down the right-field line at Fenway. I was surrounded by fans, nearly every one of them wearing a Red Sox cap, shirt, or jacket. There were fathers sitting with sons, and grandfathers sitting with sons and grandsons. I thought about how not a single person in that stadium had ever witnessed a Red Sox championship. New Yorkers are truly spoiled. Not only had the Yankees won twenty-six World Championships since acquiring Ruth, but even the New York Mets, who didn't even exist prior to 1962, had won two Championships—one of them a seven-game series in 1986 against the Red Sox. The Mets, for goodness' sake!

I'm convinced that what you think of yourself as a person, your self-worth, may very well be shaped by the success, or lack of success, of your favorite team. My team, the Yankees, always won. I had to feel good! What I found during my years in Boston, though, stunned me. So often when people spoke— prominent professionals in law, medicine, finance—they'd say, "Sure Boston is great, but it's not New York." In many ways, I thought Boston was better! Better hospitals, better schools. The city doesn't have to take a backseat to any, yet I sensed a New England–wide inferiority complex. In my analysis, of course, it was all because of baseball. New Englanders expect their Red Sox to fail, and therefore they are certainly disappointed, but never surprised, when they do. Year after year. It could make anyone feel second-rate.

🏈   🎾   🏀

After the 2003 season, the Yankees traded for Alex Rodriguez, the Texas Rangers' All-World shortstop. The Yankees already had Derek Jeter. They didn't need a shortstop, especially not one carrying a $252 million contract. But that has never stopped Steinbrenner. The acquisition was all the sweeter, of course, because it came on the heels of Boston's much-publicized failure to close a deal for A-Rod. At the start of spring training, Matt Lauer, one of the hosts of NBC's *Today* show, interviewed Rodriguez. He asked him if he was ready to hear Boston fans yelling "Yan-kees suck!" Rodriguez responded that he expected the fans to be more specific when he made his Fenway Park debut in pinstripes. He expected to hear, "A-Rod sucks." (I filed this interview away in my memory bank, in part because it made me feel a little old. I can remember a time when "sucks" was not appropriate for television, much less a national morning show.) I was at Fenway in April 2004 when Rodriguez came to the plate for the first time there as a Yankee. He was wrong; the crowd didn't chant "A-Rod sucks." Instead the fans stood and booed. I had never before seen a standing boo. It wouldn't be the last I'd see this season, though.

Before his Fenway Park Yankees debut, Rodriguez spoke with reporters in the dugout. I asked him if he thought too much was being made of "this Yankees–Red Sox thing." He said no, that the rivalry tells you how healthy the game is, how much people love the game of baseball. He thinks the Yankees–Red Sox rivalry epitomizes what makes the game so special. Boston won that night. In fact, the Red Sox won three of the four games in that series. But it was April. *The Red Sox always win when it doesn't count,* I thought. How cruel the baseball gods are to these New Englanders!

W*ere* to these New Englanders, that is. In spite of New York's acquisition of A-Rod, the Red Sox beat the Yankees in the American League Championship Series. It was an astounding reversal of the cosmic order. HELL FREEZES OVER! read the back page headline of one of New York's tabloids. Curt Schilling, Boston's ace, took the mound in Game One at Yankee Stadium. Schilling had come to Boston specifically to take the Red Sox to the World Series. Pitching on a bad ankle, he failed miserably and the Yanks won the game 10–7. Schilling had ligament damage and would need surgery after the season. The series appeared destined to be a rout. Especially when the Yankees beat Pedro Martinez in Game Two.

A month earlier, at Fenway Park, the Yankees had beaten Martinez. In fact, the Yankees have fared rather well against the future Hall of Famer. When that game ended, Martinez admitted that he just couldn't beat the Yankees, that "the Yankees are my daddy." It was a remarkable statement, and it certainly made its way back to New York. As he walked in from the visitor's bullpen at Yankee Stadium prior to Game Two of the ALCS, fifty-six thousand Yankees fans started chanting, "Who's your dad-dy?" T-shirts were made bearing the slogan, and signs popped up throughout the ballpark. That night, the Yankees beat Pedro and the Red Sox again.

I was curious what Martinez would say afterward, if anything. He had blown off reporters before his two previous starts, so there was no telling what he would do now. He showed up and was immediately asked about the "Who's your daddy?" chants. Martinez started to say that he felt honored. Some reporters laughed, but Pedro continued, asking very matter-of-factly, "Why are you laughing before you hear my answer?" He then started to talk about how fifteen years earlier he was sitting under a mango tree in his homeland, the Dominican Republic, and didn't have fifty cents in his pocket for a bus ride. And tonight he was standing on the mound at Yankee Stadium and everybody knew who he was. He felt important. I appreciated his answer. Some reporters made fun of his mango tree reference, but for me it put a lot of stuff in perspective.

It also reminded me of a trip I took in 1985 to the Dominican Republic. I went with a camera crew to report on a remarkable little town for the NBC *Game of the Week* pregame show. The town is San Pedro de Macoris. It has a population of about two hundred thousand and has produced more major-league baseball players, per capita, than any city on earth. Sammy Sosa, Pedro Guerrero, and Alfonso Soriano grew up there. Some people have joked that the city's Spanish name translates to "Land of Many Shortstops," and indeed Alfredo Griffin, Tony Fernandez, and Luis Castillo all call San Pedro de Macoris home. Spend five minutes in the town and you will see why the infielders who come out of there are such slick fielders. They play on a hard dirt and rock infield. For the story, we lined up about twenty kids on the ballfield and went down the line asking each what he wanted to do when he grew up. The manager of the boys' team had coached them to say "doctor" or "lawyer," but every last one of them answered "baseball player." It was easy to understand why. In this dirt-poor town, the homes of the major leaguers who lived there looked like fortresses. They were surrounded by high fences with gates. I can only imagine what happened down there when Sammy Sosa was making his home run charge in 1998. Any kid who was even thinking about becoming an accountant must have picked up his glove and headed for the dirt and rock infield.

The hotel we stayed at was in Santo Domingo. If you bought a Coke at the hotel, it cost $2. Out in the countryside, you could buy a couple of six-packs for the same price. As we walked down the street, we were always followed. People would walk behind us for several blocks serenading us with music until we gave them money. One of the NBC producers finally broke down and bought a six-foot-tall bamboo floor lamp from a salesman. He was very proud of the purchase until he got home and realized there was no on-off switch. I thought of this when Pedro Martinez—who comes from Manoguayabo— spoke about not having fifty cents in his pocket. He made $17.5 million in 2004. Fifty-six thousand fans thought they were rattling him as they hooted it up with their daddy stuff, but Martinez, even in defeat, was the one having the last laugh.

Last laugh or not, down two games, it seemed certain the Red Sox were dead and gone when the scene shifted to Boston for Game Three. And if you didn't believe it after Game Two, by the time Game Three ended you certainly did. The Yankees won that game by the astounding score of 19–8. The following night, with the Yankees going for the sweep, Yankees closer Mariano Rivera came in to seal the deal. The Yankees led by one run, and the Red Sox were down to their final three outs. Rivera is the most successful relief pitcher in postseason history. Yet somehow Boston rallied. The Red Sox tied the game in the bottom of the ninth on a Bill Mueller base hit, forcing extra innings. They won in the twelfth inning on a two-run homer by David Ortiz. Game Five was almost a replay. This time the Yankees' bullpen blew a two-run lead when the Red Sox had just six outs left. The Sox won this one in fourteen innings. Again, it was Ortiz with the winning hit, a single. The game took nearly six hours to play.

Down three games to two, the Red Sox returned to Yankee Stadium with one foot in the grave—literally. In Game Six, they turned again to Curt Schilling. His ankle had to be stabilized, so doctors devised a unique medical procedure. They couldn't test it out on Schilling, though, so they first practiced on a cadaver. Doctors stitched up the dead guy's ankle and it didn't seem to bother him any, so they did the same to Schilling. It worked. Schilling pitched a gem. The game may well be remembered, though, for two controversial calls. In the fourth inning, Boston's Mark Bellhorn hit a home run to left. The left-field umpire blew the call, though. The ball bounced off the chest of a fan and back onto the field, and the ump ruled that the ball was in play. The umpires conferenced and reversed the call, getting it right. Then in the eighth inning,

Alex Rodriguez hit a little ground ball to pitcher Bronson Arroyo. Arroyo went to tag Rodriguez, and A-Rod slapped the ball out of his glove. Derek Jeter came all the way from first to score. The umpires huddled again and ruled Rodriguez out, moving Jeter back to first. The rules state that you cannot slap a fielder's glove. You can slide into a second baseman to break up a double play or barrel over a catcher racing home from third, but there is no slapping in baseball.

For the first time in over eighty years, it seemed that the breaks were going Boston's way. Some yahoos in the stands at Yankee Stadium threw objects on the field in protest of the Rodriguez call. It got scary for a minute. Baseball has a policy that teams can't show controversial plays on a stadium scoreboard. If this replay had been shown, though, the fans would have understood. It was clearly the right call, and everyone watching on television saw that it was. But, without a replay, it was not clear to the 56,128 fans at Yankee Stadium. (I ran into umpire Joe West the following evening and suggested that showing the replay on the stadium screen would have helped. He didn't agree. He explained, "If you show the ones we get right, then if you don't show a replay, the fans will think we got it wrong.")

Boston ended up winning Game Six 4–2, thereby becoming the first baseball team to trail 3–0 in the playoffs and force a seventh game. Before Game Seven, I ran into Billy Crystal. He's the number one Yankees fan—and even has me beat in Mickey Mantle adoration. The game was played on October 20. It would have been Mantle's seventy-third birthday. Game Seven on the birthday of number 7. My lucky number. I took all this to be a good omen for the Yankees. It wasn't. They were crushed 10–3. Their starting pitcher, Kevin Brown—another high-priced off-season acquisition—didn't make it through the second inning. He received a standing ovation when he went out to warm up before the game, and received a standing boo when he walked off the mound in the second inning. It reminded me of A-Rod's Fenway greeting. The season had come full cycle. Javier Vasquez—still another expensive pickup—came in to relieve. I was sitting next to Tom Keegan, a former sportswriter turned radio host, in the right-field press seats. He said to me, "Vasquez gives up a lot of homers." First pitch to Red Sox leadoff man Johnny Damon: ball game. A grand slam.

Later in the game, I ran into comedic actor Bill Murray in the press bathroom. We first commiserated over the loss of Rodney Dangerfield, who had died the previous month. Then I told Murray that with Boston leading the game by seven runs, it would only make it more painful for Red Sox fans when they inevitably lost. Murray laughed. He was probably being polite. But I was tickled that maybe I had said something that he thought was funny.

After the game, Rodriguez told reporters, "I was horseshit." He was not alone. Gary Sheffield—another 2004 acquisition—came up in the sixth inning and swung out of his shoes. The Yanks were trailing 8–1 at that point. Sheffield apparently was trying to hit a seven-run homer!

Much of the postseries analysis centered on the fact that the Yankees lacked chemistry. The feeling was that the Yanks were a bunch of corporate stars, but the Red Sox were a gritty, down-and-dirty team. It made a lot of sense, but the fact is that if Rivera had recorded three outs in the ninth inning of Game Four, this discussion wouldn't be taking place. Nobody talked about the detrimental Yankees star system when New York was dominating the Red Sox three games to none.

The story ends with the Red Sox sweeping the St. Louis Cardinals in four games and winning their first World Series championship since 1918. The Cardinals had won 112 games en route to the Series, but their pitching flamed out and they were overmatched by Boston. There were no seventh-game heroics in this series. The Sox, though, were more than willing to take victory any way they could.

Even in the delirium of their victory, what was on everyone's mind in New England when the Red Sox staged their grand parade? They had just beaten the Cardinals, but of course nobody mentioned St. Louis. Boston catcher Jason Varitek told fans, "Every Red Sox fan from now on can walk into Yankee Stadium with their head high." And during the parade, Manny Ramirez carried a sign that read: JETER IS PLAYING GOLF, THIS IS BETTER. Talk about a one-track mind.

Believe it or not, I've always wanted the Red Sox to win it some year. Their fans deserve it. And yet there is one serious problem that victory brings. What will become of Red Sox fans now that their team is no longer the perennial underdog? For the diehards, their whole lives are predicated upon the failure of the Red Sox. With victory in hand, what do they have to live for now? In truth, though, now that it has happened, I'm a little disappointed that Boston won. It's not because I grew up a Yankees fan, but rather because the Sox spoiled a great punch line, even if the joke was getting a bit stale. When you think about it, maybe New England should remain fixated on the Yankees. Let's see: the score is now 26–1. At the rate of a World Championship every eighty-six years, it'll be another 2,150 years before they draw even—assuming the Yanks never win another World Series. If you're keeping score at home, it'll be the year 4154 when it's all square. I wonder if the Red Sox will have a new Fenway Park by then.

11

ON EDGE

FEBRUARY 1998, VOLLER ATH-LETIC CENTER, ROBERTS WES-LEYAN COLLEGE, ROCHESTER, NEW YORK. Point Park University basketball coach Bob Rager enjoyed a pregame Italian meal. It was loaded with garlic. During the game, Rager and the officials got into all sorts of arguments. At one point, a referee approached Rager, and the coach simply exhaled in his face. The ref called a technical foul, making Rager the only coach to get a technical for breathing!

I'm not the kind of guy who enjoys tiptoeing around people, but as a sportscaster I've had to deal with a number of people who automatically put me on edge. Some of these guys I actually like, but some I can't stand. When he was playing, everyone tiptoed around John McEnroe. It was impossible to know when McEnroe was going to explode. I used to find his outbursts on the tennis court entertaining. Everyone did. Oh sure, sports reporters all said what a baby he was, but he grabbed our attention. And he made tennis fun.

I'll never forget a 1979 U.S Open match between McEnroe and Ilie Nastase. The two of them were nuts, whining and complaining. At various times, Nastase just lay down on the court. It got so bad that one of the best umpires in the game, the late Frank Hammond, had to be replaced in the middle of the match to prevent a near riot. I thought it was hilarious. It really was better than anything the National Hockey League or even the World Wrestling Federation could come up with. Of course I had to go on the air and pooh-pooh the whole deal.

Whether or not they thought he was a bad sportsman, many of the other pros loved John. It was his honesty. Martina Navratilova told me that what she liked about McEnroe was that he was no phony. She said others on the tour were. They'd play up to the crowd or the media. Not John. She loved that about him.

I also saw McEnroe in the 1981 U.S. Open Final. He absolutely embarrassed Bjorn Borg, beating him 4–6, 6–2, 6–4, 6–3. When Borg walked off the court that day, I said to my wife, "Borg is walking out of tennis. He'll never play again." And he didn't, at least not on tour. With his lobs, baseline winners, and drop shots, McEnroe made him look silly. The great Bjorn Borg was rendered a hacker by this scrawny, twenty-two-year-old. What a talent.

But, boy, could he also be a jerk. His on-court persona existed off the court as well. My uncle Joe told me a story about a friend of his who lived in McEnroe's apartment building in New York. The guy ran into McEnroe in the elevator, stuck out his hand, and said, "Hi, I'm Joe Smith" or whatever. McEnroe responded, "So?" Quintessential McEnroe. Brutally honest to a fault. This poor schlep had to sulk off without so much as a handshake, and after the encounter he felt he had to peek into the elevator every time to make sure McEnroe wasn't there.

I know the feeling. During Mac's playing days, the media, me included, was afraid to approach the guy. We all had the sense that if we asked him something he considered dumb, he would explode the same way he did at the chair umpire. Reporters might pretend to be big and tough, but when it comes right down to it, most aren't. I've been in news conferences where there's been a controversial issue and all the reporters are afraid to bring it up. It's all about access. A reporter doesn't want to push an athlete or a team too far out of fear that he won't get an interview next time. You can't really walk up to a right fielder and say, "Your teammates think you're the worst fielder in the history of baseball and you're hurting the team. What's your reaction?"

As much as I didn't care for McEnroe at times, I do think he's probably the greatest tennis announcer ever. His honesty carries over into the broadcast booth. If a player hits a dumb shot, he says it. And his analysis is dead-on. There aren't many former athletes who "tell it like it is." They don't want to offend the stars of today. But despite his skill as an announcer, he wasn't in Athens for the Olympic tennis matches. I asked him why he wasn't going to call those matches. Most broadcasters in his situation would make up a story. It's about commitments, the time, whatever. Not John. He said it was about the money. NBC wouldn't pay him enough. He said he can make more from one special appearance than he would make the entire two weeks of the Olympics. No beating around the bush for Johnny Mac.

          ●   ●   ●

Bill Parcells is another guy who has earned a spot in my "tiptoe" hall of fame. I first met Parcells over twenty years ago. He was then a skinny assistant coach for the New York Giants. When he wants to be, Parcells can be the most charming guy you'll ever meet. I think that's what makes me feel so on edge around him. One minute he's all buddy-buddy, the next he's pitching a hissy fit. In our first encounter, I was doing a TV show with hockey star Phil Esposito. Espo had just retired and I hired him to do a fifteen-minute chat show with sports stars. The program aired on Saturday nights at 11:30 P.M. on WCBS-TV. It went head-to-head with *Saturday Night Live,* but believe it or not we actually had an audience. A sponsor, too. I was paid to produce it, and the show made a little money.

The show was called *SportsPeople,* and that's what Phil and I would do: interview sports people.

It was 1981 and we were interviewing the head coach of the Giants, Ray Perkins. While we were at the Giants' training camp at Pace University in Westchester, Perkins's assistant, the pre-Tuna Parcells, told Esposito to run as hard as he could and take a flying leap at the tackling dummy. Parcells said the dummy would be hard to bring down, which of course was a practical joke. The dummy offered no resistance whatsoever. So Phil tackles the dummy and goes flying head over heels. We all got a good laugh. In truth it wasn't a bad bit for a fifteen-minute local-yokel sports program. (By the way, one time the entire show aired without audio. Would you believe it was the show featuring John McEnroe? We had this great footage of him going nuts at a referee, and the show was mute. The ratings were published two days later, and we had our best numbers of the year. I think people like watching a train wreck. *Saturday Night Live* could have had Steve Martin dancing like King Tut, and viewers chose to watch a John McEnroe interview with no audio on *SportsPeople.*)

In 1983, Parcells was named head coach of the Giants, and I have had numerous occasions to interview him since. He was always funny, insightful, confident, and also rough, edgy, and opinionated. The Giants played Denver in the 1987 Super Bowl. The game was in Pasadena and I was staying at the same hotel as the Giants. One day I walked by the hotel bar and Parcells was just standing there talking with the Giants' public relations director, Ed Croke. I walked over and starting talking with Parcells. That would never happen today. Now you can't get within miles of an informal chat with a Super Bowl coach anytime during the week of the big game. That may be the biggest way sports has changed for reporters: access. When McEnroe played at the U.S. Open you could actually approach

him—if you dared. Today it seems you can't get within a borough of the big stars. Then again, when McEnroe was playing,
the media seeking access was quite a bit smaller. ESPN was just
beginning and there weren't guys from a thousand other cable
stations and variations of News 12 dragging around their cameras and shoving microphones in the athletes' faces.

Parcells has a knack of making everyone in the media think
that he is getting something special from him, a little something. It's his way of establishing allies. Generally, it was good
stuff. After the Giants' 1991 Super Bowl victory over Buffalo,
he said to me, "Power wins!" I had to think about that for a moment. His team had just won Super Bowl XXV because the
Buffalo kicker missed a field goal in the final seconds.
Throughout the game, Buffalo had marched up and down the
field on the Giants' defense. New York certainly didn't look all
that powerful to me. But hey, the great Tuna told me that
"Power wins!" So I'm telling you, just in case someone asks.
You'll know.

In 1988, Parcells came to the WNBC studio to make his
Super Bowl prediction for one of my sportscasts. He told me
the Washington Redskins would easily beat the Denver Broncos in Super Bowl XXII. He was right, of course. Parcells proceeded to remind me of that for years to come. I was working
as the sideline reporter for NBC Sports at a Patriots-Jets game
in 1996. Before the game, Pats owner Bob Kraft stopped by
and gave me a big hello. Just then, Parcells, who was then
coaching the Patriots, walked by. Kraft told his coach that he's
known me for years, and Parcells responded, "Yeah, me, too. I
once gave him a great Super Bowl prediction." Incidentally, I
interviewed Kraft on the telecast, and Bob told me that if Parcells were to coach the following year, it would "definitely be
with the Patriots." The next year, Parcells was coaching the Jets.
That's the way it is in sports. Sportsmen make all kinds of

statements, but who really holds them accountable? Come to think of it, it's kind of like being a weatherman.

After Parcells was named the Jets' coach in 1997, NBC hosted a reception in the Rainbow Room in his honor. Parcells held court with a group of television people. He boasted how he had changed the press parking rules at the Jets' training complex at Hofstra University. Before Parcells, media personnel could park where the players parked. It was actually pretty cool. You might get out of your car right next to Mark Gastineau. You could actually say, "Hi, Mark," and not feel as though you committed some kind of crime. Well, this arrangement didn't sit well with Parcells. He explained to us at the reception how there were now areas where the media couldn't drive their cars. I said something smart-alecky like, "Where? Long Island?" Coach Parcells wasn't amused.

The first Jets game I worked in the Parcells era was opening day in Seattle. It was the weekend that Princess Diana died. The night before the game I'm walking into the hotel with two other NBC people when Parcells walked by. Here was my buddy who goofed with me and Phil Esposito, gave me the great Super Bowl prediction, and confided in me that "Power wins!" That night in Seattle, though, he barely looked at me; he just mumbled, "Hi, fellas." I didn't expect him to ask how my flight from New York was, but I thought it would be nice if he actually acknowledged my existence. I'm sensitive that way, but I was willing to give him the benefit of the doubt. He may have been deep in thought, preparing for the game. Anyway, the next morning at the Kingdome, I was standing outside the Jets' locker room talking with assistant coach Ron Erhardt. It was a couple of hours before game time. I had known Ronnie since he was an assistant in Foxboro way back when I was calling Patriots preseason games. We were chatting away when Parcells poked his head out of the locker room. I thought, *Okay, here comes the "Have a nice flight?" question.* Instead Parcells sticks his arm straight out, points at me, and yells, "You're not allowed to talk to my assistant coaches." New rule: The media couldn't talk with his assistant coaches. I understood the rule. The head coach wanted to speak for his staff. (Byron Scott instituted the same rule when he coached the New Jersey Nets.) The thing is, though, Erhardt and I were most likely talking about the weather, or a movie, or the Lady Di tragedy. We weren't talking about football, and I clearly wasn't learning any state secrets. But that was Parcells. Erhardt apologized to me for "getting me in trouble." I appreciated that, but he really didn't get me in hot water.

If anyone got me in trouble that day, it was me. As a sideline reporter, I was only permitted to speak with the coaches. And that was at halftime. Without a microphone or camera. Makes for great TV, huh? The Jets had a fabulous first half; they were leading Seattle 27–3. I was permitted to walk next to Parcells and ask him a couple of questions as the team returned to the field. It was then that I made the cardinal mistake of anyone who does what I do for a living. I didn't listen to what he said. I was already thinking of my next question. Parcells was telling me how even though they had the big lead they weren't going to sit on the ball for the second half. My follow-up: "Are you going to be aggressive in the second half?" He looked at me and barked, "What did I just say?" At that moment I wanted just one tiny rock to crawl under, but of course on the Kingdome artificial turf I was out of luck. It was not as though I had asked First Lady Mary Lincoln, "Other than that, how was the play?" but it is something I'll never forget. If you're a young broadcaster, put this on your top ten tricks of the trade list: Listen to what your interview subject says. By the way, the Jets went on to win the game 41–3. They practiced what their coach preached, regardless of whether the sideline reporter was paying attention.

I t's no coincidence that Parcells and Bobby Knight are good friends. I imagine that they call each other and brag, "Did you see how I embarrassed that dumb reporter at the news conference?" They're incredible coaches. Hall of Famers both. But, boy, do they have issues. Knight even more so than Parcells.

I've only been around Knight a couple of times. The first time was unforgettable. It was 1979. I was announcing a college basketball game of the week with Tommy Heinsohn on HBO. Marty Glickman had put together a fabulous package of weekday games involving Magic Johnson's Michigan State team, Larry Bird's Indiana State team, Duke, North Carolina, and Indiana. The game at Indiana pitted the Hoosiers against Michigan State. Tommy Heinsohn had a pregame interview arranged with Knight. I got the sense that the people surrounding Knight were afraid to breathe, let alone speak. It was truly like walking on eggshells. You know when someone says something, self-consciously giggles, and then looks at his boss to see if what he said was okay? Multiply that discomfort by one hundred and that's what it was like being around Knight.

We set up in the locker room for the interview. Indiana had been struggling, and Heinsohn's first question to Knight began, "Bobby, it has to be tough going for you thus far this season . . ." Knight stared Heinsohn down and said, "Tommy, it's been a lousy FUCKING year." Now this was 1979. Today, the broadcasters might just bleep out Knight's adjective of choice. But back then, in the pre–*Best Damn Sports Show Period* days, we were all stunned. Somebody yelled, "Cut." Then came that self-conscious giggling from his flunkies. And then Knight said, "Hey, this is cable, isn't it?"

This is just one little isolated incident, but I've always been a big believer in the little things being windows to the big picture. Knight was just trying to keep everyone off balance. A few years later, I was hosting the NBC Sports studio show the day he flung a chair across the court. I called his behavior "unfathomable." The people working behind the scenes chuckled over my choice of words. But all these years later, I still feel the same way. In May 1986, I was shooting a *Sports Fantasy* episode at the Indiana Motor Speedway, the site of the Indy 500. There just happened to be a Bobby Knight roast going on at the track. The audience was in stitches. Knight was taking shot after shot at the media, some of it in very crude terms, and his fans ate it up. Now, of course, this was a roast, but what's the line about the truest things being said in jest?

I've often wondered how people justify Knight's rap sheet. In 1979, he was tried and convicted in Puerto Rico for hitting a policeman at a Pan Am Games practice. He was sentenced to six months in jail, but efforts to extradite him were dropped. *(Anyone can hit a cop once.)* A couple of years later at the Final Four in Philadelphia, Knight was involved in a shoving match with a fan. *(Those fans can be pesky, you know.)* There was the chair-throwing incident in 1985. *(You have to get the referee's attention somehow. Arenas can be awfully noisy.)* In a 1988 TV interview he said, "I think that if rape is inevitable, relax and enjoy it." *(Anyone can say something stupid.)* Through the 1990s, there were a number of incidents involving players, refs, fans, and obscenities. *(Coaching is a tough business, isn't it?)* It all came to a head in 2000 when Knight was investigated for allegedly choking one of his players, Neil Reed, at a practice three years earlier. *(Maybe the player's neck got in the way of Knight's grip?)* This last incident was too much and Indiana had little choice but to fire him. The previous spring the Hoosiers were bounced in the first round of the NCAA tournament. I've wondered if Knight would have been axed had they won the national championship that year. Of course, one school's problem is another's reclamation project. So Texas Tech University hired him in 2001. Three years later, Knight got into a shouting match at a grocery story with the chancellor of the university. He was only reprimanded. What did the reprimand mean really? The basketball team was doing better. It reminds me of a line baseball player and author Jim Bouton once said to me: "Sure, Charlie Manson, you might have killed a few people, but you're batting over .300. You're having a helluva year." If you win, little else seems to matter.

12

SPANNING THE WORLD
OF FOOTBALL

SEPTEMBER 1998, ROUND ROCK, TEXAS. Westwood High School quarterback O. J. McClintock was a talented and elusive runner. In one game, the defense could not get ahold of him as he ran upfield. But someone did manage to grab the back of McClintock's athletic supporter. Somehow, he pulled it completely out of McClintock's pants. It unraveled like a ball of string. McClintock scored a touchdown, and all that the defense had to show for their efforts were the threads of his jock.

NOVEMBER 2000, AUTZEN STADIUM, EUGENE, OREGON. Oregon was playing Arizona in college football. Oregon's senior safety Ryan Mitchell went back to defend a pass and ran out of bounds—directly into the band. He landed in the percussion section. He wasn't hurt, but he set off a lovely cacophony of sounds. Talk about a guy having his bell rung!

AUGUST 2000, ALLTELL STADIUM, JACKSONVILLE, FLORIDA.
With seven seconds remaining in the game, Fred Lewis
intercepted the ball to preserve a victory for the Giants.
His teammate, a rookie linebacker named Jack Golden,
tried throwing Lewis to the ground in celebration. The
clock was still ticking, though, and Golden's celebratory
tackle knocked the ball loose. It rolled into the end zone
where Jaguar Brandon Christenson recovered it for a
touchdown. Thank goodness for Golden this was only a
preseason game.

DECEMBER 2000, LINFIELD COLLEGE, MCMINNVILLE, OREGON.
In a Division III playoff game, Central College of Iowa
and Linfield played into overtime. Linfield got the ball
first and scored a field goal. Central College then had its
chance. It too advanced the ball into field goal range. It
was a rainy day and the kicker slipped. The ball didn't
even cross the line of scrimmage. Linfield's fans ran
onto the field to celebrate the victory. While they were
rejoicing, Central College picked up the loose ball and
ran for the winning touchdown! Quipped the winning
coach, Rich Kacmarynski, "Countless hours were spent
in the coaching office and out on the practice field per-
fecting that play."

OCTOBER 1997, WICHITA, KANSAS. At the start of a high
school football game, the quarterback stopped barking
signals, took the ball, and yelled out that he had "the
wrong football." It wasn't the game ball, he said, but a
practice ball. His coach called back, "Hey, I've got the
right ball over here." Very calmly, the quarterback
started walking over to his coach to exchange the balls.

As he walked past the line of scrimmage, he took off, running full speed into the end zone. The touchdown counted.

NOVEMBER 1999, TEXAS CHRISTIAN UNIVERSITY, FORT WORTH. At halftime of a TCU–Southern Methodist football game, the SMU marching band dropped grass seed onto the field in the pattern of a "Diamond M," SMU's seal. TCU won the game 21–0, but it was the SMU band that left a lasting impression—as the seeds eventually sprouted Diamond M grass.

SEPTEMBER 2000, OREGON STATE UNIVERSITY, CORVALLIS. During a college football game, a possum wandered onto the field. The TV play-by-play call from Tom Kelly and Craig Fertig was terrific: "He's just over the 50, at the 45. Nobody going after him. He's on a breakaway at the 40, the 35, to the cheers of 41,000 he's at the 25. He's a straight-line runner, doesn't have many moves. He doesn't need them! Do you think anyone's going after him? Look at the crowd! The crowd's going crazy, it's a possum! He's breaking to the outside, smells the goal line. Touchdown! Good Lord!" As entertaining as this was, it wasn't the highlight. Oregon State beat USC that day for the first time in thirty-three years! It must have been a good luck possum.

OCTOBER 1989, PORTLAND STATE UNIVERSITY, OREGON. The Vikings wanted to get their fans involved, so, in a game against Cameron University, they gave the fans cards that read RUN and PASS. The fans held up their cards, majority ruled, and, for one series, the Portland State offense responded accordingly. The plan worked and the Vikings scored a touchdown. I don't mean to knock Cameron—I know the school's not exactly competing with Harvard for admissions candidates—but I would have thought at least a couple of the school's football players could read!

13

SHRIEKERS AND STREAKERS

MAY 2000, DODGERS STADIUM, LOS ANGELES. In the bottom of the ninth inning the Atlanta Braves called on their controversial closer John Rocker. Some Dodgers fans threw water bottles. Another ran onto the field. He stopped between first and second base, dropped his pants, and mooned Rocker. The following day, in a television interview, the fan thanked his friends for buying him beers. Without their "help," he said, the incident would never have happened!

Some of the funniest "Spanning the World" clips fall into two widely different categories; let's just call them the shriekers and the streakers. The shriekers are the folks who bungle "The Star-Spangled Banner" at the beginning of sporting events. In fact, the very first edition of "Spanning the World" had a montage of these lowlights. The streakers, of course, are those who, in an effort to draw attention to themselves, race across the court or playing field in all sorts of undress. Believe me, what they draw attention to is generally not worth the price of admission. I've never built an entire show around streaker clips. Were I to do an all-streakers "Spanning" on NBC, I'm afraid Don Pardo's closing words—"if there is a next time"—would come back to haunt me. That said, if there's a cable exec out there interested in talking, I've got some ideas. *Spanning Gone Wild!*

I often begin "Spanning the World" the way the games themselves begin, with the national anthem. Well, not actually the national anthem, but rather some singer's botched version of it. I don't mean any disrespect to the singer, and certainly none to the song or the country—it's just funny. Everybody chuckles when somebody screws up the song. Sure, it's one of the hardest songs to sing well, but that's just the way it is. As long as it is sung before sporting events, people will screw it up and I'll use the clips on "Spanning the World." And, what's more, everyone will laugh. It's a win-win. Except for the poor slob who messed it up! The anthem is generally performed before the telecast begins; in television parlance, they try to "bury" the anthem. Producers think that the anthem slows things down. Too bad. If they bury it, how can we find the good stuff?

There was the late Cab Calloway, who popularized the song "Minnie the Moocher." He forgot the words to the anthem, so he just made some up: "Whose bright stripes and bright strars [*sic*] and the ev-ugly light." I've seen referees help out anthem singers who forgot the words. Portland Trailblazers coach Maurice Cheeks once helped a youngster get through it. Another time, at a basketball game in New Orleans, the public address announcer had to join in to sing a duet with a lady who forgot the words. As she stood at the microphone and the announcer sang from courtside, the referee walked up behind her and pointed to the scoreboard on which the words were displayed. Now that was the ultimate team effort.

There was a lady in Los Angeles who held one note so long, with her mouth open as wide as Kentucky, that she looked like she might swallow the microphone. Guys seem to enjoy that clip. At a hockey game in St. Louis, a poorly dressed guy played the anthem on a kazoo. I can't imagine that this is what Francis Scott Key had in mind when he saw those bombs bursting in air: some fat, slovenly guy blowing his kazoo before a hockey game. At a baseball game in San Diego a couple of years ago, five women wearing blue evening dresses lip-synched the anthem. Unfortunately, the audio man played the wrong tape. It was a male barbershop quartet. The women lip-synched the whole song anyway!

*　　　*　　　*

One of the dangers of singing "The Star-Spangled Banner" before every game is that it can become a rote exercise and its special meaning can be lost. I think this is why sports teams have guest singers. By keeping the anthem fresh, they hope it won't be seen—as it is by the TV production guys—as an obligatory waste of time before the first pitch or the opening tip-off. But if they were to just play a tape or have an in-house master, these incidents wouldn't occur.

Carl Lewis, winner of nine track-and-field Olympic golds, sang the song before a 1993 New Jersey Nets game. He totally lost it on "rocket's red glare." He was about six octaves too high. Lewis stopped and said, "Uh, oh," before finishing the song. Years later, I wanted to show a collection of botched NBA anthems on a Dick Clark bloopers show. The NBA wouldn't allow me to use the clip. I guess they thought it didn't put the league in a good light. At a dinner, I told Carl Lewis about the NBA's refusal. I got the sense he didn't appreciate my effort to replay his attempt, either.

Sometimes the screwup is not so funny. In November 2003, Spain was taking on the host country, Australia, in the Davis Cup tennis finals. The Aussie trumpeter played the Spanish national anthem before the matches. Or so he thought. He had actually played an old anthem, one dating back to the Second Republic in the 1930s. Spanish fans in attendance booed, and Spain's sports officials demanded an official apology.

Then there was Roseanne Barr's infamous anthem. She shrieked through the words at a Padres baseball game in 1990.

She hit all the notes, but none at the right time. Apparently, it was the Francis Scott *Off*-Key rendition. When the song mercifully ended, she was met by a chorus of boos. In response, she grabbed her crotch and spit. Nice. Her "Star-Mangled Banner" upset more people than any other. It seemed the entire country was outraged. President Bush called the display "a disgrace." Robert Merrill, the magnificent opera singer who passed away in 2004 and was a fixture singing the anthem at Yankee Stadium, compared Barr's performance to "burning the flag." And dogs throughout the San Diego area howled.

In fairness, though, there's no shortage of botched anthems sung by fabulous singers. Even Robert Merrill had been known to blow a word here or there. At the 1968 World Series, José Feliciano broke new ground. He performed an a cappella version that drove people nuts. Robert Goulet has been called the "king of botched anthems." The truth is, though, that he messed up only one word. In May 1965, he sang before the Cassius Clay–Sonny Liston rematch. Instead of "dawn's early light," Goulet sang "dawn's early night." One word, that's it, and yet he has become a legend in the mangled anthem department. Perhaps aware of this precedent, the Celtics once declined the offer of Stevie Wonder to sing before a playoff game versus the Lakers. Citing tradition, the Celtics opted to go with the local favorites, the Winiker brothers.

During the 2003 baseball playoffs, the Yankees were playing that contentious series with the Red Sox. I was on the field at Fenway Park for a newscast. Pop singer Michael Bolton was also on the field. He was there to sing the anthem. I had seen him perform at the Millennium New Year's Eve in Puerto Rico, and he was terrific. He put on a great show, and I told him so. I also mentioned, in my own inimitable way, that if he screwed up the anthem I would have material for "Spanning the World." Bolton then turned to a friend—a big guy, perhaps his bodyguard—and said that the national anthem is the one song you don't want to mess up. He explained that performers can be onstage and screw up their own songs. That was no problem. But the anthem? No way.

After my 6:30 newscast, I left Fenway to get dinner with friends around the corner. The game wasn't scheduled to begin until 8:30 P.M. As we were walking back to the stadium, we heard the "the home of the braaaaaaaave" wafting through the October sky. When I got to the press box, I ran into Suzyn Waldman, the Yankees announcer and sometime anthem singer. I heard her say to Red Sox executive Dick Bresciani, "Well, at least I never screwed up the anthem!" My heart sank. Waldman told me that Bolton stopped in the middle of the song, after "O'er the ramparts we watched." He resumed after consulting a crib sheet, but not before a stadium full of fans let him hear it. Can you imagine: you're singing a tribute to America and sports fans boo you? I felt like I had jinxed Bolton and worried that he might send his friend over to break me in half. My producer told me he was saving the tape for our next "Spanning." He said it was really funny. I told him to burn the tape, that there was "no way in hell I'm ever showing it." I have no idea if Bolton blames me for putting negative thoughts in his head. But he should.

I learned an important lesson about gratuitous sex early in my broadcasting career. It was soon after I started working at WCBS in New York. Though I was still the weekend sports guy, I was filling in during the week and sitting next to the late Jim Jensen, a legendary New York anchorman. I was showing highlights from a Rangers-Flyers hockey game in Philly. After the Rangers scored a goal, my producer and I edited in video of a big-busted woman rising to her feet. My line: "The Rangers go up by a pair." When the newscast was over, Jim lectured me. He said, "We don't do things like that at CBS." I was taken aback. But he was right. It was a sophomoric stunt, and though it seems rather mild by today's standards, truthfully I've never done anything like that since.

Streakers are different, though. The king of the streakers is Mark Roberts, a forty-year-old man from Liverpool, England. At the 2004 Super Bowl, Roberts ran across the field at the start of the second half. The practice in this country is that broadcasters, for the most part, don't show streakers; the theory is that the attention might embolden would-be exhibitionists and encourage them to follow in the bare footsteps of others. There was no need to show Roberts on this day, though. Viewers had seen enough already. This was, after all, the evening when Janet Jackson's wardrobe "malfunctioned," exposing her breast to the world.

Roberts faced trial in Houston, the Super Bowl's host city, several months later. He could have been sentenced to six months in jail. I'm sure his act would have been appreciated there. Instead, Roberts was fined a thousand dollars. He claimed, "The whole reason I did it was to entertain people. . . . If making people laugh is a criminal offense, I should be sentenced to prison for life." Of course Roberts failed to mention the gambling Web site he had scribbled on his chest during his run. I'm sure the advertising fee he collected for serving as a naked, mobile billboard more than covered the fine.

I've seen Roberts at numerous other sporting events. During a rain delay at Wimbledon in 2002, he decided to enliven the dreary crowd. He ran onto the court naked, flipped over the net, and started doing the moonwalk. A bare-assed moonwalk: isn't that redundant? As he cavorted around the court, the TV cameras showed the Duke of Kent and Princess Alexandria having a good laugh. It took three security guards to catch him, and when they did, they threw a red blanket over him and carted him off to the Wimbledon Police Station. He was arrested for "breach of the peace," and it was reported that he'd be questioned further. I wondered what exactly they intended to ask him. Another time, at a soccer game in Seville, Spain, Roberts ran onto the field just as the second half was to begin. He was dressed like an official and flashed a red card at the real referee. Then he flashed the crowd. Completely naked, he ran downfield and tried to score a goal. Five armed guards can claim the save.

Roberts isn't the only guy who enjoys doing this. During one stage of the Tour de France a couple of years ago, some wacko ran naked alongside the pack of cyclists. At a minor-league baseball game, a naked guy grabbed a flag and ran across the outfield. When I showed this clip on "Spanning," I suggested that he must have been the official flag barer. A streaker at the 1994 Ohio State–Michigan football game ran into the end zone and struck the Heisman Trophy pose. At a South African rugby match in September 1991, a streaker joined the scrum and tried to tackle one of the players. He wasn't hurt, but talk about putting your body on the line! The streaker at a Calgary Flames game in October 2002 wasn't so lucky. Wearing socks and only what God and genetics gave him, he climbed over the Plexiglas and jumped onto the ice. Unfortunately, he hit the ice headfirst and had to be carried off on a stretcher. The authorities considered a charge of indecent exposure but settled on interference with public property.

Even some women get into the act. At Wimbledon in 1996, a woman ran onto Centre Court topless before the start of the men's final. Mark Roberts has also streaked Wimbledon, but still, the All England Lawn Tennis and Croquet Club is hallowed ground. At least that's what the people who run the tournament want us to believe. Players have to wear white, and the spectators are silent when the ball is in play. Until recently, there were no microphones permitted on the court, even after a championship match. There is a Royal Box, and the women players traditionally had to curtsy as they passed it. So basically, the place is a library where tennis is permitted. Well, the English bet on everything, and I've always wondered if someone didn't make out big on this occasion. Odds were long that any woman would streak the match.

●　　●　　●

She would probably prefer the title "performance artist" to that of "streaker," and streaking really wasn't her game. Known simply as Morganna—in a time before single-name appellations were fashionable—the "Kissing Bandit" would run onto a ballfield and simply kiss a famous player before being chased away. (Her full name is Morganna Roberts. I'm assuming there's no relation to the guy from Liverpool.) She had long platinum blond hair and wore hot pants and tight T-shirts to enhance her ridiculously oversized, but supposedly all-natural, chest. Morganna's first victim was Pete Rose; she was just seventeen, and a friend bet her to do it. At the 1979 All-Star Game in Seattle, she got George Brett. In 2001, with nineteen arrests to her credit, she retired.

I interviewed Morganna several years ago in her hometown of Columbus, Ohio. She enjoyed telling the story of how she wasn't really guilty of trespassing during the games. She was just leaning over the railing and, gravity being what it is, the next thing she knew she was on the baseball field. She even used the "Gravity Defense" in court. I found her to be very nice and quick-witted. Among her one-liners, she once said of Pete Rose, "I tell people my career started with a bet, and Pete's ended with one." Of Steve Garvey, who ran away from her, she said, "I think he thought it was the start of a paternity suit." I have a picture of Morganna and me from that interview. She was expert at arranging herself. Just before the shutter snapped, she positioned herself so that she—or rather they—would be downright perky and pointed in the right direction. For several years after our interview, she would send me Christmas cards. Over the "M" in Merry, she would draw a pair of nipples. Now that's the Christmas spirit!

14

THE MAGIC OF TELEVISION

APRIL 2000, QUALCOMM STA-DIUM, SAN DIEGO. Padres third baseman Phil Nevin chased a foul pop-up next to the stands. A nearby TV cameraman swung his camera to get a shot of Nevin. The camera smacked Nevin in the head and knocked him to the ground. He didn't catch the ball, but he got his close-up! And nobody got hurt.

It's live. It's human. And there are lots of moving parts. So by its very nature goofy things are bound to happen in radio and television. I interviewed the late Charles Kuralt when I was just out of college. Kuralt made a living at CBS going from small town to small town and reporting on quirky things—egg-eating contests and the like. He had developed the Ten Basic Rules of Television. His rules were kind of like Murphy's Law for TV. One rule stated that if there is cigarette smoke in the room, it will always find a way to drift directly in front of the camera lens. Another one stated that if you're in the Antarctic getting ready to do your on-camera stand-up with no civilization anywhere within thousands of miles, just as the camera starts rolling a Good Humor ice cream truck will pass by and ring its bell!

Everyone who works in broadcasting has a favorite story. If I had to pick mine, it would be the time I walked into a news anchorman's office—I won't say who to protect the guilty—and read his list of New Year's resolutions. The list was taped to the wall above his desk. He wanted to jog a certain distance every day and to maintain his weight at a specific level. And right there, number three on his list, he wrote: "Stay on top of current events." The guy was a news anchorman, for goodness' sake! I thought, *Yeah, not a bad idea to read the papers every now and again.*

Another one of my favorite stories involved the great motorcycle daredevil Evel Knievel. He was born Robert Knievel, but everyone knew him as Evel. He made his name jumping his bike over lines of cars at Las Vegas casinos. In 1974, Knievel was about to embark on his greatest stunt yet. He planned to use a rocket-powered motorcycle to leap over the Snake River Canyon in Idaho. I'm not sure anyone outside of Idaho had ever heard of the canyon, but this stunt seemed to catch the nation's collective imagination. Knievel was nearly as good a promoter as he was a stuntman. He toured the country to generate interest in his Snake River adventure. When he came to Boston, I was only too happy to give him a little airtime. I remember asking him what I should call him. Evel? Mr. Evel? But most of all I remember asking during our live interview if WBZ-TV could film his little jump in Idaho. I knew the TV station would never foot the bill for such an escapade, but that didn't stop me from asking. Knievel said that if we paid him, we could certainly film it. "Pay for it?" I answered indignantly. "We don't pay for news." I explained, "When President Nixon holds a news conference, we don't pay him." To which Mr. Evel retorted: "Yeah? How many cars can he jump over?" Apparently as many Snake River Canyons as Knievel could jump. He never made it over. His parachute deployed too early. And that was that.

◆　　●　　◉

Some of the goofy stuff that happens on television is planned, but most of it is not. When I was working in Dayton, the weatherman would announce his forecast outdoors. At the time, this was innovative and the station was very proud of the idea. It even promoted the weathercasts: "Watch the weather outside, where it's happening!" This was great until it snowed. The station was located right next to a two-lane highway. Pranksters would time their drive-bys perfectly to pelt the weatherman with snowballs live during his weathercast. Where it's happening!

Another story from Dayton involves one of its suburbs called Tipp City. I looked into its history once. The town used to be known as Tippecanoe, in honor of William Henry Harrison who ran for president with the slogan, "Tippecanoe and Tyler too." In time, Tippecanoe was abbreviated to Tipp City. Fascinating stuff, I know. Anyway, Tipp City held a contest one year to name Miss Tipp City, probably in conjunction with the annual Mum Festival Parade. Now in television news it is customary to use a "locator." If the footage is from Guam, the newsman always states that it's from Guam, but producers think that's not enough. So the word GUAM is also written somewhere on the screen, kind of like LIVE. Well, just as Miss Tipp City was crowned, the words TIPP CITY appeared on the screen, and, wouldn't you know it, they were placed right across her chest. I always thought that's what local news is all about.

In addition to LIVE and the locator line, it is standard TV practice to use a "dropline." The dropline defines the speaker. Mine is "Len Berman, Sportcaster." A local news channel might use, "Jane Doe, Nosy Neighbor." Almost everyone gets a dropline, with the exception of the president of the United States, the mayor, or the governor. They don't receive any identification on the screen. The assumption is that viewers know who these people are. It's probably a poor assumption, but it may be too depressing to think otherwise, so we'll play along. My favorite all-time dropline comes from a 1992 or 1993 episode of the *Jerry Springer Show*. At that time, Jerry's talk show still had a modicum of credibility; only every other episode featured a mud-wrestling match between some creep's girlfriend and his put-upon wife. On this show, there was a guest whom I'll never forget (except her name). I'll call her Nancy. This was her dropline:

NANCY NUTJOB
Claims to Be from Venus

Classic. Well Mrs. Nutjob rambled on about her experiences coming from such a far-off land. And, this being a serious talk show, Jerry brought on an expert. There's an expert for everything. The expert was asked for his opinion on Nancy Nutjob, and, I swear, this is what he said: "Well, all I know is what I've heard her say here today, and my conversations with people from other planets." My kind of expert. I was laughing so hard I nearly peed.

Several months later I ran into Jerry Springer at a cocktail party NBC threw in New York for the final episode of the sitcom *Cheers*. Turns out that Jerry grew up in the Bronx and is a big Yankees fan and a good guy. Anyway, I asked him about the lady who "claims to be from Venus." He said her family was backstage during the taping and appeared rather normal. Her kids said Mom was great, "she just tells us all the time how she's from Venus." Personally, I hope she really is from Venus and that she's got some sports blooper videos to send me. They'll make for the first episode of "Spanning the Galaxy." Perhaps I can get Springer to do the voice-over.

*   *   *

When I was just starting out in TV news, stories were still shot on film. The film would be put through a processor for developing and then edited. When there was a late-breaking story and not enough time to edit the film, we'd just air it raw. One night in Dayton there was a late-breaking car accident and our photographer was Johnny-on-the-spot. He filmed the rescue crew carrying the accident victim from his car to the ambulance, including the little incident where the medical workers dropped the wounded man off the stretcher. Oops. The poor guy was dumped onto the ground, and you see the rescue team scrambling to stuff him back onto the stretcher before anyone notices. Of course nobody saw this mishap except everyone who happened to be watching the late news that night! Come to think of it, this was during the *Bay-Berman Report* era, so it's safe to say almost nobody saw it.

Today, we take all the technological advances for granted. I've done live shots from Australia that aired on my newscast in New York. A decade earlier, that would not have been attempted. Back in 1974, the Boston Celtics played the Milwaukee Bucks in Game Seven of the NBA Finals. It was an afternoon game played in Milwaukee. The Celtics won another championship that day. I grabbed some postgame interviews for that night's newscast. Sounds simple, and these days it is. But back then, here's how it worked. There were no live shots and no tape. The interviews were shot on film. I then hopped on a plane from Milwaukee, changed planes in Chicago, and flew on to Boston. The pilot radioed ahead to tell my station exactly when we'd land. I was driven to the studio. The film was processed and developed—just in the nick of time to get it on in the last two minutes of the eleven o'clock newscast that Sunday night. Can you imagine? An afternoon game for the NBA championship, and we barely got the interviews ready for the late news.

One year I was sent to Hawaii to announce a basketball game for HBO. Since the crew was there, HBO figured it would put together a surfing show as well. I had never seen professional surfers in action. I still haven't. I walked onto the beach to tape the on-camera portions of the program with the local surfing expert, whom I'll call Kahuna. So the tape rolls, and the first words out of my mouth were "Kahuna, it's been great working with you." I had never met the guy. We shot the close of the program first, and we didn't even shoot any surfing. The producers just took some old footage and dubbed in music. Weeks later, they added my voice-over. It was like putting together a jigsaw puzzle. But hey, Kahuna, wherever you are: the check cleared. So it was *really* great working with you.

Years later when I was hosting the NBC football pregame show, I had to toss to a Bob Hope promo for his special that night. Hope started the promo by saying, "Hey thanks, Len." It wasn't live, and we'd never met. But I always thought it was kind of cool that Bob Hope thanked me for something.

I've been a guest of Dick Clark numerous times. He's the king of the blooper show genre, having produced and hosted several different bloopers shows through the years. One time I was asked to share some "Spanning the World" clips on his NBC bloopers show. I was told that I would be flown to California to tape with Dick on a soundstage. I said I was looking forward to the live audience. On these shows, they always cut to the audience laughing hysterically. Well, guess what. That's not how it's done. Those audience reaction shots are edited in afterward. The producers explained that it would be too expensive for the show to gather (and clean up after) an audience every week so they had been using the same audience for years. Dick Clark wears the same coat and tie every show to match the look. So I didn't get my live audience, but instead I got the world's greatest excuse. If my material bombed—à la Conan— I could say, "But the audience was dead."

THE MAGIC OF TELEVISION

It is said that "Everybody loves a parade." The best part about winning a championship is that the town goes nuts. The worst part? The town goes nuts. Actually, it's generally not too bad. There are parades and rallies where the fans get to heap love on their conquering heroes. These celebrations would be better, though, if it were only the athletes and their fans who showed up. But there's also the mayor, the governor, the borough president, the city council president, the head of the department of sanitation, the dog catcher, you name it . . . and they all expect their turn on the podium.

When the Celtics won the title in 1974, it was the first time I worked in a city that could claim a champion. I was the primary sportscaster at WBZ-TV, and I had announced some of that season's Celtics games. A big parade was planned to celebrate the team. When I asked the station's news director for my assignment at the big parade, though, he told me I didn't have one. It was a news story, not a sports story, he explained. Got it.

Six years later, in May 1980, the New York Islanders defeated the Philadelphia Flyers to clinch the Stanley Cup championship. Bobby Nystrom scored an overtime goal to win it. I interviewed him during a postgame show on WCBS. The Islanders proceeded to win the next three Stanley Cups as well. They won their second cup on their home ice after beating the Minnesota North Stars in five games. I was standing on the mezzanine level, watching the game with sports columnist Mike Lupica of the New York *Daily News*. We said to each other what a cool moment it is to hoist the cup, really one of the sweetest moments in sport. The Nassau Coliseum was sheer bedlam. Fans were going nuts, you couldn't hear yourself think, and yet I remember Lupica and I just having this matter-of-fact conversation. Our conversation was kind of like one between two comedians. If the second comedian thinks the first's joke is hilarious, he won't even crack a smile. He'll just nod and say, "Good one."

Looking back on it, the Islanders didn't get much in the way of celebrations. Four championships and all they got were trips down the Hempstead Turnpike on Long Island. The players and the Stanley Cup were loaded onto the back of flatbed trucks and rolled down the highway for about a mile. That was it. It didn't quite befit the number one media market in the country—yet I thought it was great. I took my kids to watch and everything.

The first really big parade that I was part of was in 1986 when the Mets won the World Series. They were treated to an old-fashioned ticker-tape parade up lower Broadway in Manhattan. Since no one has ticker tape anymore, though, people threw all kinds of junk out their windows. One tradition held true, though: the city wildly overestimated the number people who were actually present. WNBC broadcast the parade live. There were a couple of glitches. First, we hardly ever captured the Mets players on camera. We saw paper, we saw fire trucks, we saw fans, and occasionally we saw a Met. But just about the time we caught a glimpse of a real live baseball player, it always seemed to be time to cut away to commercial. And then the parade reached City Hall. I was in the studio with Channel 4 anchorman Chuck Scarborough. No one told us that the Mets were going inside for lunch, that there wouldn't be a ceremony for another hour or so. I think all ten of Kuralt's Rules may have been realized during this broadcast. So there we were, filling time. Filling and filling and filling. I must have recounted every pitch of every game during the season. Scintillating television, let me tell you.

The next year the Giants won the Super Bowl in Pasadena, California. Now, next to the Yankees, I think the Giants are the most beloved sports franchise in New York. (I would rank the current teams in descending order: Yankees, Giants, Knicks, Mets, Jets, Rangers, Nets, Islanders, Devils.) The Giants, after years of futility, had finally reached the promised land. So what kind of ticker-tape parade did they get? None. New York wasn't about to honor them because they play their games at the Meadowlands in New Jersey. Instead, the Giants had some kind of rally at Giants Stadium. The highlight was when linebacker Harry Carson dumped a Gatorade bucket on coach Bill Parcells. The Giants had been doing this all season long. This time, rather than Gatorade, though, when Carson tipped the bucket, out poured confetti. Did I mention that that was the highlight?

The Rangers won the Stanley Cup in 1994, their first in fifty-four years. The following year, the New Jersey Devils won it. There are a million Rangers fans for every Devils fan. The Rangers were New York's first professional hockey team, and they played at the great Madison Square Garden. The Devils were a team that was born as the Kansas City Scouts in 1974, became the Colorado Rockies in 1976, and moved to New Jersey in 1982. Not much in the way of New York tradition. They play in a big barn in East Rutherford, New Jersey, that rarely sells out, even during the playoffs. When they won their cup, though, WNBC decided to televise their parade live. Apparently, we didn't want to piss off the twelve people in New Jersey who cared. I was on the scene at the Meadowlands, and Matt Lauer, who was then one of our news anchors, was in the studio. The station decided to give Matt a hockey expert to be his cohost, so they brought in Neil Smith, the general manager of the Rangers. Devils fans hate the Rangers, so having Neil Smith there must have really pissed off the twelve people watching. Anyway, the big Devils ceremony consisted of one of the goofiest celebrations in sports history. It was a parade in a parking lot. The hockey players sat in convertibles and drove around the arena parking lot. We had our cameras lined up at strategic spots, and as the parade turned the corner Matt Lauer would invariably ask me, "Which Devil are we looking at?" Since we always caught the first car with our camera, I answered three different times, "Matt, it's still Ken Daneyko."

◆   ◆   ◆

One job title that hasn't necessarily made it on to my résumé is Official Sportscaster of the Howard Stern Show. But I've been on his radio program a few times—twice as a play-by-play man and at least once as the subject of a farcical rumor. In the mid-1980s, Stern was speaking with the WNBC radio traffic reporter, Jessica Brown. He said, "Everyone knows you're having an affair with Len Berman." Now at this point, my wife was driving on the Meadowbrook Parkway on Long Island. She was listening to the program and when she heard that she nearly drove off the road. For the record, I wasn't having an affair with Jessica Brown. In fact, I don't believe I've ever even met her. But that was Howard Stern. And I didn't hold it against him.

So when Howard called and asked me to announce a boxing match, I readily agreed. The match pitted Geraldo Rivera against Frank Stallone, Rocky's brother. It could have been worse; it could have been a pair of lesbians duking it out in a vat of Jell-O. You couldn't believe the hoopla surrounding this fight. It took place early in the morning at a gym in Times Square. When I arrived, crowds had gathered in the street; traffic was jammed. Several hundred people clamored to get in to watch the fight, but no one was allowed in. It was crazy, but that was the effect Stern had on his audience. So I sat down to announce the fight—clearly a career highlight—and Howard welcomes me to the broadcast. Then he starts in with, "Who has the bigger penis, you or Marv Albert?" I did the prudent thing. I said nothing, just looked at him. It's radio and Stern didn't want dead air, so he moved on. Frank Stallone, by the way, won the fight in a unanimous decision. Along the way, he broke Geraldo's nose. There was no call for a rematch. (On another broadcast, I called a basketball game between Stern's sidekick, Robin Quivers, and his lawyer, Dominic Barbera.)

In 1975, while I was working in Boston, I developed the idea of a *Sports Fantasy* program. The late George Plimpton was probably my inspiration. Plimpton made a name for himself through participatory journalism. He pitched to Willie Mays, boxed with the great Archie Moore, suited up with the Detroit Lions, and played in pro-am golf tournaments, the circus, and even the New York Philharmonic. I loved the Alan Alda movie based on Plimpton's best-selling book, *Paper Lion,* about his punishing 1963 training camp experience in Detroit. The idea behind *Sports Fantasy* was simple. While the word *fan* may be short for fanatic, it could just as well be short for fantasy. Everyone who follows a sport either played the game or fantasizes about what it would be like to play it. So with *Sports Fantasy,* viewers could write in and do stuff with their favorite pros and I would air the highlights during my sportscast.

To introduce the segment to the audience, I donned the uniform and gear of a Boston Bruins goalie and challenged Phil Esposito to try to score against me. Espo was the leading scorer in the NHL at the time, and I . . . well, I'm not a very strong skater, or netminder for that matter. (When it comes to the feet, I'm really not much good at all. In fact, I once broke my arm standing still on roller skates. I just tipped over.) Esposito scored at will, allowing me to stop his shot once. One viewer wrote that he "hoped I didn't get a sunburn from the red light going on so much." I then asked viewers to mail in their fantasies. I had no idea what to expect. Within a month, there were two thousand letters in my mailbox—and the stack grew from there. And, mind you, this was just a local TV show. These letters all came from Bostonians looking to compete with local athletes. One kid challenged Celtics center Dave Cowens to a foul-shooting contest. A bunch of softball players took their licks against Red Sox pitcher Bill "Spaceman" Lee at Fenway Park. Boxer Marvin Hagler didn't think he got much respect, so when he took on an MIT student in a little fantasy match, he dropped him in the first ten seconds! Hagler later legally changed his name to Marvelous Marvin Hagler. I guess he figured he'd get more respect. (I kind of like the concept. I'm toying with Nobel-Prize-Winner Len Berman.)

We had some goofy fantasies as well. A guy took his pet dog to the track to race against a greyhound. We dressed his dog up in racing silks, held a post parade, and crammed the little guy into the chute for the match race. Around came the mechanical rabbit, the chute popped open, and out charged the two dogs. Well, one of them charged. The other, the viewer's pet, just ambled out and started sniffing the ground. Then he started running the wrong way around the track. He'd discovered a shortcut, and when he crossed the finish line, we declared him the winner. Another time a guy wanted to scuba dive in the tank at the New England Aquarium and hand-feed the sharks. There were insurance issues, so he fed the turtles instead. Needless to say, the animal stuff didn't go so well.

But *Sports Fantasy* did. We even got written up nationally in *TV Guide*. In the May 24, 1975, issue there was an article headlined, HOWARD COSELL HAD BETTER DUCK IF A BOSTON SPORTSCASTER MAKES ONE VIEWER'S DREAM COME TRUE. The viewer wanted to throw a lemon meringue pie in Cosell's face. It never happened. Nor did another viewer's fantasy: this guy wanted to stand on the pitcher's mound at Fenway Park and have us drop a baseball out of an airplane so he could catch it.

⚾   ⚾   ⚾

When I moved to New York, I brought the *Sports Fantasy* program with me. Esposito was now a high-scoring Ranger, so I again suited up. He scored at will, I got the sunburn, and off we went. I always had the viewer sign a legal release to protect the station if he or she got hurt. Thankfully, no one ever got hurt or sued. I was, however, once worried about an athlete. Mets catcher Gary Carter agreed to try to throw out a viewer attempting to steal second base. The viewer wasn't the speediest of base stealers. Carter could have thrown to second, taken a return throw, and still gotten this guy with his second toss down to second. Carter came up throwing and immediately grabbed his knee. I had visions of the backpage tabloid headlines: BERMAN RUINS METS SEASON. Thankfully, he was okay.

Another time, a woman wanted to challenge Mike Newlin of the New Jersey Nets to a game of Horse. It wasn't that she had such confidence in her shooting prowess—she just thought Newlin was cute. So I set it up, and I set her up as well. Newlin beat her handily. Then I informed her that he had shot lefty, with his off-hand. No one ever tried to use *Sports Fantasy* as a personal dating service again.

One of my all-time favorite fantasies involved John McEnroe. A viewer from Long Island wrote that he wanted to serve match point to McEnroe. It was 1979 and John was not yet a megastar. He graciously agreed to film with us before a practice session at Madison Square Garden. So I set it up as though our viewer had earned match point and he served to McEnroe. Mac's return was out. That wasn't part of the deal. The viewer jumped the net and proclaimed victory. McEnroe said, "I want a rematch!"—to which the viewer responded, "Sorry, I've got commitments!" He was kidding, of course, but didn't that just top off the fantasy. Not only did he get to serve match point and beat McEnroe, but he also got to tell him to buzz off! In any case, we filmed a mulligan. The viewer served again and McEnroe hit it out again. "That was a blankety-blank return," McEnroe said in the "postmatch" interview. He didn't use profanity; he actually said the words *blankety-blank.* He was embarrassed. He hadn't given the guy a break, he had simply hit two balls out. And he wasn't real happy about it. That moment was one of the most endearing glimpses I've ever seen of McEnroe. In the ensuing years, he'd often come off as brash and loud and crude and all of the other stuff critics like to say about him, but not at that moment. That's my most vivid memory of McEnroe, other than his wiping Bjorn Borg off the court at the 1981 U.S. Open.

In the mid-1980s, I started doing the fantasies on national television for NBC *SportsWorld.* These ran for six years, and I had big-name participants: Michael Jordan, Wayne Gretzky, Arnold Palmer. A Lutheran minister from South Dakota stood in goal against Gretzky in Edmonton. Before he started his breakaway from center ice, The Great One got down on his knees and prayed—for forgiveness for scoring against the minister. Jordan participated in a two-part fantasy. First, he had a dunking contest against a viewer. Jordan won. (What? Are you surprised?) The second part was a game of wheelchair basketball. A Chicago teenager took on "Ground Jordan," who also sat in a wheelchair for the game. The kid won, and Jordan came across as a big winner as well. Another viewer challenged Palmer to one hole of golf and actually beat him! When Arnie went to shake the guy's hand, he was smiling through clenched teeth. One thing was obvious about the fantasies. The athletes wanted to look like good sports, but with the cameras rolling, their competitive juices would take over.

At halftime of a Notre Dame basketball game, a college kid put on an Indiana University jersey and tried to make the "winning" foul shot while the sold-out Notre Dame crowd hooted and hollered. The Irish fans yelled out, "Choke!" and "Air ball." But wouldn't you know it, the kid made the shot. The arena went deadly silent. The only noise was announcer Al McGuire's wild call of the action. Another kid's fantasy came true on my show. He had written in that he dreamed of being in the Baseball Hall of Fame. We commissioned the same people who make the plaques for Cooperstown to make one for this kid. We filmed his acceptance speech, reverberating the audio as though the sound was coming from a loudspeaker. "Today-*ay-ay*," he said, "I consider myself . . . the luckiest teenager in Plano, Texas!"

People frequently encourage me to bring back *Sports Fantasy* as a television show. It would fall within the reality TV genre, but I wonder who really wants to watch some kid going one-on-one against Shaq when there are Playmates eating live cockroaches on another channel. I think the times may have passed this concept by.

Sports fans think that spending time with famous athletes must be the most fun, but with the exception of Mantle and a few other legends, I've gotten the biggest kick out of meeting celebrities from outside the sporting world. Comedians and musicians are particular favorites. I met Jerry Seinfeld when he was basically an unknown. He approached me in the makeup room at WNBC-TV and said, "Hi, Len." I didn't know who he was, but Al Roker, who was then the local weatherman on WNBC, filled me in. Seinfeld was then an up-and-coming stand-up comic and came on our newscast to promote his HBO special. Another time, Jerry Lewis walked into the studio and said "Hi, Len" before I could say hello to him. To me Jerry is a legend, so I thought that was pretty cool. I also met Milton Berle, who loved talking about sports, especially football. After he underwent open-heart surgery, I wrote him a get-well note. I'd spent just five minutes with him, but Berle had me feeling like he was my very own uncle Miltie. On a flight to L.A. one time, Don Rickles saw me and told that he's a fan of mine. Don Rickles, the Merchant of Venom! He started in on me for the entire plane to hear. "What a hockey puck!" he yelled. "He needs five producers to come up and tell him that Pete Rose is forty-two years old." I used to carry little NBC souvenirs around, so I reached into my bag and gave Rickles a ballpoint pen. Years later, somebody went up to him and mentioned my name. Rickles said, "Yeah, he gave me a dopey pen once."

It was on another airplane that I met former President Gerald Ford. I was waiting to use the lavatory and he stepped out. I still don't know the proper etiquette regarding whether one shakes hands with a president who just exited a bathroom. Surprisingly, Emily Post has been of no assistance in this area.

I met Walter Cronkite at a football playoff game. The game was played at Giants Stadium, and at halftime I visited Jon Tisch's luxury box. Jon now runs the Loews Hotel company, but we used to work together at WBZ-TV in Boston. His father co-owns the Giants with Wellington Mara. As such, lots of famous people gravitate to the Tisch box. On this particular day, I was speaking with Jon when Frank Gifford and Walter Cronkite walked over. Now Frank is a genuine football hero, one of the all-time greats. I had spoken with him on any number of occasions, but I had never met Uncle Walter, the most trusted man in America. When I was growing up, watching

Walter Cronkite was like going to synagogue. My family tuned in every night and we weren't permitted to talk until he had intoned, "And *that's* the way it is. April 19th, 1965. This is Walter Cronkite, CBS News. Good night!" So suddenly I was chatting with Frank and Walter, and Frank said that he just got back from calling a *Monday Night Football* game in Kansas City. He said he couldn't believe the number of stations he got on the TV in the hotel. This was before satellite TV became big. He goes on and on about all the stations, until Cronkite interrupted to say, "Yeah, I bet none of them are like Channel 35." Gifford had no idea what Cronkite was talking about—but, sadly, I did. Channel 35 is the free, public access porno channel in New York City. I'll give Uncle Walter the benefit of the doubt—I'm sure he discovered Channel 35 when researching a news story about media indecency. Anyway, that's *my* story and I'm sticking to it. But I have to admit that as I left Giants Stadium that day all I could think of was "And *that's* a set of hooters. . . . Walter Cronkite, CBS News."

The singer Patty Scialfa was on WNBC's *Live at Five* once. Her husband came along. Maybe you've heard of him. Outside of the baseball world, he's known as The Boss. Bruce Springsteen! I'm a fan, and I spoke with him in the green room. NBC used his song "My Hometown" during the opening video sequence before Game One of the 1984 World Series. I told him I thought it was terrific. He said he was honored that they had used his song. Springsteen couldn't have been nicer. Another time, Robert Plant was on *Live at Five*. I don't know much about Led Zeppelin, but I do know the band sang "Stairway to Heaven," the song considered by many to be the greatest rock-and-roll song of all time. (I personally think the Rascals' "A Beautiful Morning" is as good as it gets.) I told Plant that it must be pretty cool to have written the greatest rock song ever.

He said something to the effect of "enough already," and then told the story of how he was driving on the freeway in California when he stumbled across a radio station doing a fundraiser. The deejay said that for a $50 donation he would play "Stairway." Plant said he called up the station and offered them fifty bucks *not* to play it!

Ringo Starr was another guest on the show, so I can always say I shook hands with a Beatle. By the way, while I've never met Paul McCartney, he did make an appearance on "Spanning the World." He had a front-row seat behind home plate at a 2001 baseball playoff game at Yankee Stadium. Between innings, the Beatles song "I Saw Her Standing There" was played over the public address system. The song is irresistible, and fans sang along with the recording. This is the song that ends with the lyrics, "Now I'll never dance with another (whoooh) / Since I saw her standing there." The "whoooh" is basically a long "oooooooh" and when it came to the end, McCartney stood up, raised his beer, and sang out, "Oooooooh." It was a great moment, and Fox's television cameras caught it.

I named McCartney "Spanning's" Fan of the Month. A few days later, I received a phone call from his public relations firm. McCartney had heard that he was Fan of the Month and he wanted to see the tape. What a career highlight this must have been for McCartney! Forget the Beatles' world-changing *Ed Sullivan Show* appearance or performing before the Queen— he'd made "Spanning the World"! So, of course, I told the PR lady that this would cost him. My wife is a huge Beatles fan; she once jumped the barricades at one of the Beatles' Shea Stadium concerts and had to be dragged off to the first aid room. Today Paul McCartney has a dubbed tape of "Spanning the World," and Jill has a couple of autographed photos from a Beatle—most lopsided trade since Red Sox owner Harry Frazee traded the hearts of Bostonians for a Broadway musical.

While I'm on the subject of celebrity, I ought to address my own minor celebrity. First of all, I really don't consider myself a celeb. I thought a fourth-grade girl summed it up best. I returned to my old elementary school in Queens for one of those Principal for a Day programs. The kids wrote me letters the next week, thanking me for coming. This one girl wrote that "it was cool that somebody sort of famous came to visit." So that's it. I'm sort of famous.

And apparently not too memorable. In 1995, I was asked to speak to the graduating high school class of York Preparatory School, a small private school in Manhattan. Among the handful of graduates that day was Liv Tyler, the actress and daughter of Aerosmith frontman Steven Tyler. I'm sure I delivered a riveting speech encouraging the students to follow their dreams, to strive to become a rock star or even a dorky sportscaster. Several years later, Liv was a guest on *Late Night with Conan O'Brien*. I asked one of Conan's producers to ask her if she remembered who spoke at her high school graduation. She said, "No."

One measure of celebrity is whether people ask for your autograph or to have a photograph taken with you. Surprisingly, I get both requests fairly frequently. And unlike a lot of athletes, I've never said no. I figure that if a fan thinks I'm important enough to ask me for an autograph, I'll go along with it. I get embarrassed, though, at Yankees spring training games when I'm standing in the dugout next to big-star players and a fan asks me to sign. I figure the players must be wondering, "Who does this guy think he is?"

Believe me, it's nice being sort of famous, but there is a flip side. When your mug is on TV all the time, people think they know you. At least they are pretty sure that you kind of look vaguely familiar to them. When I was starting out in Boston, I was in a Baskin-Robbins ice-cream shop and a lady asked me if I was Len Berman. I said yes, but she later called the TV station to complain about "how unfriendly Len Berman was." I guess I didn't smile and announce, "Yes, I am" in an animated sports-caster voice. One guy once asked me if I was in the garment business. I said, "No. I'm Len Berman, on Channel 4." The guy shook his head and said, "No." He thought I was mistaken.

Then there are the people who just can't get my name right. I was actually asked once if I was Walter Cronkite. I've gotten Brent Musburger a few times. And Chris Berman, too. O. J. Simpson, in fact, once said "Hi, Chris" to me. I responded, "Hi, Ahmad"—as in Ahmad Rashad, the football star who, like O.J., also had moved into sports broadcasting. Chris is an ESPN sportscaster, and though we are not related, articles often say we are. A *Los Angeles Times* article written some twenty years ago stated that he and I were brothers. Decades from now, when some sorry soul is writing his Ph.D. dissertation on the history of the ancient art of sportscasting, he'll probably note that the Brothers Berman were on the scene. And in the footnotes, "*Los Angeles Times,* 1982." Chris and I joke about this all the time, telling each other, "Mom says you need to call her more often."

The name I get the most often is Marv Albert. Marv is a New York guy and before me he did the sports on WNBC. So I can understand the confusion. But I don't like it—it's an ego thing. One time after landing at LaGuardia Airport, some guy walked by and said, "Hi, Marv." I'm always at a loss when this happens, but this time I also had my hands full of luggage and was particularly flustered. I wasn't in the mood to explain who I really was, so I just kept walking. He wouldn't give it a rest. He came over to me a few minutes later to tell me how disappointed he was with how unfriendly I was. I still didn't answer. I'm sure the guy went home and told his wife what a jerk Marv Albert is!

At least he got Marv's name right. I've been asked if my name is Merv. At a grocery store, a lady asked me if I was Herb Alpert. She probably wanted to know where my Tijuana Brass was. My kids were with me that time. They've helped me keep it in perspective, telling me to just say hello no matter what name I'm called.

In August 1990, David Letterman invited me on his show. I was thrilled. In his early days at NBC, he taped right across the hall from where we do the news and I became a big fan. He wanted to talk about Major League Baseball's banning of Pete Rose and he asked me to show a few "Spanning" clips. He said on the air, "You dress nicer than Marv Albert." I accepted the compliment, but I've since wondered—first Howard Stern, then Dave—"Are all these guys hung up on Marv?"

I know, though, that names can be tough. It's definitely not just me. At the NBA Finals in Houston one year, I was walking out of the arena with an NBA Hall of Famer. A fan came up and said, "Clyde, I've always liked watching you play." The fan may have enjoyed watching Walt "Clyde" Frazier play, but apparently he wasn't paying close enough attention. I was walking with Earl "The Pearl" Monroe, not Clyde. A few years ago, I made a similar mistake. I went to see *The Producers* on Broadway, and before the show, on the way to the men's room, I saw Redskins coach Joe Gibbs. Gibbs owns a NASCAR team, and I had interviewed him several months earlier at his garage in North Carolina. Outside the theater bathroom, though, the name that came to me was Dan Reeves, who then coached the Atlanta Falcons. I called out, "Dan." Gibbs, of course, ignored the call. So I figure if I can be an idiot when it comes to getting someone's name right on the spur on the moment, I'll cut everyone else some slack—even if it does bruise my ego from time to time.

JUICE AND JAYSON

MAY 1998, TEXAS STADIUM, ARLINGTON. Rangers manager Johnny Oates engaged in a heated argument with the umpires. A fan jumped out of the stands to add a piece of his mind. He was quickly led away by police. Television cameras focused on his buddies "passing the hat." They were collecting bail money for their departed friend!

O.J. Simpson and Jayson Williams were two of my all-time favorite athletes; not only were they extremely talented, but they were also brilliant interview subjects: always good-humored, frank, and cooperative. The camera loved them. Today, Williams is best known for his involvement in the accidental shooting of a limousine driver, and Simpson for the murder of his wife, Nicole, a crime for which he was acquitted in 1995. So now whenever I tell a friend that a sports figure I like reminds me of O.J. or Jayson, he says, "Aren't you a great judge of character!"

But really, O.J. Simpson was perfect. He was beautifully built, incredibly athletic, and articulate. In short, he was The Juice. Not only could he speak intelligently, but he was charismatic. In 1974, when I started announcing preseason football games for the New England Patriots, I sat down with a Patriots assistant coach to do some homework before the game. I wanted to sound semi-intelligent when I was talking about the players from the other team, even though almost no one had ever heard of most of them. After all, these were guys suiting up for an exhibition football game. The assistant and I started talking about various players around the league. I made some brilliant observation such as, "Hey, that Simpson guy is a pretty good running back, huh?" The previous season, in 1973, he had broken the two-thousand-yard barrier in rushing. The record has since been eclipsed, but O.J.'s still the only player to rush over two thousand yards in just fourteen games. He was also voted Most Valuable Player. The assistant said that, yes, he was the best in the league. "The best running back?" I asked. "No," he said. "The best athlete in the entire National Football League. Period!" Not bad. A couple of years later, Simpson was playing the Pats at Foxboro Stadium. Early in the first quarter, he got into a minor scuffle and the officials threw him out of the game. I thought, *How dumb is that?* Here's the greatest athlete in the league—a prime attraction—nothing really happened, and yet he was tossed? In hockey, there wouldn't even have been a penalty.

I covered my first NFL regular-season game, as a TV reporter, on September 17, 1973: the Patriots against Simpson's Buffalo Bills at Foxboro. I had started working at WBZ-TV in Boston only two months earlier. I remember being quite nervous and fearful walking into the Patriots' locker room the first time. I was worried that it would be difficult to find who I wanted to interview. I expressed my concern to the team's public relations director. He told me that it would be easy, that the names of the players are above their lockers. I then prayed that the half-naked guy taking off his pads would be standing in front of the right locker. After all, you don't want to ask a gargantuan football player, stripped down to all his manliness, about the mistake he just made on the field—especially if he's not the right naked football player.

Now people think the locker room is all glamorous and

glitzy, but mostly it's cramped and moist. Guys are running around in various forms of undress while the hot showers are running and the newsperson's hair is kinking up. It's really not at all pleasant. That's why when people turned "women in the locker room" into a big issue, I thought it was ridiculous. Women in the locker room? Heck, *I* don't even want to be in the locker room. It would be fine with me if everyone was banned and teams held interviews in a side room. I know newspaper reporters think that's a rotten idea. They want the spontaneity of the postgame reaction, but what TV reporters seek is the sound bite. For that purpose, I would have no problem waiting a few minutes and going someplace where my hair doesn't frizz to collect my brilliant quote: "I know just I rushed for a gazillion yards, but you really have to give credit to my offensive line for opening up the holes, to God for giving me strength, to my mother for giving birth to me, to the guy who got her pregnant in the first place . . ."

Anyway, I was all worried about going into the lion's den of the Patriots' locker room after the game, but then during the game O.J. put on a show that changed my plans. He rushed for 250 yards, which was then an NFL single-game record. Not bad material for my first NFL postgame interviews. So instead of interviewing the Pats, who had just set a record for defensive futility and wouldn't necessarily be so accommodating, I decided to try to interview Simpson. I timidly walked into the Bills' locker room. O.J. was in a side room, taped up, iced up, and beat. I stammered something about wanting to ask him a few questions, but the Buffalo PR man interceded. "No time, Juice, plane to catch." O.J. would have nothing of it, and to my amazement and delight he said to me, "Let's go." O.J. sat there and patiently answered as many dumb questions as I could think of. No rush, no attitude. At that moment, he was my hero.

Through the years, I interviewed O.J. several more times. He was always great. He just knew how to give a good sound bite. I think it's an art form, and if it doesn't come naturally, it is really hard to master. The key is to answer the question, add a bit of substance, and complete your thought in twenty seconds or less. Willie Randolph, when he played for the New York Yankees, was a master. He would look you in the eye, give a good answer, and then shut the hell up. You gotta love a guy like that. O.J. was damn good as well. I guess that's why he went into television and the movies. He had a way of making a dumb question come to life through his answer. I remember once asking him during a sit-down interview why he wore the number 32? Talk about a penetrating question. Well, that's what you get in a sit-down in-terview. When you're asking questions on the fly, players can just turn around, put on their underwear, and ignore you. But sitting down, they're already clothed and miked up. It's harder for them to get away when you come at them with the tough questions, like why they wear number 32. O.J. said he didn't want to wear "some dump truck number like 38." That's what I liked about O.J. He gave a colorful answer to an innocuous question, and I remember what he said twenty years later! I'm still not sure what that meant, but it sounded good. He had a glib answer for everything. I asked him how he felt about having never played in a Super Bowl. "So what?" he said. "I know guys who played in Super Bowls who tried to pawn their rings!"

The last time I talked with Simpson was in February 1994, four months before his fateful white Bronco car chase. My fam-ily and I were down in Florida for spring training. Whatever it is you think about reporters covering spring training, you're right. It's a cushy assignment. You don't see reporters and pro-ducers fighting to see who gets to cover training camp in hockey. We were staying at the Boca Beach Club. One after-noon, after I had conducted my usual array of scintillating spring training interviews with the Yankees and Mets—"So, uh, you think you're gonna win it this year?—my wife pointed to a pretty woman sitting in the next cabana with two beautiful children. She figured the woman must be married to an athlete. It was Nicole Brown Simpson. A short time later, O.J. sauntered by. He was there to play in a charity golf tournament. We started chatting and he introduced me to Nicole. She struck me as a little shy and content to stay out of the sun, in the rear of the cabana. Nicole and I talked for a few minutes, but I can't remember anything about the conversation. O.J. spoke about the latest *Naked Gun* movie that he had made and about how the cast was so close. The whole time we were talking, maybe a period of thirty minutes, people on the beach made a steady procession to O.J.'s cabana. He signed tons of autographs and posed for pictures with everybody who asked. He was polite and friendly, almost to a fault. Even when someone rudely interrupted our conversation, or thrust a piece of paper in his face, he was more than gracious. Two of my kids were with me, witnessing this parade. After it was over, I told my son Daniel, "If you ever get to be in the public eye, *this* is how you should behave!"

That was February of 1994. In June, Nicole and Ron Goldman were dead. The trial, of course, was major news for months. WNBC had an "expert attorney" who would go on the air every night and sum up the proceedings. Off camera, he told me, "O.J. doesn't stand a chance. Just wait until they trot out the DNA evidence." I guess I always believed him, so I was pretty stunned that day when the not guilty verdict was read. I was even more stunned, though, by the polarized reactions of people across the country. I remember seeing a video of a group of white people groaning in disbelief when the verdict came down. This reaction was countered by that of a group of African Americans at Howard University. When they heard the verdict, they broke into wild cheers. That really set me back: how could race alone determine these completely different reactions? I've since heard lots of discussion about this. A prevailing theory is that African Americans have felt persecuted by police their whole lives and that they perhaps bought into the defense argument that Los Angeles Police Department officers planted evidence to "get O.J." I wonder if African Americans really believed O.J. to be innocent, or if they just saw this as payback for all the African Americans before him who've been screwed over by police.

A couple of years later I emceed a dinner for the Police Athletic League. Sitting at my table were Joe DiMaggio, Giants coach Jim Fassel, and the New York City police commissioner Howard Safir. Not a bad group of dinner companions. Talk turned to O.J. and we all deferred to the comments of Safir. Safir said that he thought the prosecutors "had enough evidence to convict O.J. ten times over." He couldn't believe what happened in that courtroom. He said he's seen murderers convicted where they never found the body and here they couldn't get Simpson with all the DNA evidence they had.

What bothers me about this case is that if Simpson didn't commit the murders, who did? Years ago, when I was covering a basketball game in L.A., a director friend of mine took me to the actress Karen Black's house. She said, "The only difference between the good guy and bad guy is whose story you know." When she said this, she was lying on the floor looking up at her glass coffee table. I'm pretty sure the quote wasn't original, but it stuck with me. I know, or rather, used to know the great O. J. Simpson. Two people are dead, and years later nobody has been found guilty of the crime in a court of law. Back in 1981, Simpson summed up his life this way: "The public has been so good to me, everywhere I go I get good vibes from people. I'm having a ball!" How hollow those words ring now. When somebody used to ask me if I thought O.J. did it, I would answer, "I hope not." That was my story then. I'm finding it harder and harder to stick to it.

＊　　　＊　　　＊

This brings me to Jayson Williams. Jayson starred at St. John's and began his career with the Philadelphia 76ers before moving on to the New Jersey Nets. I was with Williams the last week of January 2002. I've been the emcee for the annual Thurman Munson Awards Dinner for ten years, and in 2002 Williams was one of the honorees. Munson was the great Yankees catcher who died in 1979 while practicing takeoffs and landings in a small plane at his hometown airport in Canton, Ohio. I never formally met Munson, but the first time I ever walked into the Yankees' clubhouse he was sitting at a table playing cards with his teammates. He looked up at me and just glared. I think that was a "hello." Through the dinners, though, I feel as though I've gotten to know him well. His widow, Diana, is one of the finest people you'll ever meet. He is described by family and friends as tough on the outside, a softie on the inside. His teammates loved him—I mean *loved* him. Willie Randolph still attends the dinner twenty-five years later.

So I was doing my six P.M. newscast from the dinner in 2002, and Williams and Yankees manager Joe Torre, another honoree, were my guests. I never missed an opportunity to put Jayson on the news. Four years earlier, in 1998, the NBA All-Star Game was in New York. Williams was the star. Everyone wanted an interview. He took me to his house in western New Jersey and gave me a guided tour. He had built the home with his father, and he was understandably proud of it. What a place! We went everywhere, even his bedroom. And no, I didn't see any guns. On the drive from practice to his house, it was just the two of us. No microphones, no cameras. And, oh, the stories he told. He talked about a current teammate who was on the injured list. Jayson said he wasn't hurt; he "just wanted to take a little vacation" right in the middle of the season. That really burned Williams. He told me a dozen stories like that. The real inside stuff, the stuff you never get in the papers or on *SportsCenter*.

That's the way Williams was: just terrific. First of all, he was funny. This is a guy who could charm any group of people. He had a million stories. He tells one where he was sitting on the bench with Yinka Dare at a Nets game, and Dare points out Christian Laettner, of the Minnesota Timberwolves. Laettner had a "C" on his jersey, signifying that he was the team captain. Dare asked Williams what the letter stood for, and Williams says "Caucasian." Laettner, of course, is white. At that point, Benoit Benjamin, another teammate, reacted and said something like, "Aw man, that's ridiculous. Everyone knows Caucasian starts with a 'K.' "

Williams not only knew my name but would address me by it. That's a thing with me. I'm sure most of the athletes who play in New York know who I am. After all, I'm on TV three times a night five days per week. I've been at the same station for over twenty years. Yet some athletes walk right by and pretend they don't know me. And then there are those like Patrick Ewing and Derek Jeter. They'll say "Hi," but never, "Hi, Len." (Jeter, I'm told, doesn't call any reporter by name and still refers to his manager as "Mr. Torre.") Anyway, Jayson went on the news with me and Torre and cracked everyone up as usual. I said to him, "Now that you left the Nets, the team got good." And he quipped that since he had joined NBC as a basketball commentator, the network lost its contract to televise the NBA: "I'm on a roll. . . . I'm the Jimmy Hoffa of the Nets."

During the Munson dinner there was an auction. Two reporters from a radio station auctioned off a Giants football package: go to a game, stand on the sidelines, sit in a luxury box, hold a jockstrap, whatever. In the middle of the auction, Williams stormed up to the stage and grabbed the microphone and said, for everyone to hear, "You guys suck." He took over, and everyone laughed. The bidding had reached about $1,500. Through the sheer force of his personality, Jayson drove the price to about three grand. Then, suddenly, he stopped and said, "Screw it. I'll pay $10,000 for it." With that, he walked off the stage.

A couple of weeks after the Munson dinner, Williams shot and killed Gus Cristofi, a limousine driver to whom he was giving a house tour. Apparently it was an accident. Now, I'm certainly not a criminologist, but I have to figure that if Williams didn't try to cover up the shooting and if he hadn't tried to make it look like a suicide, he would have gotten off scot-free. Jayson would have gone on the stand, and with that magnetic personality of his, simply said, "I screwed up. I was showing off my shotgun. I have no idea how it happened. It just went off." As it was, he was convicted of four lesser charges for covering up the evidence. As of this writing, he is set to be retried on the manslaughter charge. Instead of owning up to the mistake in the first instance, there was the cover-up: wiped fingerprints, washed-off blood, attempts to make it appear a suicide.

On a large scale, this is one of my gripes about society. People don't take responsibility for their actions. It always seems to be somebody else's fault. Or it's my upbringing, my environment, or the fact that my undershorts were too tight. I remember a story on the news about a kid who jumped out of a hotel window. Apparently he was aiming for the swimming pool but missed. His mother was interviewed. She said it was the hotel's fault. I thought, *What should the hotel have done?* Should the hotel have had someone there to move the pool closer to the building when the kid started to jump? I was once called for jury duty; the plaintiff is fortunate I wasn't picked. The judge outlined the matter. It was a slip-and-fall case. A minister was suing the Salvation Army. There was a sign that read WET FLOOR. So, in summary, the plaintiff's case was this: the floor was wet; a sign read WET FLOOR; the minister ignored the sign; he fell; and it was the Salvation Army's fault. I agree. The Salvation Army should have had a sign that read YOU'RE AN IDIOT!

Maybe it's just because their actions are so high profile, but athletes often seem to be the worst when it comes to claiming responsibility. It was the coach or my teammate or the sun got in my eyes or the umpire screwed me. And on and on. It's so rarely "my fault." So maybe, when an athlete gets charged with a crime, he just draws on his experiences in the locker room. Blame somebody else. I may have screwed up, but it wasn't my fault.

16

SPANNING THE WORLD
OF BASKETBALL

JANUARY 1994, CASPER, WYOMING. The Natrona High School boys basketball team trailed by one point in the final seconds. The coach drew up a very simple play. Just before a teammate inbounded the ball, Jason Holt fell to ground and started barking like a dog. All the players on the opposing team stopped to look at him. Meanwhile, the pass was made to another teammate and Natrona scored an easy, game-winning basket.

MARCH 1993, LAWRENCE, KANSAS. To wish the Kansas basketball team well in the NCAA tournament, hundreds of fans lined up on a bridge over the Mississippi and staged a sunrise "spitfest." When it came to their team, they rightfully had high expectorations! The Jayhawks made it to the Final Four.

JANUARY 2004, FLEET CENTER, BOSTON. As Celtic Paul Pierce was cutting through the lane, his defender,

Indiana's Ron Artest tried a new tactic. He pulled down Pierce's shorts! No one whistled—not the refs and not the fans. Undeterred, Pierce pulled up his shorts, took a pass, and hit a three-pointer.

FEBRUARY 2004, GUND ARENA, CLEVELAND. The game clock malfunctioned during a Cavaliers-Celtics game. During the stoppage, Boston's Paul Pierce went to center court and, with his back to the basket, heaved an over-the-head half-court shot. Pierce missed badly. Then the Cleveland mascot gave it a try. Swish. Three points for Moondog!

DECEMBER 2001, PHILIPS ARENA, ATLANTA. At halftime, a Hawks fan was blindfolded and led to the foul line. He was told to hold a basketball high over his head for somebody to grab on the fly and dunk it. So the fan just stood there with the ball held aloft. He waited and waited and waited. It finally dawned on him: he wasn't part of the act. He was the entertainment and the joke was on him!

NOVEMBER 1994, ALAMODOME, SAN ANTONIO. Fireworks were ignited inside the arena before a Spurs game. The fans loved it—until the smoke set off the sprinkler system. Huge torrents of water came shooting out of water cannons into the stands. Fans went scurrying every which way, and there was a fifty-minute "rain delay."

APRIL 2004, PHILIPS ARENA, ATLANTA. At a Hawks game, rapper DMX's song "Party Up" was played over the loudspeaker during a time-out. Among other choice lyrics are "How the fuck you gonna cross the dog with some bum shit?" The Hawks later apologized for their choice of songs. After all, it was "Family Night" at the game.

MARCH 1998, PALACE OF AUBURN HILLS, DETROIT. After Joe Dumars scored a basket for the Pistons, his teammate Rick Mahorn went over to the referee and the public address announcer and told them that Dumars had just scored his 20,000th NBA point. The feat was announced to the crowd, and Dumars received a prolonged standing ovation. One problem. Dumars had only scored 15,715 points. Mahorn was playing a joke on him. Dumars retired before he ever got to 20,000 career points. But at least he got the ovation.

JANUARY 1993, OAKLAND ARENA, OAKLAND, CALIFORNIA. As part of a promotion, if the Warriors scored 120 points against the Miami Heat, ticketholders would all get free pizza. In the final seconds, Golden State had 119 points. Tim Hardaway heaved a half-court shot. The shot was good—free pizza for everyone! But the refs ruled that the shot came too late (even though replays seemed to show otherwise). The fans booed, and the refs needed a police escort off the court. It wasn't victory that the fans craved, but pizza!

17

MR. OLYMPIAN

JULY 1992, BARCELONA. At the Summer Olympics, German diver Albin Killat was competing in the three-meter springboard competition. He jumped off the diving board, did three somersaults in the air, and then–splat! He landed flat on his stomach. It was an Olympic belly flop! The Cuban judge gave Killat a score of two points out of ten. The British judge gave him a zero! Killat didn't win a medal.

The week before the 1980 Winter Olympics opened in Lake Placid, New York, the United States Olympic hockey team played the Russians at Madison Square Garden. The game was a total wipeout. The Russians won 10–3, and they made the Americans look silly. One of the Russian skaters did a 360, spun completely around, and scored a goal. It was as if men were playing against boys. That night, I went on the air and opined, "Why bother playing this Olympic hockey tournament at Lake Placid? Just wrap up the gold medals and ship them to Russia." That, of course, was not one of my better predictions. Maybe you've heard of the Miracle on Ice?

That *was* the beauty of the Olympics. In 1980, the Iron Curtain was in place, and these Games pitted the good guy Americans against the big, bad Russkies. They were professionals and we were a bunch of kids. (At the time, sixty-six Americans were also being held hostage in Iran.) It all seems kind of quaint now when our NBA stars beat up on Angola 364–12 in

Olympic basketball games. (Although by their having to eat humble pie in 2004, these Games are at least mildly interesting.) This is not to say that the thrill of victory is gone from the Olympics. Anyone who watched Sarah Hughes skate to the gold in Salt Lake City knows that's not the case. Seeing Sarah and her coach, Robin Wagner, scream like schoolgirls when they realized Sarah had won the gold is as pure as it gets in sports. Sarah, of course, *was* a schoolgirl: just sixteen years old at the Salt Lake Games. She went out there with a nothing-to-lose attitude and skated the routine of a lifetime. Twenty-four-karat Olympic gold!

⬤　⬤　⬤

My first Olympic memories were of Jim McKay, the ABC Sports host. He *was* the Olympics. I thought he had the coolest job in the world. At the 1968 Games in Mexico City, he was there when Tommie Smith and John Carlos raised their fists in a black power salute on the medal stands and when long jumper Bob Beamon leapt twenty-nine feet. No one had even cleared twenty-eight feet before. But here's what I remember most from those Games: in the 10,000-meter race, runners were dropping like flies, unable to cope with the high altitude. When the race ended, even the television audience was gasping for air. What was next? A Coca-Cola commercial! It was the best product placement I've ever seen. Amazing things happened in that watershed Olympics, and I remember a TV commercial.

My most unforgettable Olympic memory, though, is from the 1972 Games in Munich. People remember exactly where they were when President Kennedy was shot, or when the *Challenger* exploded. I remember exactly where I was when Jim McKay said, "They're all gone." Eleven Israeli athletes were massacred by Palestinian terrorists. It still brings a lump to my throat when I think of him saying that.

M y own Olympic "career" began on an ominous note. I took off for Atlanta from New York's LaGuardia Airport on July 17, 1996. I was covering the Summer Games for WNBC-TV. At the same time, TWA Flight 800 took off from Kennedy. When that flight went down, killing all 230 people aboard the Paris-bound 747, everyone feared it was terrorism, and many worried the act was related to the upcoming Opening Ceremony. Tom Brokaw was on my flight. When we landed in Atlanta, he turned right around and headed back to New York. We all waited and wondered what was next?

Throughout the Games, everyone was a bit jittery. After one late newscast, I returned to my hotel room. It was from there that I heard the bomb go off. I had been in Centennial Park just minutes before it detonated. It was chaos that night. Yet the 1996 Summer Games survived. In fact, they all seem to survive. There are always dire predictions about the traffic or the weather or the security. Thankfully, the doomsdayers are usually proven wrong. Atlanta had hosted the Super Bowl in 1994 and the traffic was awful. People couldn't move. So how did it work out during the Olympics? First, when the Games began, many residents left town. Those who stayed tended to leave their cars at home, and the Olympic organizers set up special traffic lanes for Olympic vehicles. (Authorities estimated that more people departed from the Sydney airport than arrived in the days leading up the 2000 Games.)

The Olympics are the most heated, compressed, and televised sports event on earth. For seventeen days, it's almost as if the world stands still for the Olympics, resuming only after the

Closing Ceremony. For the athletes who train for years, though, their glory can be fleeting. A gold medal winner could have walked through Centennial Park in Atlanta, with his medal around his neck, and nobody would have recognized him. How do I know? Because it happened to Derrick Adkins, the winner of the 400-meter hurdles race. Adkins was from Long Island and I invited him to be a guest on my newscast. After the interview, people came up to me asking, "Who was that?" Now, it's not exactly like the 400-meter hurdles is the hammer throw. This is a marquee event. And Adkins had won it only the day before. Yet, he was virtually anonymous.

The anonymity never bothered Adkins. He told me, "You don't get into track and field in this country to become famous." He went a full year without anyone recognizing him on the street. Then he went on his honeymoon in March 2004. He took a cruise around Hawaii and the European crew members all made a big fuss over him. Track and field *is* a big deal in Europe. The track athletes who cash in are those like Carl Lewis and Marion Jones who win a whole lot more than one event. Lewis won a total of nine gold medals in the four Olympic Games between 1984 and 1996, and Jones won five medals in Sydney (three gold and two bronze), although the BALCO mess has called those medals into question. Adkins's gold did trigger a performance clause in his Reebok contract, and his appearance fees went up at track meets in Europe. But people have the notion that if you win a gold medal in the Olympics, you're set for life. It's simply not true. Adkins works for the CEO of a company that operates running-shoe stores. More important, Adkins, who suffers from clinical depression, works with young people at the Nassau County Mental Health Association. He tells the kids that it's okay to seek help if they're feeling the symptoms of depression. Some sports fans might not agree, but Derrick helping those kids is much more meaningful than his Olympic medal.

The night Adkins won his medal, he was just ever-so-slightly overshadowed. My cameraman and I had gone to the stadium to watch his event. We were about to leave when I suggested that we should hang around for a few minutes. Michael Johnson was about to race. It was the single biggest story of the Atlanta Olympics. Johnson was going to try to win a rare double. He had already won the 400-meter race, and he was about to run the 200. In the moments before the gun went off, the eighty-five thousand people in the stadium all rose, section by section. A hush grew over the crowd. When Johnson crossed the finish line, he glanced at the clock. He had not only won, but he had set a world record. Johnson raised his arms in triumph, and the stadium was bedlam. I was standing only about twenty-five feet from the finish line. It was an awesome scene. Meanwhile, in the press area, Derrick Adkins was having his news conference. There were TV monitors set up in the room. Everyone stopped to watch Johnson's race. When they saw what happened, the reporters all bolted out of the room. Said Adkins, "My press conference was over."

          🏈   ⚽   🏀

I worked for NBC Sports during the 2000 Summer Games in Sydney. My first assignment? Rowing. I have to admit I didn't do a lot of rowing growing up in Queens. I did find it interesting, though. I thought, *Wouldn't it be fun to sing, "Row, row, row your boat" while the crews were charging down Penrith Lakes*—but I controlled myself. (That's not to say I didn't hum the tune to myself while the races were on.) The U.S. heavyweight crew had won the World Championships, but they flamed out in Sydney. I also covered whitewater. In whitewater, the athletes paddle down rapids while they navigate through a series of gates. But since there were no American contenders, my interviews rarely saw the light of day.

The second week I was supposed to cover canoeing, another sport with no American contenders. At the last minute, though, I was reassigned. NBC's wrestling reporter had to go home to attend to personal business. I didn't know a Greco from a Roman. But I had to learn the sport in a hurry. The first night I was at the wrestling arena, Henry Kissinger showed up to watch. He would see the Greco-Roman equivalent of the "Miracle on Ice"—the single biggest upset in Olympic wrestling history. Some people called it the "Miracle on the Mat." (They're big on this miracle thing at the Olympics.) A dairy farmer by the name of Rulon Gardner defeated a Russian named Alexander Karelin. Karelin had a little winning streak going. Thirteen years. He hadn't lost a match since 1987.

It was up to me, Mr. Wrestling himself, to interview Gardner. During the NBC announcer meetings, the producers had stressed that they didn't care for the question "How do you feel?" They felt the announcers should be more creative. But after this monumental upset the only thing I cared about was how Rulon Gardner felt. I asked him seven or eight questions—all variations of "How do you feel?" Finally, after my sixth attempt, Gardner said, very matter-of-factly, "This is awesome." Gardner was what he was, and some television interviewer wasn't going to get him to blather on incoherently. After the Olympics, I received a letter from the U.S. Olympic Committee asking permission to use my interview as the on-hold track on their phone system. While waiting to talk with Olympic bigwigs, callers got to hear my slew of "Uh, how do you feel?" questions over and over.

Gardner's upset should have been my standout memory from the 2000 Olympics. Instead there were two others. I didn't get to interview too many other U.S. wrestlers because they didn't win gold medals. They were expected to, but they didn't. It was the first time since 1968 that no American freestyle wrestler struck gold. Actually, that isn't technically correct. Brandan Slay got his gold after the Games were over. His opponent in the finals, German Alexander Leipold, had won four-nothing, but Leipold later failed a drug test. On the mat, though, Slay had been disappointed with the officiating, and when the match ended, he wouldn't shake either Leipold's hand or the referee's. Another American wrestler, Sammy Henson, lost in the finals. So he had to settle for silver. He sobbed on the medals stand. A third, Terry Brands, was so upset with his bronze that he took it off on the medals stand and put it in his pocket. Needless to say, the crowd wasn't very happy with the U.S. team. Boos rained down in the arena. Many of the fans were there to support the Iranian wrestling team, so I could understand an anti-American bias, but most of the spectators were Australian. And they were booing, too. The phrase "ugly American" kept popping into my head.

My other lasting memory? I met the King of Sweden. I've met kings before. Who hasn't? Don King, the late Alan King, Larry King. But a real king? This was a first. NBC had decided to do a feature story on team handball. (A headline in the *Sydney Morning Herald* had earlier asked of the sport: WHAT THE HELL IS THIS?) Team handball is part basketball, part volleyball, basically soccer with hands. Born in Scandinavia, the sport is more than one hundred years old. The night we went to the game, the Swedish fans went wild for their team handball guys. They chanted some song in Swedish. Naturally, the song was about frogs without ears and tails. Perfect! The King of Sweden, Karl Gustaf, and the lovely Queen Sylvia took in the match. They had front row seats—it's good to be king. I cornered King Karl Gustaf for an interview and asked His Majesty if he cheers for his team. "Of course," he answered. I asked what he yelled in support. He said he couldn't say it on television. Funny, this king. So I played along and asked if he ever yelled out "My kingdom for a goal!" He was walking away by that point—who could blame him?—but his hand motion suggested, "Yeah, something like that." And then he was gone. I had one last question, but it was too late. I wanted to know if he was ever tempted to scream when a player screwed up, "Off with his head!"

⬥   ⬥   ⬥

NBC tapped me again for the Salt Lake City Winter Games in 2002. I was assigned to report from ski jumping—another one of those Queens, New York, favorites. I'll let you in on a little secret. The ski jumpers are never very far off the ground. It's the camera angle that makes it appear like they are soaring. From where I was stationed at the bottom of the hill, though, it was incredible as the jumpers soared toward me. The surprise winner of the 90-meter event was a Swiss jumper by the name of Simon Ammann. He looked like Harry Potter. When I interviewed him, he was so excited about his victory that the words just tumbled out of his mouth. Most of them were completely unintelligible, but I looked at him and nodded earnestly anyway. Finally Ammann stared into the camera and yelled, "Gold medal! Ahhhhhhhhhhhhhhhhh!" Now *that* I understood. A few days later he also won the 120-meter event. When I interviewed him a second time, my producer told me to ask him about Finland's Matti Nykanen. Nykanen is the only other ski jumper to win Olympic gold on both the 90- and 120-meter hills—but you knew that. So I asked Ammann how it felt to match Nykanen's record. He looked at me in bewilderment. Finally, I said, "Just do the yell."

So he looked in the camera and screamed once again, "Gold medal! Ahhhhhhhhhhhhhhhhh!" There you have it. That's the real thrill of victory!

In 2004, I headed to Athens for the Summer Games. I was initially asked to be a sideline reporter for the tennis and wrestling matches, but when I got to Athens, NBC added play-by-play assignments for the archery, fencing, and shooting competitions. An NBC executive facetiously explained the reasoning behind my new assignments: "Anything with a weapon, assign Berman." Perhaps they thought that since I grew up in Queens I could handle the rough stuff. But what did I know about fencing? Very little. I can tell you this, though: fencing is not a very good television sport. The uniforms are wired so that when a sword touches them, lights go on. The problem is that often both fencers touch at the same time, so both lights go on. What's worse, the fencer who touches first doesn't automatically get the point. The touch is awarded to the person on offense. It can sometimes take fifteen seconds before the referee awards the point, to *droit* or *gauche*. (That's right or left for Anglophones.) In that time, we've shown three replays and Mr. Fencing Announcer still has no idea who the hell scored. My solution? The referee should push a button, indicating *droit* or *gauche,* and then he can go into his little riposte and parry explanation. That way, everyone will know the score as soon as it happens, as they do in most sports. (That's the fun thing about announcing these obscure sports. I spend a lifetime ignoring them, and then in five minutes I've figured out how to improve them.) The highlight of fencing: A young lady from Beaverton, Oregon, named Mariel Zagunis won the gold in sabre. It was the first

American fencing gold medal in one hundred years. As the athletes were celebrating, I uncorked the following line: "The letter Z used to stand for Zorro. It now stands for Zagunis." Pretty clever, huh? Just wait 'til I'm assigned to curling!

Incidentally, unlike fencing, archery competitions make for surprisingly great television. The competitions are head-to-head, so as an announcer you can build the drama. "Korean Park Sung-hyun is trailing by eight points with one arrow left. . . ." The truth is, it's almost a given that a Korean woman will win the gold—since 1980, Korean women have won more Olympic gold archery medals than athletes from all other countries combined. But it's still dramatic when the archer shoots a final bull's-eye to win the match. I opened the gold medal telecast by saying, "You could call the Korean women archers the New York Yankees of archery, but that wouldn't be fair to the Koreans. The Yankees actually lose the World Series." (That was, of course, also before the Yankees lost the unthinkable, a playoff series against the Red Sox.)

At the Athens Games, it was "all Rulon, all the time." I interviewed Gardner at the Parthenon before the Games, after each of his matches, and even after he was interviewed on the *Today* show the day following his final match. What a difference four years makes. Gardner was funny, insightful, likable, emotional—in short, he was one of the best interview subjects at the Olympics. And he also produced one of the Games' most poignant moments. After he wrestled his final match, winning the bronze medal, he took off his shoes and left them on the mat. The gesture is a time-honored tradition signifying a wrestler's retirement. Rulon cried, his mother cried. It was really something to see: this giant Greco-Roman wrestler wearing his skimpy singlet and crying his eyes out. The moment overwhelmed him. Rulon was happy to win the bronze, which I appreciated. I saw other athletes in Athens cry because they won silver rather than gold. One American fencer won a bronze medal and didn't react at all. No smile, nothing. She wanted gold, and nothing else would do. There's something wrong with that. What happened to the notion of just competing? These athletes are so fortunate to have even made it to an Olympic Games, and here some are destroyed if they don't wind up standing on the highest medals stand tier. It came off as childish, like a little kid not getting his way. Not Rulon, though. The bronze was just fine, and he wore it proudly the next day wherever he went. I'm now a Rulon Gardner fan for life!

After working four Olympics, I've come to the conclusion that the best place to watch the Games is definitely on television. This is especially true of the Opening Ceremony. It was hot and sultry inside the Athens Olympic Stadium on the night of August 13, 2004, and the parade of nations seemed to be interminable. I nearly dozed off. Television viewers could enjoy the ceremony in the comfort of their homes; not me. The entrance of the Iraqi athletes was the highlight of the parade. As they marched around the stadium, fans rose, section by section, and gave them a standing ovation. The good old U.S. of A. received only polite applause—a very restrained welcome compared with the one they received four years earlier in Sydney. What struck me most, though, was the reaction to Israel. None. There was dead silence. Every country got a little something, even the ones I had never heard of, such as Kirabati. But Israel? Zip. That changed, however, when an Israeli athlete, Gal Fridman, won the country's first ever gold medal, in windsurfing, and the Israeli national anthem, "Hatikvah," was played for the first time in Olympic history. Hearing the song brought a tear to my eye.

Being at the Games in person and seeing a little bit of this and a little bit of that, though, you arrive home with impressions that don't necessarily come across on television. For instance, when American fans chanted "U-S-A!" at various venues, other fans started to boo. I'm not sure the television coverage captured that. Another thing from these Games: When the U.S. Dream Team was crushed by the Puerto Rican basketball team, a Mexican radio reporter ran up to me breathlessly. He saw me wearing an NBC shirt and figured I was an American. The reporter asked me if I was upset that the Americans had lost in basketball. I told him no, explaining that I was actually kind of glad. It made for a much better story. The reporter was perplexed. He expected me to be rooting for the Americans to win. I mumbled something about my being a journalist (very Cosell-like), but I don't think my answer satisfied him. I'm pretty sure my comments didn't make it on the air in Mexico that night.

Although I pride myself on my objectivity, I must admit that I was proud that not a single American athlete tested positive for drugs while in Athens. (Cyclist Tyler Hamilton, though, was later accused of blood doping—using a transfusion to increase the number of red blood cells carrying oxygen to his muscles. Although his tests came back positive for doping, Hamilton was allowed to keep his gold medal when it was determined that an Athens blood lab had mistakenly dealt with a backup sample.) After security—there were metal detectors and Greek militia men holding machine guns (and that was just to get into my hotel!)—drugs was the unfortunate story of the Games. More than twenty athletes were kicked out of the Olympics for testing positive or for failing to show up for drug tests. Even horses, in the equestrian events, tested positive. On top of that, some Paralympians failed drug tests: three athletes were stripped of their medals. I can't help but think how stupid some athletes must be. Do they actually think they are not going to be caught? How dumb and selfish must they be to jeopardize their reputation and that of their country for the chance of winning a medal? Because no American was busted in Athens, no Mexican radio reporter breathlessly assaulted me for my reaction to my country's embarrassment. It's not that "no news is good news," it's that in many cases "good news is not news."

18

YOU SHOULDA SEEN IT!

JUNE 1989, MONMOUTH PARK RACETRACK, OCEANPORT, NEW JERSEY. The fog was so thick that basically you couldn't see a thing. That didn't stop the track from running the day's first horse race, or the announcer from try-ing to call it. Here is his call: "They race past the stands into the first turn with Hot Lights Excellence in front. On the outside Equal to None is second as they disappear into the fog. From now on . . . you're on your own!"

People think that one of the greatest things about being a sportscaster is getting to go to all the games—and it is pretty cool, when it works out. But when you do what I do, it doesn't always work out. I think I have set the record for going to sports events and not seeing anything. There's a good reason for it, though. I've done a lot of pregame shows in my life, and with a pregame show, you go on the air, do your thing, and then usually head home. I know I set some kind of record in 1984. That October, I was on the field for two playoff games in two cities in one day. And how many pitches did I witness? Not a one. First, I went to Chicago where the Cubs were hosting the San Diego Padres at Wrigley Field. I did a bunch of interviews for future use. Then I flew to Kansas City where the Royals were to play the Detroit Tigers. Again, I conducted some interviews. And when we wrapped, my producer and I went to dinner. Aaron has 755 homers and I've got this: two games, two cities, one day, zero pitches. Some record!

At other critical times, though, I was actually there, right in the ballpark, and yet I didn't see The Big Moment. The first time it happened, I was floored. It was Game Three of the 1975 World Series. The Red Sox were playing the Reds in Cincinnati, and Red Sox outfielder Dwight Evans tied the game with a two-run homer in the top of the ninth. I was working for WBZ-TV in Boston, so near the end of the game I had to head down to the Red Sox locker room and get in position to rush in breathlessly to do postgame interviews. As a TV news reporter, when the game goes into extra innings, as this one did, you're basically stuck in the bowels of the stadium waiting it out. It's not a big deal most nights. But this game didn't end with a walk-off homer or something simple. Rather, the game turned on one of the more controversial plays in World Series history.

It was the bottom of the tenth and Reds manager Sparky Anderson called on a seldom-used Bahamian pinch hitter by the name of Ed Armbrister to lay down a sacrifice bunt. Cesar Geronimo was on first and there were no outs. Armbrister squared around and the ball dropped dead in fair territory, right next to home plate. Boston catcher Carlton Fisk pounced on it and tried to fire to second base to get the force-out. In doing so, he got tangled up with Armbrister and the ball went sailing into center field. Geronimo took third, and Armbrister second. Umpire Larry Barnett ruled that there was no interference, that both Armbrister and Fisk had the right to be where they were, to do what they did. It was one of those calls that could have gone either way. Only this was the Red Sox, and for fifty-seven years nothing had *ever* gone their way. In typical New England fashion, Boston fans took the call in stride: they sent Barnett death threats. Three batters later, Joe Morgan lined a single into center field and the Reds won the game 6–5.

In the Cincinnati locker room, Armbrister waxed poetic about his "bunt and bump." So what if he changed his story a

YOU SHOULDA SEEN IT!

couple of times. Okay, he sorta, mighta stopped to admire his bunt, and in doing so he coulda possibly gotten in the way. Didn't matter. He was the hero.

Across the way, in the Red Sox locker room, the players weren't exactly waxing poetically. Ignoring the fact that Fisk could have simply turned and tagged out Armbrister, Red Sox star Carl Yastrzemski railed about the umpiring, and not just about Barnett. At the time, Major League Baseball simply rotated its umps for the World Series. There was no merit system, like in the National Football League where playoff officials are selected based on who "grades out" the best during the regular season. I'll never forget Yaz's complaint: "We have the best players in the World Series, why not the best umpires?"

Anyway, all hell broke loose, and there I was gathering all these momentous interviews, but there was one slight problem. I hadn't seen the play! I was standing less than fifty feet away from where it happened, directly behind home plate at Riverfront Stadium—yet I was clueless. That was just the first time.

•   •   •

Super Bowl XXV was another doozy. That's the famous 1991 game in Tampa where Buffalo Bills kicker Scott Norwood lined up for the winning field goal against the Giants. The Giants led by one, 20–19, and there were eight seconds remaining in the game. Norwood's attempt was a forty-seven-yarder. It had the distance, but it sailed wide right. The Giants were champs, and the Bills would go on to lose the next three Super Bowls.

I was at the game. What a day! It was played during the first Gulf War. ABC stationed a camera a mile away from Tampa Stadium—that way, in case somebody blew up the stadium, they'd have the footage. (NBC does the same thing at the Opening and Closing Ceremonies of the Olympics.) This was the first Super Bowl where fans entering the stadium needed to pass through metal detectors. Over seventy-eight thousand fans had to walk through one at a time. Officials had advised everyone to come early, but as game time neared, thousands of ticket holders were still outside. Eventually the officials just gave up and let everyone in. Before the game, Whitney Houston sang the national anthem. This wasn't one of those anthems that I like to feature on "Spanning the World." It was beautiful. All of the fans had been given American flags, and as Houston sang the anthem and jets roared overhead on a flyby, everyone waved his flag.

My most vivid memory of that Super Bowl? New York City construction workers waving their flags and crying. You'd think Scott Norwood missing the kick would be the number one moment, but then I never saw it. (Sure, I've seen it replayed hundreds of times in highlights, but it's not the same.) Again, I had left the press box to be near the field to grab some interviews. Norwood missed the kick, and I missed Norwood missing the kick! I did get to interview Norwood afterward, though. There was nobody around him. Strange. He *was* the story. And the reporters pretty much left him alone. They don't anymore. Anyone who does a retrospective on Super Bowl XXV tracks down poor Scott Norwood. You have to feel sorry for the guy.

Much as you have to for Bill Buckner. Buckner played twenty-two seasons in the big leagues and had 2,715 hits and a career batting average of .289. That's more than solid. Even more impressive was his fielding percentage. He played 1,555 games at first base and his fielding percentage was .992! How many people have that kind of percentage in *anything* that they do, let alone on a major-league baseball field with millions watching? Yet all anyone remembers about Buckner is how the ball went through his legs.

It was at Shea Stadium in New York on October 26, 1986. Game Six of the World Series. Once again, the Boston Red Sox were tantalizingly close to winning the championship. Just three outs away, with a two-run lead going in to the bottom of the tenth inning. And it all went wrong. The Mets tied the score. Then, with Ray Knight at third, two outs, and a 3-2 count, Mookie Wilson hit a little ground ball toward Buckner, playing deep behind first. The slow bouncer rolled right through the legs of Buckner. Knight scored, and the Mets went on to take the seventh game the following night. And that was that . . . *again*!

After he retired, Buckner had to move out of New England because Red Sox fans wouldn't let it go. The fans forget that even if Buckner had made the play, the game would have still been tied. And, *really,* what were the odds that Boston was going to win?

So where was I when this life-altering error occurred? Nodding off in a motel room in Buffalo! I was there to call a Patriots-Bills football game on NBC the next day. Vin Scully's play-by-play woke me up: "It gets through Buckner! Here comes Knight! And the Mets win it!" I couldn't believe it. I was the hometown sportscaster. This incredible play had just happened. And not only was I not at the game, but I missed it on television, and—to top it off—I was stuck in a motel room with nobody to talk to about it. And that's really one of the great pleasures of sports. You turn to the guy next to you and say, "Did you see that? Can you believe that?" You see it, then you get to rehash it over and over. No wonder twenty-four-hour sports radio is such a success. Rehashing 'til the cows come home.

Incidentally, my wife *was* at the game with my two sons. When Boston took the lead in the top of the tenth, though, it was late and she said, "Let's go home." They were standing on the platform of the Long Island Railroad station when the roar went up from Shea. They had all been at the game, and yet they had all missed it. It must be in the genes!

These days, this stuff happens more and more often. With a zillion members of the media accredited for the big events, there are simply not enough press box seats to accommodate them. I went to Denver for the Jets-Broncos AFC championship game in 1998. My press seat was located behind the press box in a tent! I had flown eighteen hundred miles to sit and watch the game on television. I thought that was ridiculous, so I sat on the press box floor. At least that way I could see some of the game in person.

At the 2003 World Series in Miami, several long rows of tables were set up in the press dining room, adjacent to the press box. Some of the best-known sportswriters in the country were sitting there—all watching the game on television! But at least they were in the city where the game was played. I remember one time in Boston a sportswriter wrote a game story about the Celtics when they were on the road. The writer admitted to me that he had stayed home and had watched the game on TV. Of course the dateline beneath his name listed the city where the game had been played. The Celtics were there. He wasn't.

The same thing happened to me with a Celtics game—but it was due to circumstances beyond my control. In the mid-1970s, Bob Cousy and I were announcing Celtics games for WBZ-TV. Cooz did the color commentary and I called the play-by-play. The Celtics were playing the Kings in Kansas City, but a snowstorm hit Boston and I couldn't get there. Cousy, who had been out of town, flew in to KC without any trouble. That night, Cousy and I announced what I believe may be the only two-city, two-announcer basketball game. I sat in the studio in Boston calling the play-by-play, and he sat in the Kansas City arena doing the analysis. You know, at times I called a better game that way. Sometimes announcers tend to drift away and talk about anything but the game. I couldn't. I was forced to watch the monitor. I could only see what the viewer could. On top of that, I could only hear the audio coming from the microphones at the arena. The crowd noise and the PA announcer weren't distractions as they can be when you're live in the stadium. I remember actually hearing a referee call out a three-second violation. A microphone was located under the basket. I had the correct call immediately. If I was at the game, it might have taken a few seconds to make the right call after hearing the whistle. The next morning I ran into a viewer. He wanted to know how I got home from Kansas City so fast.

While I was in Boston I also got to call Patriots preseason games on television. One summer, the Patriots and San Diego Chargers agreed to play a game in Norman, Oklahoma, home of the University of Oklahoma. Patriots coach Chuck Fairbanks and Chargers running back Little Joe Washington were both former Sooners. Norman is football country: it was the middle of August, about a thousand degrees, and there were kids on every sandlot playing peewee football in full pads. The preseason game was a great idea, except kickoff time was at eight P.M. and they had never played night games in Norman. Sure, they had illumination of some sort, but it was hardly enough for television. Calling play-by-play in the dark was not the ideal broadcasting situation. I pretty much couldn't make out anything between the thirty-five-yard line and the goal line down to the right of the press box. So my partner, former Patriots running back Jim Nance, and I spent the broadcast having some fun with the situation, trying to handle it the best we could. We would say things like, "We *think* he got tackled." The broadcast was a fumble at best. When I got back to Boston, my boss was furious. He told me that he had listened to the game on the radio, and those broadcasters called the play-by-play just fine. I wondered if they had been issued night-vision goggles!

● ● ●

Game Five of the 1976 NBA Finals has been called the most exciting NBA game ever played. The Celtics beat the Phoenix Suns in triple overtime to take a 3–2 lead in the series. The Celtics' hero was a seldom-used reserve named Glenn McDonald. With Dave Cowens, Paul Silas, and Charlie Scott having fouled out, McDonald responded to the call and scored six points in the final overtime. I was at the Boston Garden for this game. Well, in keeping with tradition, I was actually there for only the first quarter. I then had to return to the station for my newscast. The game was being broadcast by CBS, and my newscast, on the local NBC station, was probably seen by about twelve people. Twelve people who could care less about the Celtics, of course. After the game was over, I returned to the Garden. It was as if I had entered a time warp. In those days smoking was permitted in the arena, and the Garden had taken on a very different atmosphere. Incidentally, my parents were there. I thought it would be fun if they came up from New York for the game. It was the only NBA game they ever went to. They didn't leave early. They probably thought all the games were like that.

When the Yankees and Red Sox played for the American League pennant in the dramatic seventh game of the 2003 playoffs, the game stretched into extra innings. I was there so Channel 4 News could break in "live from the scene" to announce that the Yankees had won the pennant. Fox Sports had the broadcast rights to the game, and we weren't permitted to go live inside the stadium until the game was over. Of course, this regulation hadn't always stopped me. In fact, the night the Yankees clinched the World Series in 1996, I was wired to do a live shot from outside the Yankees' locker room. We must have been live for forty minutes before a representative from Major League Baseball came over to me and said, "You know you can't be live until Fox is off the air." I said, "Absolutely, no problem." It wasn't a problem for me—I had gathered and shared plenty of interviews to that point. I remember one in particular. As I turned a corner, outside the locker room, Yankee Tim Raines and his wife were sitting on a bench. They were sharing champagne right out of the bottle and crying. I know a tender moment when I see one. So I barged right in and interviewed both of them on television. Live. (But don't tell anyone.)

In 2003, though, "live from the scene" was a hill in the Bronx, overlooking the House That Ruth Built. I don't know if we would have broken in live if Boston had won the game, but, this being before the 2004 Yankees–Red Sox series, I'm not certain anyone ever considered that possibility. So as the game dragged on, I found myself sitting inside a huge TV satellite truck. Again, I was all alone. Just yards away in the jam-packed stadium, fans were watching history in the making. At one point, I heard noise from outside and wondered what was going on. It turns out the broadcast I was watching in the truck was on about a five-second delay. What I heard outside was the stadium erupting to Aaron Boone's game-winning homer in the bottom of the eleventh inning. I not only didn't see it in person, but I saw it five seconds after everyone else watching on TV! I then went on the air and told Channel 4 viewers that the "Yankees had won the pennant." Somehow I assumed that most of them already knew.

B oone's homer was the latest—but undoubtedly not the last—all-time great Yankees highlight that I missed. The first that I remember missing was even more special. It was October 8, 1956. Oh, how I wished I had been at Yankee Stadium that day. I wasn't, though. Instead I was seated at my fourth-grade desk at PS 112 in Queens. When the final school bell rang on World Series days, we would all race two blocks to the corner bar. Of course we weren't allowed inside the bar, so we'd stand at the door and call to the patrons to ask them the score. Then we'd run home a few more blocks and watch the end of the game on television. We never thought about who was hanging out in bars at three in the afternoon on a weekday. We just wanted to know if the Yanks were winning or losing.

Well, that day when we got to the bar we found that it was nearly empty. The game was in the Bronx, and it was a beautiful fall afternoon, so we knew it couldn't have been rained out. When we asked for the score, we were told that the game was over, that "Don Larsen pitched a perfect game." I turned to a friend and asked, "What's a perfect game?" Not a single Dodger had reached base—no hits, no runs, no errors, and no base runners, all of which meant the game was played in no-time flat. Two hours and six minutes to be exact. Nowadays, with the pregame show, the introductions, and all the commercials, two hours into a World Series game, you're lucky if they're in the fourth inning! So Don Larsen had pitched a perfect game and I had spent my afternoon learning about why rocks have different colors. I should have known right then and there that I was destined to miss some big sports moments.

Here are a couple of other memorable moments that I missed. The Yankees won the World Series in 1996—first time

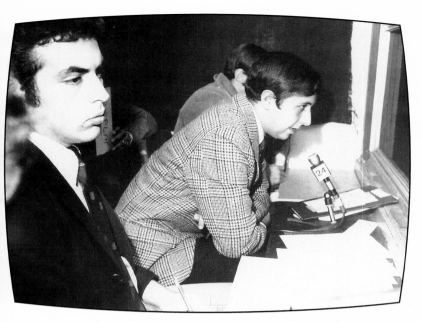

Announcing the first ever high school football telecast in Syracuse, New York, 1970. (COURTESY OF THE AUTHOR)

Anchoring the news in Dayton, Ohio. What a stud-muffin!
(COURTESY WDTN-TV)

Interviewing Sparky Anderson after a World Series game in 1972. Talk about the old days—that camera is shooting 16mm film. (COURTESY OF THE AUTHOR)

Getting my first Emmy Award from one of my heroes, Curt Gowdy. "But what about the game?" (COURTESY OF WBZ-TV)

Announcing a "Sports Fantasy" in Boston with Arthur Ashe. He'd rather Dan Rowan was at the microphone. (COURTESY OF WBZ-TV)

Hosting NFL '83 with Pete Axthelm, Bill Macatee, and Dave Marash. There was no NFL '84. (COURTESY OF NBC SPORTS)

With Dick Enberg at Super Bowl XVII. The Redskins finished the year beating the Dolphins. Much better than how the year began with Canadian Football League telecasts. (COURTESY OF NBC SPORTS)

A tip of the cap from the 1984 World Series MVP, Alan Trammell, but not to the fans who rioted. (COURTESY OF THE DETROIT TIGERS)

With the kissing bandit herself, Morganna. She liked to use the "gravity defense." (Courtesy of NBC Sports)

"You'll be okay, kid. Second base is down there." (See chapter 25.) (Courtesy of Topps Company, Inc.)

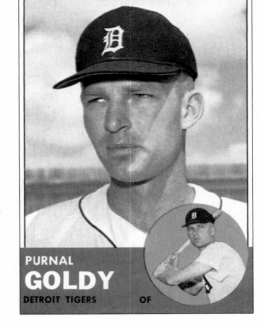

PURNAL
GOLDY
DETROIT TIGERS OF

With Wilt Chamberlain and Bucky Waters. At least Wilt's entire body wound up in this picture.
(COURTESY OF NBC SPORTS)

Bill Raftery and me announcing Big East games. "The games will sell themselves."
(COURTESY OF BOB STOWELL)

We got thousands of letters for "Sports Fantasy." Many of them legible. (COURTESY OF NBC SPORTS)

My football show with Lawrence Taylor lasted one season. His restaurant in New Jersey didn't last too much longer. (COURTESY OF WNBC)

With my hero Mickey Mantle. No, we didn't discuss his favorite Yankee Stadium moment on the air. (COURTESY OF WNBC)

Mickey Mantle autographed baseball. Perhaps he was thanking me for caring. (COURTESY OF MARQUEE PHOTOGRAPHY)

*Sandy Koufax and Ralph Branca, two pretty fair Dodger pitchers.
I somehow failed to mention to them how much I hated Brooklyn.*
(COURTESY OF ANN BRANCA)

*With another one of my boy-
hood heroes, Bob Cousy. A
killer on the tennis court.*
(COURTESY OF BRIAN BALLWEG AND
THE BOYS CLUB OF NEW YORK)

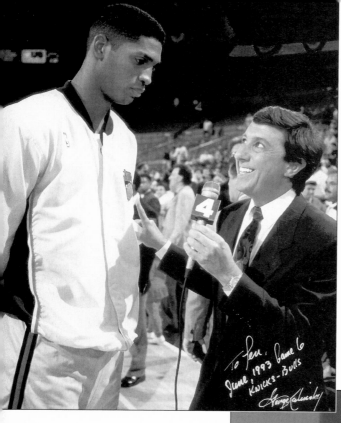

No, I didn't ask Charles Smith about those shots he missed against the Bulls. (COURTESY OF GEORGE KALINSKY)

On the sidelines with Patriots owner Bob Kraft. He told me Bill Parcells would be back in New England. It didn't quite work out that way. (COURTESY OF THE NEW ENGLAND PATRIOTS)

Simonn Amman, ski jumper. "Gold medal . . . Ahhhhhhhhhhhhhhhh!"
(COURTESY OF BOB VASILOPOLUS)

With the man himself. Just a couple of Syracuse guys talking bloopers on television.
(COURTESY OF DICK CLARK PRODUCTIONS)

Jay-walking with Leno at a station function. (COURTESY OF WNBC)

With Al Roker and his wife, Deborah Roberts, at my daughter's bat mitzvah. To quote Al, "This is great. They should have parties like this for black people. I'd call it a 'bro mitzvah.'" (COURTESY OF MARQUEE PHOTOGRAPHY)

Before there was Bonnie Blair there was Irving Jaffee. (Courtesy
of Brian Ballweg and the Boys Club of New York)

***Receiving a Thurman Munson Award from his widow, Diana.
Thurman glared at me once.*** (Photograph by Camera One/Courtesy of
AHRC NYC Foundation, Inc.)

Getting my Sportscaster of the Year Award from Joe Garagiola. Twenty-eight years earlier he made the perfect call. (COURTESY OF IVAN BOWYER)

The Yankee manager being honored by a Jewish organization. Joe Torre isn't Jewish but he's definitely a mensch. (COURTESY OF AMIT CHILDREN)

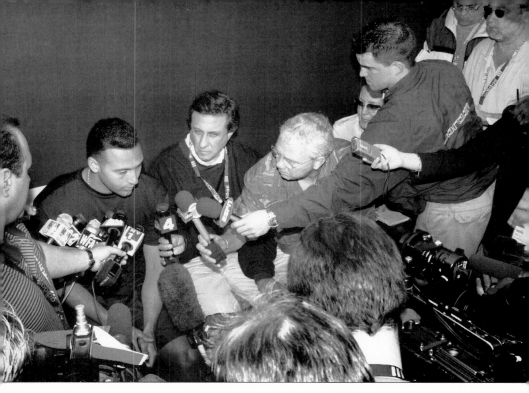

Derek Jeter and me just hanging out. Yeah, right. (COURTESY OF NEW YORK POST/REX USA)

Interviewing Jason Giambi, spring training, 2004. "Did I take steroids? No." (COURTESY OF ERIC HAUSMANN)

Did this idiot sportscaster really just ask me about Manolo Blahnik shoes? (Courtesy of Eric Hausmann)

in eighteen years. I was there, stuck in the bowels of Yankee Stadium behind the home-team dugout. The world saw the final pop-up to Yankees third baseman Charlie Hayes. I didn't. (But, as you know, I did go on live soon thereafter.) When the Rangers won the Stanley Cup championship in 1994, ending their fifty-four-year drought, I was there—waiting in the "rotunda" adjacent to the ice. That's where they keep the elephants when the circus is in town. As the Rangers skated around the rink, hoisting their precious Stanley Cup, I didn't see a thing. But I was there when Rangers defenseman Brian Leetch took the congratulatory call from President Clinton. As I wondered how often the president took time to speak with hockey players, *l'odeur des elephants* brought me back to reality.

●　●　●

Now before you start thinking that I've spent a life in sports and missed everything, that's not exactly the case. I happened to be in Yankee Stadium on September 30, 1956—eight days before Larsen's perfect game. It was the last game of the regular season, and the Yankees had long since wrapped up the pennant and were waiting to play the Brooklyn Dodgers in the World Series. I don't remember much from this game—Boston beat the Yankees 7–4 (I looked it up)—but do I remember Bob Sheppard announcing over the public address system that because Tigers slugger Al Kaline didn't have any RBIs that day, Mickey Mantle had the most runs batted in in the American League. And since he had the most homers and the highest batting average as well, it meant he had won the Triple Crown. Now that's extremely rare. Only two players have accomplished that since Mantle, and no one has done it since Yastrzemski won the Triple Crown in 1967. So I may not have been there when Larsen blanked the Dodgers, but I was there when my hero clinched the Triple Crown!

TELLING IT LIKE IT IS

JULY 1989, OKLAHOMA CITY. I was standing next to the rabbi at my cousin's bar mitzvah. The rabbi turned to the congregation and asked, "Do you believe in miracles? Just look at the 1968 New York Mets." The rabbi did not know that I was a sportscaster. I leaned over and whispered, "Rabbi, it was the '69 Mets." Without missing a beat he whispered back, "Well, it was the '68-69 season!"

For over three decades, as both a coach (1950–1966) and a general manager (1966–1984), Red Auerbach led the Boston Celtics. During his coaching days, when I would watch him from afar, I thought Auerbach was a warm-and-fuzzy character. In time, I came to learn just how far off that estimation was. Gruff and old school would be more accurate adjectives. As a kid, I thought it was cool that he'd sit on the Celtics bench and, when victory was assured, light up a cigar. All eyes would be on the coach. Boston's up by eighty points with five seconds remaining—is Red puffing yet? How about now? I thought it was neat, but the Celtics players didn't think so. They thought their coach was showing up the other team. Today, we have a different view of what constitutes sportsmanship and one-upmanship. Not to mention a different view of smoking in arenas!

Auerbach's Celtics were supposed to win. It was pure and simple, the natural order of life. And they did win: an incomparable nine times from 1957 to 1966 and seven more times during his reign as general manager. In leaner years, if the Celtics were losing and our TV cameras caught the players laughing on the bench, Auerbach was pissed. Losing teams are supposed to act upset, he would say. Everything with Red's Celtics was "us against the world." He had this notion that the New York Knicks pulled the strings at the NBA because the NBA offices were located in Manhattan. If something was good for the Knicks, then the league would approve it. If something was good for the Celtics, it might get voted down. That was Red's view. I remember when Portland won the NBA title in 1977. The Celtics were the reigning champs. Auerbach barked of the Trailblazers, "Aw, they were lucky." When Boston won, it was skill and hard work.

When I started working Celtics games, one of my first jobs was to read a promo for wristband night. I wouldn't do it. Me? I'm a *journalist*. Journalists don't shill for products or teams. Red quickly disavowed me of that notion. He said in so many words, "Your job is get fannies into the seats! Don't give me this journalism crap." Welcome to the Real World, Mr. Big-Shot Journalist. Another time, my job was to interview Red during halftime of a Celtics–Washington Bullets game at Cole Fieldhouse at the University of Maryland. We didn't know that there would be a marching band on the court at the time. Not just a couple of instruments, but an entire marching band playing loud marching band music—indoors! I couldn't hear my own questions, and I have no idea what Red heard.

Somehow, though, I survived those initial fiascoes, and WBZ-TV, with Auerbach's blessing, tapped me to call Celtics games on television. We were in the press box during a baseball game at Fenway Park and Auerbach introduced me to Senator Ted Kennedy. He told the senator that I'd be announcing his games next season. Kennedy didn't react. I think he was underwhelmed. (I seem to have that effect on elected officials. When

I met Hillary Clinton at a cocktail party, she said she didn't know much about sports, but that her "husband watches sports twenty-four hours a day." Somehow, I doubted that.) Congressman Dick Gephardt, however, once told me he liked my voice. (Of course, he was running for president at the time.)

I called Celtics games for five seasons in all, four of them as the play-by-play man on television, but I'm not sure I ever earned Auerbach's good graces. In 1978, there was a halftime ceremony at Boston Garden for John Havlicek, who was retiring after sixteen seasons with the Celtics. Auerbach described him as the "guts of the team." The writers who covered the Celtics planned to give him a typewriter as a parting gift. The press was appreciative that he had always been such an accommodating interview subject. At the last minute, I was asked to present the gift because the sportswriter who had been assigned the task was camera shy. I didn't come to the game expecting to work, and afterward Red was annoyed with me. I wasn't wearing a tie.

In 1973, I was the color commentator alongside Johnny Most, the legendary voice of the Boston Celtics. Truth is, Johnny didn't need a color man. He was the entire show. He would show up in the booth with only the rosters of both teams and proceed to broadcast a fifteen-minute pregame show with no notes whatsoever. Our broadcast was simulcast, airing on both radio and TV at the same time. I don't like simulcasts. In radio, you have to paint the entire word picture. On television, the picture tells the story. Here's a play on the radio: "Frazier's at the line to shoot two. He bounces the ball two, three, four times. He stops. Takes a breath. Eyes the basket, shoots . . . swish." The same exact sequence on television sounds like this: "Frazier at the line. He makes the first."

What's worse, I was supposed to be the expert analyzing the TV replays, but when we were on the road I couldn't see the replays. The television station didn't want to spend the money for a replay machine on the road, so they used the equipment they had in Boston. If you were back at the station in Boston or if you were watching the game at home, you could see the replay. But not me, not the so-called expert. So there I was working with Johnny Most and explaining plays I didn't quite see the first time, let alone the second. It was a disaster.

One game in Washington, Most turned to me during a commercial break and lectured me about disagreeing with him on the air. I don't remember what I had said, but Most didn't like it. He thought the play-by-play and color men should be in total agreement. Personally, as a viewer, I like it when the announcers have a healthy disagreement about a game. But Johnny didn't.

🏀　🏀　🏀

After a year of simulcasts, the station came to its senses and separated the radio and TV broadcasts. I was picked to do play-by-play on television with Bob Cousy. I had the honor of announcing games with "The Cooz" for four seasons. Having played thirteen years for the Celtics and having made the All-Star Game every year, Cousy was a legend in Boston—almost comparable to Bobby Orr and Ted Williams. Paired with Bill Russell, he led the Celts to the championship in 1957 and then again in each of five consecutive seasons, from 1959 to 1963. (The Celtics won three more titles in the three years after Cousy retired.) Earning the nickname Houdini of the Hardwood, Cousy was far and away the best and flashiest passer of his day.

But as great as he was on the court, he was even better as a person off the court. On road-trip flights, when the stewardess came around and asked our names, he would deliberately mispronounce his name and say "COW-zee." He didn't want anyone to make a fuss. Cousy was a fabulous basketball analyst. I learned more from him than anyone. He made the game understandable with pithy lines such as, "I'll trade you jump shots for layups all night long." Cooz would cut through all the nonsense and get right to the point. Oftentimes, his point was about money in pro sports. He should know. He was an all-time all-timer, and his top salary in his NBA career was just $35,000. That's why he'd rip your throat out if you were opposing him in the playoffs. That extra few grand of playoff money actually *meant* something back then.

I once stood across the net from him on a tennis court. It was long after he had retired from basketball, but I saw that competitive fire in his eyes. I can only imagine what the opposition saw when he walked onto the court during his prime. Actually, he told me that there were nights when the Celtics were so confident that they would win that they basically coasted for the first three quarters. Then they'd huddle up and say something like, "Let's stop screwing around," and proceed to blow the other team off the court.

Cousy and I would talk about life as much as basketball. One thing he taught me: when you're all uptight and your blood pressure is racing, try to slow everything down. Brush your teeth slower. Pull up your pants more deliberately. Everything. It works, and I do it to this day. Cousy represents the absolute best part of what I do for a living. I idolized him from afar, met him, worked with him, and was never disappointed. At the end of the day, it's a privilege to call him a friend. That's about as good as it gets.

◆   ◆   ◆

I like to think that my broadcasts have always been impartial. But I know that when I was calling Celtics games, friends who are Knicks fans would tell me that my broadcasts were pro-Celtic. Part of the reason, I think, is that the New York broadcasters would concentrate on the Knicks Walt Frazier, while I was more apt to concentrate on Celtics guard Don Chaney.

While I might tilt my emphasis for the home crowd audience, I don't think that I could ever be accused of being a "homer"—that is, an announcer who openly roots for the team whose games he is announcing. I don't blame the homers, though. Why wouldn't they want to root? In most cases the team either pays their salaries or has the right to approve their announcers. The most extreme homer is Kenny Harrelson, who broadcasts Chicago White Sox games. I love "The Hawk," as Harrelson is called. In his playing days, he was a colorful outfielder for the A's and Red Sox. I got to know him when he was announcing Boston games. He later became general manager of the White Sox and is now their TV play-by-play man. When a White Sox player hits a homer, his call will be something like this: "There it goes . . . deep to left. YOU CAN PUT IT ON THE BOARD!" This is punctuated by the stereo call of "YESSSSSSSS!!!!!" with his broadcast partner. When an opponent hits a homer? Harrelson, sounding disinterested and bored, says, "There it goes. Home run."

We can debate the propriety of homer broadcasters all we want, but the more important question is whether a play-by-play guy working for a team can really tell the truth. Red Barber was fired as a Yankees announcer after the 1966 season. He asked the cameraman to pan around Yankee Stadium to show that only 413 fans were there for a late-season game. The cameraman knew better. He wouldn't do it. Yankees management was irate, and Barber was out.

When the late Al McGuire was announcing college basketball games for NBC, I remember him yelling on the air, "Stop jerking around and get this game over with." He was railing about how long it took to play the final moments of a college game. Between fouls, commercials, and time-outs, the final minute could take half an hour. I loved McGuire's little bit of honesty.

When I first announced some basketball games for HBO, Marty Glickman told me that if the game was terrible I was permitted to say so on the air. I was even allowed to tell the viewer to go do something else and come back in time for the next program: HBO was unique in sports broadcasting in that it was commercial free. We could say, "This game stinks. Go find something useful to do with your life," without upsetting any advertisers. I never followed Marty's advice. I didn't have the balls. Another HBO executive told me I really shouldn't say stuff like that, but I liked the concept.

While I was at HBO in the late 1970s, I was also asked to host some boxing matches. There have been times in my boxing career when I wished I could have been as forthright as Glickman suggested. I mean, how many boxing matches are total mismatches? Lots—especially when big names are involved. The boxers and their managers don't want to risk huge paydays by fighting tough opponents every other month, so they schedule lots of patsies. But if you're announcing a pay-per-view fight, it certainly doesn't help your announcing longevity if you begin the broadcast by saying: "Welcome to Caesar's Palace, suckers. I can't believe you just dropped $39.95 for this piece-of-crap fight." (Likewise, when calling a Royals–Devil Rays game, you can't open the broadcast by saying, "The Royals are hosting the Devil Rays. They're a combined trillion games out of first place. Isn't this a complete waste of time?")

The blow-by-blow man for HBO at this time was the legendary Don Dunphy, known as "the voice of boxing." One time Dunphy and I were in Landover, Maryland, for a Sugar Ray Leonard fight. We stopped for a sandwich before going to the arena. When the check came, Dunphy said, "I'll flip you for it." He said that that was the way he's always treated restaurant bills over the years. He flipped and he lost. The bill couldn't have been more than ten bucks, but the great Don Dunphy was buying me dinner. I knew right then and there that I liked the fight game.

I wasn't so sure on the night of October 12, 1978, though. HBO decided to broadcast live from Rahway State Prison in New Jersey. The show was promoted as "Boxing Behind Bars." It was a history-making telecast: a boxing match had never before been televised from the pokey. An inmate by the name of James Scott was going to fight light-heavyweight contender Eddie Gregory, later known as Eddie Mustafa Muhammad. Gregory told me he wasn't uncomfortable going into the slammer to fight the inmate, that he himself had spent time in jail, but "for small stuff." He explained that he had "beat[en] up four cops once." You know, petty crime! As usual, my job was to host the telecast, but once the fight began, I was sent to the Drill Hall where eleven hundred inmates were watching the fight on a large-screen television. I was supposed to gauge their reactions.

I really don't think they wanted their fellow inmate, James Scott, to win. They were jealous of all the publicity he was receiving, and I think they would have been perfectly happy if he had been decked. That wasn't going to happen, though. What else did Scott have to do but train? All day long. In his cell, push-up after push-up, sit-up after sit-up. He won the fight in a twelve-round decision. Thankfully the inmates didn't riot. After the fight, one inmate shared his opinion that "Winners never quit, and quitters never win." He couldn't quite get the phrase right, though. He stumbled around with the words for a while. Then I just looked into the camera and said, "Words to live by." Thankfully they were, and I got out of there alive. For their part, the fans had a short trip home.

◆ ● ◉

My next big play-by-play gig was announcing Big East basketball games, first with Big East commissioner Dave Gavitt and then with Bill Raftery. I was named the initial television voice of the fledgling basketball conference. We began on a syndicated group of stations and then got picked up by ESPN. When it was formed in 1979, the conference had only seven schools. One of the first televised Big East Monday night games of the week was played on a *Wednesday*. It pitted Seton Hall against Princeton, a school that wasn't even in the Big East. The public address system didn't work, the referees showed up late, and at the end of the game the lights at Seton Hall's Walsh Gym were shut off. We broadcast our postgame show in the dark. From such humble beginnings, the Big East developed into a powerhouse conference boasting the talents of Patrick Ewing, Chris Mullin, Eddie Pinckney, Pearl Washington, and others. The conference had great games, great teams, and great players who actually stayed in college for four years.

In the early days of the conference, one of the biggest rivalries was between Syracuse and Georgetown. Because I was a Syracuse alumnus, Georgetown supporters thought my broadcasts were biased toward the Orangemen. At the same time, the athletic director of Syracuse complained to the Syracuse newspaper that Raftery and I were biased against Syracuse. We pissed everyone off, so we must have been doing a good job. I think local teams at the time expected to hear their local announcers play the part of cheerleader. Our broadcasts were being heard around the country, so we left our pom-poms at home.

Like Auerbach, coach John Thompson had built up an "us against the world" culture at Georgetown. Hoya Paranoia, it was called. The media couldn't go into the locker room and couldn't talk to the players. Sometimes we felt lucky we were even permitted in the arena for the game! I spoke to Thompson about these policies while we were waiting for a plane at the Syracuse airport. He explained, "The referees of the games are grown men. They're not really allowed to talk to the media and explain themselves. And yet my players are kids. They're hardly as mature as the refs. I don't want these kids being placed in the position of having to defend their actions when the referees get a free pass." It was an interesting perspective.

In 1984, I brought my seven-year-old son, Daniel, to a Georgetown game in Washington. After the game, Thompson grabbed him by the hand and took him to meet the Hoya players in the locker room—the very place from which I'd been barred. The guys were great with my son. They showed him around the locker room and introduced him to all their teammates. Afterward, Daniel emerged from the locker room with a huge smile on his face. He had this to report: "Daddy, they have penises the size of fire hoses!" Thank you John Thompson and Georgetown for knocking me down another peg in the eyes of my kid!

One day, early in the history of the conference, Raftery and I were driving from the Washington airport to Landover, Maryland, for a game. Dave Gavitt, then the commissioner of the Big East, and the conference's current commissioner, Mike Tranghese, joined us. Tranghese said, "You don't really have to sell the conference on the air." I was rather stunned. I had worked for the Celtics under Auerbach where the whole idea was to be a pitchman during the broadcasts. Believe it or not, the Celtics didn't always sell out their games back then, and Red had made it very clear to me that part of my job was to tell fans about the upcoming game where they could get free calendars. But the Big East guys explained, "We've got a good product. It'll sell itself." I really appreciated that. Just announce the games. It was what Gowdy meant when he told me that "sportscasting would be the greatest job in the world, if only they *let* you broadcast."

And, boy, were Gavitt and Tranghese right. A few years later, when Georgetown met St. John's at Madison Square Garden in 1985, the game pitted the country's number one ranked team against the number two team. Georgetown was led by Patrick Ewing, and St. John's by Chris Mullin. The two stars would split that season's player of the year honors, with Mullin taking home the Wooden award and Ewing getting the Naismith prize. I had the honor of calling that game. It was one of the biggest college basketball games ever, and at the time it was the top-rated telecast in the history of ESPN. Since most people didn't have cable then, fans lined up around the block to get into bars showing the game, even in places as removed from the Big East as Florida. Georgetown won. Georgetown also beat St. John's in the Big East Championship game, and a few of weeks later, three Big East teams—Georgetown, St. John's, and Villanova—made it to the Final Four. In the semifinals, Georgetown once again defeated the Johnnies. But in the championship game, Villanova, with near-perfect execution, beat the heavily favored Hoyas 66–64. It was one of the greatest upsets in NCAA history.

In 1982, I was hired by NBC Sports to host the network's NFL pregame show. Tom Brokaw had left the *Today* show to anchor NBC *Nightly News,* and Bryant Gumbel had left NBC Sports to take Brokaw's job on *Today.* NBC initially asked Bob Costas to take over for Gumbel, but he declined. And so, the job was mine. Network sports—pretty cool! I thought I had made it. Well, it didn't take long for things to fall apart. For starters, the NFL players went on strike. I was stuck with a pregame show, but no games. For a while NBC filled the time with Canadian Football League games. They weren't a big hit. But how could they be? The CFL was the only league on earth that had two teams with the same name. There were the Saskatchewan Roughriders and the Ottawa Rough Riders. Sure, Ottawa broke up the name into two words, but that didn't help the play-by-play guy much: "The Roughriders win the toss and the Rough Riders will defend the goal to the east." (In 1996, Ottawa renamed its Rough Riders the Renegades. Spoilsports.)

Eventually the strike ended and the NFL played a short season. I got to host Super Bowl XVII in Pasadena. John Riggins and the Redskins beat the Miami Dolphins. Then came the 1983 season. Halfway through, Marty Glickman tipped me off that I wouldn't be around for NFL 1984. Bob Costas would be taking over the following year. Talk about dead man walking— I was a lame duck for half the year. I got paranoid. The executive who just passed me in the hall wasn't as friendly as he used to be, was he? I asked for a telephone line directly from the studio to the edit room, so I could be in close communication for some of the highlight editing. The producers told me fine, but they never installed the line. More paranoia. It was the most unhappy time of my life. When I started out in broadcasting, I had three professional goals: become a major-market sports director by the time I was thirty; make fifty grand per year, also by the age of thirty; and make it to a network. I had accomplished all three. You know the line about not wishing too hard for something because it may come true? Well, I was miserable. To this day, it's difficult to think about that time, and it's even more difficult to write about it.

I could pen a nasty tell-all about that period, but I despise those books. What's the point in taking potshots at former colleagues or bosses? Tell-alls come off as bitter. It cuts both ways, though. Sugarcoated tomes about how everyone was wonderful come off as phony. So I'll leave it at that and say only that it was during this period that I had the honor to meet and work with two of the legends of broadcasting: directors Harry Coyle and Ted Nathanson. They've both passed on. Teddy was the football man. He gave me a lesson in broadcasting diversity. He'd be upset if a pregame package featured only white athletes. I remember my visit to a football training camp in the early 1970s. At lunch the black players ate with other blacks and the whites with whites. It made a big impression. This was supposed to be a football *team*. Too bad Teddy Nathanson wasn't with me then; he'd have straightened them out.

Harry Coyle was NBC's legendary baseball director. He virtually invented the sport on television. I remember him telling me before the 1984 World Series that the ideal scenario would be a seven-game series with the home team winning every game. He asked me how many times that had happened in World Series history? I had no idea. "It's never happened," Harry crowed. (It has since—in 1987, 1991, and 2001.) As the director, Harry would be stationed in the production truck and communicate with the cameramen and technicians over headsets. Once when Harry was directing a big baseball game, he bellowed in the truck, "Get the runner!" All the cameramen in the stadium swung their cameras, swishing and panning every which way, to get the runner. At least five cameras, all trained on the same base runner. It wasn't quite what Harry had in mind. He was calling for the "runner"—the kid who fetches stuff for the guys working in the production truck. Harry wanted a hot dog!

Coyle subscribed to the KISS theory of broadcasting: Keep It Simple Stupid. I can only imagine what he would think of today's sports broadcasts. With all the graphics, sound effects, and jump cuts, one sometimes forgets that a game is being played. Today, directors have all sorts of cameras at their disposal. In the 2004 baseball postseason, Fox even implanted tiny cameras in the dirt in front of home plate pointing back at the hitter. They called them Diamond-Cams. I didn't think the shot added much—in fact, I thought it kind of made the players look like video games—but the cameras were another toy at their disposal and the directors made the most of them. Much of the time, a simple shot from the mezzanine level behind home plate is all that is needed. With one camera, you can follow the action from the windup to the play at the plate. Instead, though, directors zoom in for tight shots of the pitcher, the hitter, the fielder, the base runner, and, then, for the dramatic play at the plate, the director might cut to a camera by the first-base dugout. In the end, all you see is bodies and dirt flying. I think Harry would agree that all the technology is great for MTV, but for a simple play in a simple game like baseball, no thanks.

In any case, my unhappiness and paranoia passed. And five years later there was another NFL strike. *Football strike?* thought the NBC execs. "Get Berman!" So once again, I was back at the network for the NFL pregame show. At the start of my first show, I thanked Bob Costas for filling in for me the past five years.

Through the years, I've also done some play-by-play for NBC Sports: college basketball, NFL football, and even baseball (well, sort of). In 1985, I was assigned to work a Cincinnati Reds baseball game. I had called a few baseball games on radio in college, but this was my big opportunity: Major League Baseball play-by-play. I did my homework and I was ready. Mike Shannon, one of the Cardinals' announcers, was my color commentator. We interviewed Johnny Bench for the opening of the broadcast and then it started to rain. Games never get rained out in Cincinnati. The Reds played on Astroturf and Riverfront Stadium had terrific drainage. But this one got washed away. NBC sent the entire country to the other game being televised, and I was sent home. That was the end of my baseball play-by-play career. I didn't call a single pitch, and I haven't called a game since.

Dick Enberg and a variety of color commentators called the big national football broadcasts, and I was assigned regional NFL games. I broadcast eight games a season between 1984 and 1986. I spent a lot of time in Cincinnati and Cleveland for Bengals and Browns games. I loved dealing with Cincinnati coach Sam Wyche. Wyche would share his playbook with me. Wyche once told me the Bengals had a weebee offense planned for the goal line. I had never played football, and I had no idea what a weebee offense was. He explained: "If we get down close to scoring, the big offensive linemen will say to themselves, 'We be going into the end zone.'" I liked that. For another game, he told me the first eight or nine offensive plays he intended to run. Not only did I appreciate the trust, but it made me look awfully sharp when I turned to my co-announcer, Gene Washington, and said, "Gene, I would look for a Kenny Anderson pass here to Chris Collinsworth." Before a game in Cleveland, Wyche told me that if the Bengals offense got inside the five-yard line, I should expect a tackle-eligible pass. The quarterback would throw the ball to some hulking lineman in the end zone. So, of course, the Bengals move the ball inside the five and I totally blanked. It was a gimme and I dropped the ball. Wouldn't I have looked brilliant if I had said to Washington, "Know what I'd do here? I'd call a tackle-eligible pass"? Hell, I might have even been written up in *USA Today*'s sports media column! But I blew it. The next thing I knew, the tackle was jumping around in the end zone with the football. This was just one of a million times that I've thought afterward about what I should have said but didn't.

I haven't done football play-by-play since 1986, but in 1997 and 1998, I worked as a sideline reporter for NBC Sports. I hated the job, but the boss of my television station wanted me to get involved with the Jets' telecasts, so I had no choice. When I was a sideline reporter, I wasn't allowed to stand near the bench area. I wasn't allowed to talk to the players. What was I permitted to do? I was allowed to report injuries, but the only way I could find out about an injury was when a team's public relations man in the press box phoned the network's TV truck and told my producer, who then relayed the information to me through my earpiece. So there I was Johnny-on-the-spot reporting fresh information that was processed three or four times through an elaborate game of telephone. If I actually figured something out on my own, NFL rules said I couldn't use the information. The rules were ridiculous. I was a *sideline* reporter, but I wasn't allowed to really walk the sidelines between the twenty-yard lines and midfield. The area between the two twenties was off-limits. At one game the league actually assigned somebody to keep me in my place. When I started to walk across the twenty-yard line, he pushed me back. God forbid I might see or hear something worth reporting. One player could turn to a teammate and say that the other team stinks. You wouldn't want top-secret information like that getting out.

In one game, Jets quarterback Neil O'Donnell got hurt. What I did ran completely afoul of the rules. I was standing in the off-limits portion of the sideline, right next to the Jets' team doctor. "Hey, Doc, how is he?" I asked. The doctor knew me and whispered, "Separated shoulder." Well, in the context of sports, when the starting quarterback has a separated shoulder, it's rather newsworthy. But, of course, I wasn't allowed to say anything. The doctor was supposed to tell the coach, who would tell some sideline functionary, who would call the PR man in the press box, who would call the producer in the television truck, who would then tell me in my earpiece, "Neil O'Donnell has a separated shoulder." The season might end before I ever got to report this bit of news. So I said screw it and went on the air with something brilliant like, "First indications are a separated shoulder." I punked out. It wasn't "first indications." It was the truth. The doctor had told me so. But you know what? The NFL and the free world didn't cease to exist because I reported the story.

Another time, linebacker Pepper Johnson went out with a knee injury. The official word was that he had "a sprained knee" and that he may or may not return. Sprained knee? From where I stood, the guy looked dead. I wasn't sure he'd return to life, let alone the second half. But of course I couldn't say anything. I happened to run into Johnson's mother in the elevator during halftime. She was in tears, and I kind of figured his season was in jeopardy, which it was. So again, violating all the rules, I went on the air with the stunning news, "It may be worse than it looks." Again, the world didn't stop spinning on its axis.

As an announcer I know I shouldn't say this, but I've always felt there should be a second audio channel for sports telecasts. On the first channel, viewers could hear the play-by-play and color commentary of the announcers. The second channel, however, would broadcast only what the fans hear in the stadium. Viewers would have a choice of which one they want to listen to. Why? Because some of us just talk too damn much. And it's not just the talking. It's the analysis. Does every single play have to be analyzed and replayed and hashed over? In baseball there's just too much airtime between all the spitting and scratching and throws over to first to keep the runner close. And football is set up perfectly for babbling announcers. There's an entire thirty seconds or so between every play. God forbid some announcers should permit any "dead air."

I tried out my philosophy when I did some boxing announcing for TVKO, the pay-per-view arm of HBO. I figured that most of the boxing audience was watching the bout in bars, fraternity houses, or other group settings. They probably couldn't hear what I was saying anyway. I also thought that they could see most of the action and didn't need me to tell them what they just saw. A right to the head—that's radio. On television, they could see the right to the head. My job sitting ringside was to give an indication of whether the blow meant anything or not. Needless to say, my approach to boxing announcing wasn't well received by everyone. One newspaper critic actually put a stopwatch to the telecast and pointed out how I had gone thirty or forty-five seconds at one point without saying a word. He didn't think that was good at all. I wasn't paid by the word, as many sportswriters are, but my lack of verbiage was a big deal to this critic.

SPANNING THE WORLD
OF INDIVIDUAL SPORTS

MARCH 1990, FLORIDA. The tee shot of LPGA golfer Dale Eggeling took a big bounce and landed in the lap of a guy sitting in a golf cart. In golf, the rule is "hit it where it lies." Eggeling walked over and found her ball in the guy's lap. Waving her hands, she shouted, "I'm not touching that!"

JULY 2001, WIMBLEDON, ENGLAND. Pete Sampras was playing at Wimbledon when a ball hit by Englishman Barry Cowan bounced right up Sampras's shorts and stayed there. Sampras sat down on the court and summoned the ballboy to come retrieve the ball. It's not easy to turn down the request of a tennis superstar, but like Eggeling, this ballboy wisely declined.

OCTOBER 1995, MOLINE, ILLINOIS. It was fight night and Lonnie Horn was battling Craig Houk. Horn not only knocked out Houk, but he knocked off Houk's toupee in the process. At one point the toupee was sticking straight up in the air, making it the first hairpiece in boxing history to receive a standing eight count!

FEBRUARY 1991, NEW YORK. Boxer Wali Muhammed was penalized two points for biting James Salerno in a tight clinch. The TV camera caught a close-up of Muhammed munching on Salerno's left forearm. After the fight, Muhammed denied the incident. "Why would I bite him?" he asked. "I'm a vegetarian!"

MARCH 1996, BUFFALO. There was a full-scale snowstorm at the racetrack in Buffalo. No one could see anything. Not the fans, not the TV cameras, not the race announcer. But that didn't stop the horse race. Track announcer Peter Szymanski made the call: "Into the far turn . . . come out . . . hello . . . horsies, where are you?"

JULY 2002, WIMBLEDON, ENGLAND. John McEnroe and Chris Evert were broadcasting live. They were discussing Venus Williams when an elderly male fan approached them on camera and asked for their autographs. Evert said, "We'll have to do that a little bit later." McEnroe added, without missing a beat, "Unless you have something to say about Venus!"

JULY 2003, SILVERSTONE, ENGLAND. At the British Formula One Grand Prix, while the cars were screaming around the race course, a protester carrying signs and wearing a kilt ran onto the track. Cars had to swerve to avoid hitting him. The guy was arrested and charged with trespassing. It turns out he was a priest and his signs urged people to read the Bible. He later showed up at the

Olympic Games in Athens, where he disrupted the marathon. The guy should thank God he wasn't kilt.

SEPTEMBER 1991, YONKERS RACEWAY, NEW YORK. Fast Traffic and Fulla Potholes were two of the entrants in a harness race. You guessed it: there was a six-car, er, horse, pileup.

MAY 1994, HUSKY SOFTBALL STADIUM, SEATTLE. At the University of Washington, a softball player hit a long foul ball clear out of the stadium. On the fly, it hit a passing bicycle rider right on top of his head. The cyclist wasn't hurt, but it's another good reason why you should wear a helmet.

APRIL 1996, NAZARETH, PENNSYLVANIA. At a CART race, Paul Tracy had a little mishap in pit row. He bowled over three crew members. None of them was hurt. So what was Tracy fined for? Running over the air hose.

JULY 1990. Chi Chi Rodriguez chipped the ball onto the green. A dog ran over, took the ball in his mouth, and scurried off. How was it scored? A birdie? An eagle? No, a beagle!

VALENTINE'S DAY 2000, DAYTONA MOTOR SPEEDWAY, DAYTONA, FLORIDA. During a practice session leading up to the Daytona 500, the Viagra car caught on fire. Happy Valentine's Day.

OCTOBER 2003, RIO DE JANIERO, BRAZIL. An unhappy soccer fan showed up at his favorite team's practice session and proceeded to throw live chickens onto the field. He was making a statement about what he perceived to be a lack of toughness on the part of the players. They made a statement in return. They chased down the fan and started pummeling him.

MARCH 2004, ANAMA, BRAZIL. A soccer referee reached into his pocket to pull out a red card to eject a player. By mistake, the ref pulled out a pair of red panties! He said he had no idea how they wound up in his pocket, but he reportedly was so red-faced that he called off the rest of the game with twenty minutes remaining. Word is that his wife was watching the match and the panties weren't hers. We're told divorce proceedings started immediately!

21

MARATHON MAN

AUGUST 1992, SAN ANTONIO, TEXAS. The "Fun Run" was only open to people named Bill. The participants all wore T-shirts with BILL proudly printed on the back. You just couldn't beat the excitement and drama of the "Running of the Bills."

I could never run a marathon. But then, I could never do just about anything I report on. I used to run about two miles a day, and during the 1970s I actually contemplated trying to run the Boston Marathon. So I upped my regimen to three miles. I found it to be a complete struggle. Marathoners tend to "hit the wall" around the twentieth mile. I hit mine around the third. I can't imagine running 10 miles, let alone 26.2. The thing I love about the marathon, though, is that everyday working stiffs can race right alongside world-class athletes. Well, not actually right alongside because elite athletes now get a head start.

I sometimes wonder if the origin of the marathon might explain why so many bizarre things tend to happen along the 26-mile, 385-yard course. That distance, to begin with, is ridiculous. You've probably heard the story: a guy named Pheidippides supposedly ran that distance from the town of Marathon to Athens in 490 B.C. He arrived with the news of some great Greek army victory over the Persian army. Pheidippides made his announcement and then dropped dead. Isn't that a cheerful beginning to the sport?

◦　◦　◦

I covered the Boston Marathon for WBZ-TV from 1974 to 1978, and I've since covered the New York City Marathon on and off for a quarter of a century. While I never pulled a Pheidippides and dropped dead, there were some uncomfortable moments to say the least. Remember that labor dispute at WBZ in 1976, when the TV technicians ruined the station's first-ever live shot? A few weeks earlier, those guys had showed up at the Boston Marathon. This was an event that I always loved reporting from—but not that year.

The race begins in the tiny town of Hopkinton; it ends on Boylston Street in front of the Boston Public Library in the heart of downtown Boston. The whole town of Hopkinton comes out once a year to celebrate the race and to send all of these running lunatics on their way. And after the runners clear out, Hopkinton goes back into hibernation for another year. The start of the marathon always reminds me of the 1993 Bill Murray movie *Groundhog Day*. There were these self-important poobahs who ruled the day. Same as in Hopkinton. The poobahs run the show at the start of the marathon, and then the other 364 days of the year they go back to doing whatever poobahs do when they're not poobahing.

When the locked-out technicians saw me at the start in Hopkinton, they did all they could to interfere with our coverage of the race. Every time the "replacement" cameramen tried to shoot some footage, the locked-out guys would hold up large pieces of paper directly in front of the camera lenses. I freaked. I was having a hard time imagining going on television to describe the "marathon masses" without any footage. One of the local policemen witnessed my plight and thought he'd give me a hand. So he tried to shoo the union guys away. One big problem: The policeman had his police dog with him. As far as the union guys at my station were concerned, Mr. Big-Shot Television Sportscaster—who also happened to be in a union—had sicced a police dog on his station compatriots. That, of course, is not exactly what happened. But it didn't matter. The damage was done. And to this day some of those technicians probably would not talk to me. Clearly, this was one of the darkest days of my career.

I wasn't the only guy dealing with cameramen on race day 1976. Paul Newman was also there that day. Everyone went nuts trying to get a glimpse of the movie star or to take his picture. He was watching his wife, Joanne Woodward, run the Boston Marathon for the made-for-TV movie *See How She Runs*. It was the story of a middle-aged housewife whose life was changed by her decision to run in the Boston Marathon. (Thank goodness they weren't filming *Sportscaster's Dog Day Afternoon* that day.) Some residents of sleepy Hopkinton actually blame Newman for turning the Boston Marathon into the spectacle it is today. It was not only his presence in town that day, but also his wife's film, they say, that got people excited about the race. I'm not sure that's true. The New York City Marathon is the "biggest sporting event in the world." And so far as I know Newman never showed up in Staten Island on race day. Then again I never had a union problem in New York, either.

Despite that 1976 fiasco, some of my fondest sports memories were formed at the starting line in Hopkinton. I could walk right up with a cameraman and a microphone and speak with the great marathoner Bill Rodgers, who won Boston four times, in 1975 and then again in 1978, 1979, and 1980. Moments before the gun would fire, I'd be standing there interviewing him about his game plan for the race. Access is one of the great things about the marathon. You can't approach a World Series starting pitcher just before he throws the first pitch or a Super Bowl quarterback just before the kickoff. Taking it a step further, you can't run the base paths as your hero takes his home run trot or rub shoulders with the quarterback while he stands over the center. But you can in a marathon—you can run the same course at the same time with all the big-shot star athletes and nobody will come out and arrest you. I couldn't run a five-minute mile for a full mile, much less 26.2 miles, but I could keep up with Bill Rodgers the day *after* he won a marathon. I did just that in April 1975. He jogged along with me and spoke about the feeling of running and winning such a fabled race. The most remarkable thing about this may be that the day after Rodgers won the marathon, he went out and ran some more. I told you these guys are nuts.

If there was a face of the Boston Marathon, it was Johnny Kelly's. He won the marathon in 1935. And for good measure he won it again ten years later, in 1945. He also ran the race in 1955, 1965, 1975, and 1985—and all the years in between. He was the goodwill ambassador for the sport of running in Boston. He was at every race, always smiling, always talking about how great it was to run. In 1991, he ran the Boston Marathon for the sixtieth time. Kelly was eighty-three years old at the time. As he crossed the finish line, there was a banner stretched across it that read JOHNNY KELLY 60TH BOSTON MARATHON. His wife, Laura, was there to greet him. He hugged her and the two of them fell down onto the pavement, with Johnny on top. Fortunately, nobody got hurt. He ran one more Boston Marathon, his sixty-first, the following April. At the age of eighty-four, he finished in under six hours!

No wonder Johnny Kelly lasted on this earth until October 2004. When his incredible body finally gave out, he was ninety-seven years old. Johnny Kelly was one of my all-time favorite sportsmen. He represented everything that was good about the marathon—and sports in general.

So did K. Switzer. In 1967, Switzer entered the Boston Marathon. Only when Switzer got to Hopkinton did the poobahs realize that the K. stood for Kathryn. A woman had never officially run Boston before. As the race began, stodgy old New Englanders could be seen trying to rip the number off her shirt. But K. Switzer was too swift for these old fogies. She finished in four hours and twenty minutes, but, more important, she opened the race up for women. Actually, women ran "unofficially" from 1966 through 1971. But in 1967, there was a famous picture of the race director, Jock Semple, trying in vain to tear the bib off her shirt. It just looked silly. I think it was the combination of Kathryn's craftiness and Jock Semple's futility that helped women take a quantum leap in the sport of marathon. It wasn't until 1972 that the AAU, which sanctioned the race and was pretty old-fogeyish in its own right, broke down and allowed women to enter the Boston Marathon. In 1972, Nina Kuscsik of Huntington, New York, was the first "official" women's winner of the Boston Marathon.

And then eight years later there was Rosie Ruiz—the Boston Marathon's most famous unofficial winner. On April 21, 1980, Ruiz crossed the finish line in a course record of two hours, thirty-one minutes, and fifty-six seconds. There was one problem, though. Ruiz didn't actually run the race. Here's what probably happened. Ruiz lived in New York. She had qualified for the marathon by running a respectable time the year before in New York. Some say that she actually took the subway a good portion of the New York City Marathon route. (Well, isn't a marathon all about "mass transit"?) She went to

Boston with the intention of jumping into the race with about a mile or so to go. She would finish and then brag to all of her friends about how she ran a good time in Boston.

She made a slight miscalculation. When she jumped into the race, none of the other women had reached that point. Suddenly, she was in the lead. So she finished the race first among the women and was declared the winner. She accepted all of the crowd's adulation, along with the winner's wreath, at the finish line. And then the whispers started. Bill Rodgers won his fourth Boston Marathon that day. He asked, "Who is Rosie Ruiz?" The top runners all knew one another, but nobody had ever heard of her. Moreover, nobody remembered seeing Ruiz at any of the checkpoints along the route. In those days, there was no start-to-finish coverage of the race, but rather just shots at the start and the finish. And running experts said she didn't look like she had just run a marathon, which obviously she hadn't.

Rosie Ruiz was a clerk for a New York City company called Metal Traders. I was working at WCBS-TV in New York at the time, so I called Metal Traders and was invited to come on over with my camera crew to interview Ruiz. I think it was her only one-on-one television interview after the controversy began. She told me that she absolutely ran the entire race and that she was the rightful winner. I also interviewed her fellow employees. They vouched for her 100 percent. Nobody else did, though, and ten days after the race Ruiz was disqualified. A few days after her disqualification, she held a news conference in New York. She brought along the plaque she had been given at the finish line—as well as a new excuse. She once again affirmed that she ran the race, and she also said that maybe because she had short hair, people didn't realize that she was a woman. All the doubting Thomases at the news conference continued to question the veracity of her story. Eventually, she stormed off the stage, leaving some of her belongings behind. My last memory of that news conference was a newspaper writer yelling out, "Hey, Rosie, you forgot your plaque."

Nobody remembers who actually won the women's race in 1980. It was a Canadian woman named Jackie Gareau. And she, not Rosie Ruiz, truly set the new Boston Marathon mark for women: 2:34:28. Her record lasted exactly one year. In 1981, Allison Roe of New Zealand bettered Gareau's mark by over seven minutes. By the way, I recently read that Ruiz, who doesn't go by that last name anymore, lives in Florida. She's still sticking to her story. I wonder if she ever got her plaque back.

       ✿   ✿   ✿

Of course, another Rosie Ruiz incident couldn't happen today. Each runner now has a computer chip attached to his or her sneaker. An individual's time only begins when he or she passes the starting line—which in a race such as the New York City Marathon can take up to thirty minutes if the person is stuck at the back of the pack on the Verrazano Narrows Bridge. The computer chip also tracks the runners so that anybody can go online and check the progress of a participant during the race. It's a great feature. (Perhaps it was Rosie Ruiz who inspired this technology. If that's the case, I guess she deserves our everlasting thanks and appreciation.) When my daughter, Rachel, raced in New York in 2004, I followed her progress online. Rachel took about three hours longer to complete the distance than the women's winner. But at least she ran the entire race. I couldn't have been prouder.

In 1980, I covered my first New York City Marathon. The broadcast was laughable by today's television standards. I was working at WCBS-TV and our news director, Steve Cohen, came up with the idea of televising the race. Well, not exactly the entire race. We didn't have the technology then to have the overhead or on-the-course moving shots like you see today. That year's race began at 10:30 in the morning. At 10:25 A.M., we broke into the cartoons we were carrying on the station and showed the start of the race. We stayed on the air for about ten minutes. Then it was back to the cartoons. The minute we got off the air, we jumped into a car with the legendary creator of the race, the late Fred Lebow. We received a police escort. With sirens blaring we raced to the finish line at Tavern on the Green in Central Park. Then we set up to cover the end of the race. Alberto Salazar crossed the finish line about 12:40 P.M. So once again, we dumped out of local programming for a few minutes, showed the finish, and then got the hell off the air. There you go: our first live telecast of the New York City Marathon. When the ratings came out on Monday, our Sunday morning numbers were just about the same as they always were. Not very many people watched the race or apparently cared. Steve Cohen wrote a note on the ratings sheet for all to see in the newsroom: "Why did we bother?"

That the race grew in popularity to the point where a live broadcast actually made sense can be attributed largely to the relentless efforts of Fischl Lebowitz. Who? Lebowitz was born in Romania, emigrated to the United States, and the rest is history. Sort of. Along the way, he changed his name to Fred Lebow and created a little running race in Central Park. That was 1970. One hundred seventy people ran the first New York City Marathon. They each ran four loops around the park. The winner got a bowling trophy. Six years later, the marathon course was refigured so that the runners would race through all five of New York City's boroughs. In 1977, when 4,821 people showed up to run, it was called the "largest marathon in the world." In 2004, there were over thirty-seven thousand entrants and the prizes totaled more than half a million dollars. The male and female winners each received $100,000 and a car.

In the early days of the marathon, Lebow or one of his assistants at the New York Road Runners Club would constantly call the various newsrooms begging for coverage of some runner or another. Lebow, with his Romanian accent, was rather pushy, to say the least. I often wondered, *Who is this guy? What is his angle? What is in it for him?* To be honest, I was a bit suspicious of Lebow. It took me years to realize that he was the real deal. He was just promoting a great race. Nothing more, nothing less. He was truly a visionary.

There was another pushy bearded fellow who Lebow always reminded me of. In my early Boston years, this guy from the public affairs unit at WBZ would frequently come by to pester us in the newsroom. The Federal Communications Commission requires television stations to do some kind of community good or public service while they are raking in their millions. That task generally falls to the station's public affairs department, where anything deemed good for the local community is tossed. Of course, the unit didn't have any kind of a budget to do its good work, and that's where the pushy bearded fellow came in. His name was Vinnie, and when he entered the newsroom, the reporters, producers, and the people who assigned the cameramen would all run. He'd come in, hat in hand, to beg, borrow, or steal a camera crew to do an interview with some old lady on welfare who was suffering from gout or something. These interviews weren't ratings grabbers—the station just wanted to protect its license, which some people in the business used to call "a license to steal." Anyway, every time Vinnie showed up, we would hide. We didn't want to part with our precious camera crews. After all, we were doing the really important stuff: interviewing some local congressman or hockey player. So what became of Vinnie? Maybe you've heard of the program *America's Funniest Home Videos?* The creator and producer—and consequently, the gazillionaire—behind that program is none other than Vin DiBona. Vinnie himself. Fred Lebow and Vinnie DiBona were two guys who knew exactly what they were doing. It was the rest of us who didn't have a clue.

●　　●　　●

I've been the host of the New York City Marathon coverage on WNBC since 1999. No more cartoons. No more cut-ins early and late. We come on the air at nine in the morning, and we don't sign off until two in the afternoon. Salazar's victory in 1980, the first New York race I covered, was no big deal. An American had won the race every year since the race was founded in 1970. Salazar won again in 1981 and 1982. Since 1982, though, no American has won the race.

Yet despite the parade of African winners (eight in a row through 2004) and the dearth of top American talent, people tune in. It's truly an amazing spectacle. I can't think of a more breathtaking scene in all of sports than the sight of thirty-seven thousand bodies crossing the Verrazano. Actually, the number of runners in New York in 2004 reached an all-time high of 37,257. Now of that number, how many people do you suppose actually finish the race? Run all 26.2 miles? Just about everyone. Only 744 didn't finish in 2004.

Of course, we spend much of our broadcast sharing those gorgeous shots of workaday marathoners running side by side. Even with our exhaustive coverage, though, there are some things we don't show. Of particular note, we don't show runners throwing up at the end of the race. There's a little area just past the finish line where many of the runners go. They lean over the fence and puke their brains out. I've even seen winners do it. C'mon, don't wince. I share this news just so you don't think the marathon is all one pretty picture-postcard from beginning to end.

Although there hasn't been a Rosie Ruiz incident in New York—at least none that we know of—the race has had its share of goof-ups. In 1994, two Mexican runners, German Silva and Benjamin Paredes, were charging to the finish. On the New York Marathon course, toward the end of the race, the runners exit and then reenter Central Park. When Silva went to turn into the park, he made a wrong turn, reentering too early. Paredes followed the correct route, and Silva had to make a U-turn and try to catch Paredes in the final yards. Thankfully he did it. Silva won the race, saving a lot of people a lot of splainin'.

I loved what happened at the finish of the men's race in 2004. Henrik Ramaala of South Africa was charging to the finish line. At the finish, the mayor of New York and the race director hold up a wide ribbon that the runner goes through with his hands held high. It's the money shot, the picture replayed on every newscast and printed in every newspaper in America and around the world the following day. There's a reason why it's called the money shot. Printed on the ribbon are the names of the race's biggest sponsors. The sponsors get worldwide publicity from that picture. In 2004, though, Ramaala didn't run through the ribbon. He ran right around it. Good-bye money shot. It's probably the only marathon you've ever seen where there was no picture of the winner crossing the finish line. All the papers carried shots of Ramaala draped in a South African flag after the race was over. A short time later, Ramaala came into WNBC's television booth for his postrace interview. Before we went live on the air, I asked him why he didn't break the tape. He didn't know what I was talking about. He didn't realize that he hadn't done it. So I said to him, "Well, you didn't break the tape. That means you didn't really win." For a second, before realizing that I was only kidding him, he had a completely stunned look on his face. Only in marathon racing.

●　　●　　●

And only in marathon racing do you get stories like these. In 2004, several veterans of the war in Iraq ran in New York. Some were injured, some were whole. One of the soldiers spoke of his training for the marathon. He said that after walking dangerous patrols, he would run for miles near the Syrian border. I thought, *This guy put his life on the line for the rest of us, and then he went out to train in some area where there might be land mines.*

Another Iraqi war veteran is Melissa Stockwell. In April 2004, she was riding on patrol in Iraq when an explosive hit her Humvee. To save her life, her left leg had to be amputated below the knee. A little over six months later, she competed in the New York City Marathon in the wheelchair division. In the first New York City Marathon, there was just one female competitor. Thirty-five years later, there were about twelve thousand women, including Melissa Stockwell. I have to admit that I'm impressed with what professional athletes are able to do, particularly the superstars; when a Michael Jordan or a Wayne Gretzky rises higher than the rest of the elite athletes, it blows me away. But not nearly as much as First Lieutenant Melissa Stockwell.

Or Zoe Koplowitz. She may well be the world's slowest marathoner. Her races are timed by calendars, not stopwatches. She finally finished the 2004 race after more than twenty-seven hours after the first runner crossed the finish line. Koplowitz has an excuse. She suffers from diabetes and multiple sclerosis. She walks the full 26.2 miles on crutches—through the morning, the afternoon, and the night. Koplowitz has completed eighteen marathons, both in New York and London. In every one, she has finished last. The same week as she completed her eighteenth-career marathon, one of the big sports stories in New York focused on New Jersey Nets center Alonzo Mourning. Mourning had a kidney transplant the previous year, and he was making a comeback. But he wasn't happy. He had signed with the Nets for a chance to win a championship. But the Nets were falling apart; in cost-cutting moves, the team had allowed some players to leave, most notably Kenyon Martin. Mourning wanted out of his contract, which had three years and more than $17 million remaining. He wanted to play for a winner. In my book, Zoe Koplowitz is a winner. A few weeks later a basketball player for the Indiana Pacers, Ron Artest, went to his coach and asked for some time off. He was tired. After all, he was out promoting a rap album he had produced. What? The team should expect maximum effort from a guy making $6 million a year? By the way, Artest later earned his time off without pay. He got involved in a fight with fans in Detroit. The NBA suspended him for the rest of the 2004–2005 season. What about Zoe Koplowitz getting paid zippo? More pro athletes should take a page from her book.

22

NO INTERVIEWS, NO AUTOGRAPHS

SEPTEMBER 1992, YANKEE STADIUM, NEW YORK. Yankees first baseman Don Mattingly couldn't snare a foul pop-up down the first-base line. But he was able to grab a handful of popcorn out of the container held by five-year-old Mikey Chiaparelli, who was sitting in the front row. As Mattingly reached into his container, the little boy just looked up at his hero in disbelief. It wasn't a one-sided exchange, though. Mattingly signed a baseball for Mikey: "Thanks for the popcorn. Best wishes, Don Mattingly."

When it comes to sports, there are a couple of cardinal rules for the media. One is, "No cheering in the press box." Another is, "No autographs." They're good rules. We're not fans, we're reporters. I've broken the second rule a couple of times, though. First, when I helped the fan score Hank Aaron's signature on his Babe Ruth autographed ball. A second time was when I asked Don Mattingly for his autograph. Somebody had given my son Daniel a baseball painted with portraits of Mickey Mantle and Don Mattingly. Mantle was my hero, and Mattingly my son's. I thought it was a pretty cool collectible. So I got the Mick to sign by his portrait and then brought the ball to spring training to get Mattingly's autograph. Donnie Baseball graciously signed it for me. I tell this story in the interest of a full confession. I broke the rule. I admit it—and I feel better already. But more important, my son has a super souvenir.

Some athletes aren't as gracious as Mattingly was. This is true in terms of both interviews and autographs. To a degree,

I understand. It's not easy being a famous athlete. The first time I realized this was in Dayton back in the early 1970s. Johnny Bench was the All-Star catcher down the road in Cincinnati. One night, he made an appearance at a restaurant in Dayton. He had to walk in the front door and make his way about sixty feet to a reception room. Everyone was grabbing at him. Reggie Jackson once said, "Everyone wants a piece of Reggie." Well, everyone not only wanted a piece of Johnny Bench, they were taking it. They grabbed his arm, demanded autographs and photos. The fans would call out things like, "Hey, Johnny, my wife's cousin once met your uncle." (You actually hear that sort of thing all the time around athletes.) Anything to make a connection, to have something to brag about to friends. Now that was just one little appearance by Bench. But for some guys it is like that every day.

One of my first times in the Mets' locker room, I watched as an infielder rifled through a large stack of fan mail. He sat on a stool in front of his locker opening letter after letter. Most contained a baseball card and a stamped return envelope. The infielder basically ripped them all up and tossed them into a heap onto the floor of the locker room. Maybe he was looking for money or for girlish handwriting, as was said of Mantle. Whatever it was, I thought the guy was a jerk. Maybe his fans—or former fans—thought so too when they never got their autographs.

To a degree, though, I understand and sympathize with the dilemma athletes face. If they sign for one, they feel they'll have to sign for everyone. They could get stuck signing all day. John Havlicek told me the trick is to "sign and walk." Sign away, but keep on walking. When you arrive at the team bus or the exit, you can leave gracefully. Some stars try, they really do. After the first Yankees spring training workout a couple of years ago, a thousand fans were lined up against the fence, clamoring for autographs. Who was there trying to sign as many as possible? Yankees captain Derek Jeter. It would be nice if everyone could stop and sign for a few minutes. I know it's difficult to extricate yourself once you start, but maybe that is a price athletes must pay for being who they are.

The memorabilia explosion has complicated this. It turned a scrapbook entry into a business. If you go to any hotel where a pro team is staying, you'll see guys camped out in the lobby with suitcases full of pictures and sports cards looking to get a star to sign his wares. Some athletes decide early that they won't sign anything. Bill Russell was one of those. He wouldn't sign autographs and that was that. You could be famous yourself and approach him, but he wouldn't sign. He was within his rights.

W hen the policy becomes "No interviews," though, I find it more troublesome. Of course, I'm biased here. Autographs aren't my stock-in-trade, but interviews are. Knicks center Patrick Ewing started with a "no game-day interviews" policy. For the most part, it worked for him. But toward the end of his career, the stance backfired. The media was invited to one of those feel-good holiday stories at Madison Square Garden. The Knicks threw a party for some underprivileged kids and Ewing helped to serve the food. The media was there, but Ewing wouldn't talk. It was a game day. Some of the kids wanted autographs, but Ewing again declined. Game day. One problem, though: Ewing was on the injured list and there was no chance he was going to play. But that didn't stop him from alienating both the media *and* the kids.

Similarly, most major-league pitchers won't talk before a game they are scheduled to pitch. I can understand that. But when Roger Clemens joined the Yankees in 1999, the media was told he wouldn't do interviews between starts either. If we couldn't talk to him on the day he pitched, and we couldn't talk with him between assignments, when exactly could we approach him? Turned out, as time went on Clemens was very approachable. During the off-season after he retired from the Yankees in 2003, and then unretired to play for his hometown team in Houston, he was honored at the Thurman Munson dinner. Even though he had turned his back on the Yankees, Clemens received a standing ovation. He couldn't have been more gracious with autographs. When the night broke up, he was saying his good-byes to all of the other great athletes who were there. He made a point of shaking my hand and saying good-bye to me as well. This little gesture meant a lot to me.

Approachable athletes make my job as a reporter much easier and a lot more fun. Big stars may be good "gets"—to use the TV news lingo—but big stars aren't necessarily good interview subjects. Some of the biggest are the most guarded—guys like Michael Jordan, Tiger Woods, and Derek Jeter. They are so careful about what they say. The media would rather deal with a loose cannon, such as Charles Barkley, who's a lot more quotable. It's true that a lot of his stuff is racially tinged, but he can get away with it. When he says, "I make $3 million a year to dunk a basketball, but if people on the street saw me coming, they'd run," it's funny. It's also partially true.

For some athletes, though, being mute can work in their favor. Steve Carlton won 329 games, and during his career he probably said as many words to the media. A whole mystique built up around Lefty. If Carlton actually had spoken, what he had to say might have been boring and nobody would have been interested. Basketball star Bill Walton was another interesting character. He didn't talk much as a player and the feeling was that he was just weird. He later admitted that his unwillingness to talk was due to a speech impediment for which he had successful therapy. Then Walton went into broadcasting, and now you can't get the guy to shut up!

When athletes treat reporters with respect and help them fill their column inches, the reporters can't help but be partial to them. That's why I think there is something fundamentally wrong with baseball's system that has newspaper writers electing Hall of Fame members. The personal stuff can't help but be factored into the equation. Of course, milestone numbers can overcome this. After all, baseball writers elected Old Stone Face Eddie Murray into Cooperstown. Murray was a guy who gave the media two cold shoulders. It didn't matter if he had played a good game or not, if his team had won or lost. I remember when he was playing for the Dodgers and hit a milestone homer at Shea. The next day, he told my camera crew to "Get lost." Several years later, Murray spoke at one of those luncheons I emceed in the Rainbow Room. And, believe it or not, he was terrific. Funny and insightful—it was no wonder his teammates loved him. He carefully explained his media stance. He said that he viewed the locker room as his office. He was preparing for work, and he was entitled to his privacy.

I read recently that Larry Bird doesn't do many newspaper interviews anymore. In one story, though, he was quoted as saying that he first saw Magic Johnson play on TV against the Russian National Team during the preseason of Magic's sophomore year at Michigan State. I love when I read stuff like that. I called that game with Tommy Heinsohn for HBO in November 1978. It was the start of HBO's college basketball series. Today, if you flip through the cable channels during the season, you can watch a zillion games per night, but back then there was no ESPN 1 through 20 and no regional sports channels.

The idea of a midweek college basketball game on cable was new. Little did we know that the year would culminate with Magic and Michigan State winning the national title and Johnson leaving college for the NBA. Anyway, Tommy was a riot. A couple of times during the telecast, instead of calling Magic Ervin Johnson, he called him Irving. I thought to myself, *Gee, I didn't know Johnson was Jewish.* At halftime we aired an interview with Magic that we had taped before the game. It's funny to see it now—so quaint. Johnson wore a little hat and his letter jacket, a big "S" on it for "State." It wasn't exactly a searing interview. First question: "Where did you get the nickname Magic?" (High school. Sportswriter gave it to him.) Last question: "What do you need to work on?" (Jump shot and defense.)

Anyway, the same season that we broadcast Magic's game, we broadcast an Indiana State game. That's how I know that dating back to his college days Larry Bird was never very comfortable with the media. Bird was a senior and one of the most talked about college athletes in the nation. But he didn't do a lot of talking himself. There was no halftime interview. What happened after the game stuck with me, though. Heinsohn and I went to a local pizza joint and bar in Terre Haute, Indiana. Fans approached Heinsohn and asked him all sorts of sports questions. Many of the fans were inebriated, but Tommy treated each fan with respect. If a *New York Times* reporter had asked him the same questions, Heinsohn wouldn't have been any more thoughtful or amenable. It was a great lesson—and a rather surprising one because Heinsohn's public image was anything but patient and gentle. Few people knew that he'd sit in his hotel room during his coaching days and paint. He was an artist. What people saw of Tommy most of the time was a big, gruff guy arguing with officials. Heinsohn coached the Celtics for eight-plus seasons, from 1969 to 1978. WBZ used to film Celtics games at the Garden. One Sunday, the game was on national television, but we stationed a photographer up in the mezzanine anyway. Our photographer was great. He would point the camera toward the action but look outside the lens with his naked eye. Per usual, Heinsohn went nuts. The cameraman saw Heinsohn stalk in front of the Celtics bench, and in one smooth maneuver, panned his camera the length of the court, zooming in on Heinsohn as he kicked the team's water bucket, sending it flying. It doesn't sound like much, but this was a great highlight, and with all the cameras the network had that day, it was a shot they missed.

Well, I finally got to interview Bird in 1982 when he was playing for the Celtics. One of the questions I asked him was about his media stance during college. He said he was mostly wary of the newspaper writers. They would descend on the locker room, thirty or forty of them at once, and go directly to him. He thought it was embarrassing to his teammates, and he thought the reporters would "write stuff that wasn't true," trying to "stir things up" with his teammates. I recently listened to that Bird interview again. It was rather stunning. Bird was frank and to the point, just as he played. Phil Esposito and I did the interview together, and Phil asked Bird about his being basketball's "Great White Hope," a hardwood Gerry Cooney. Bird said, "It doesn't bother me. Basketball is a black man's game. White players are spoiled. A black person goes out and works harder to be better. And they are better." This is the type of statement that has ruined people's careers, but Bird has stood by it. In a rare interview, in June 2004, he told ESPN that basketball is a "black man's game," and he added that the sport needs more white stars because most of the fan base is white.

Espo and I also asked Bird in the 1982 interview how he would like to be remembered. Without missing a beat, Bird answered, "He gave everything he had every single night he played, through injuries, he gave one hundred percent. That's what the fans want to see, that's what they pay for. If they write one thing: 'hustle.' "

♦   ♦   ♦

I never thought of Bird as being on my All-Interview Team. But after listening to what he had to say twenty years ago, and his willingness to stand by a controversial position with so much at stake today, I wish he'd rethink his interview stance. When I think about my best, worst, and favorite interviews, there is only one clear winner. Captain of the All-Interview Team is Muhammad Ali. Undefeated and still champion. No one had a mouth or a mind that worked as quickly as his. In Ali's prime, you would ask him a simple question and were likely to get a five-minute oration of philosophy and history and poetry and pugilism that made perfect sense. He had a million quotes, such as "If you view the world at fifty the same way you did at twenty, then you've wasted thirty years of your life." He had all of his poems stored in his head, and they'd come tumbling out. Before 1971's so-called Fight of the Century, for instance, Ali said this about his opponent, Joe Frazier:

> *Joe's gonna come out smokin'*
> *But I ain't gonna be jokin'*
> *I'll be pickin' and pokin'*
> *Pouring water on his smokin'*
> *This might shock and amaze ya*
> *But I'll retire Joe Frazier.*

Of course, Ali was the one who got smoked at Madison Square Garden. He was knocked down in the fifteenth round and Frazier won a unanimous decision. So much for the prediction, but his poetry was entertaining. Ali announced to the world in 1962, "I am the greatest!" How many of today's athletes think or act as if they are "the greatest"? I always appreciated what Joe Torre said about his championship Yankees teams of the late 1990s. "Everyone wants to be the hero," Torre said, "but nobody wants to talk about it." Maybe that's the true definition of a champ. You go about your business and let the others do the talking. Not Ali, though. He talked a great game, and he backed it up. He *was* the greatest—at least linguistically speaking. (In contrast, boxing promoter Don King's colorful palaver has a familiar circularity to it: every statement always seems to include the phrase "Only in America" and to end with "Buy my fight on pay-per-view for $49.95.")

After Ali, I'm not willing to rank my favorite interview subjects, but it's clear from the anecdotes throughout this book the guys I enjoy—as well as those I don't. I will, however, rank the various sports in good-guy order. In the individual sports, boxers, jockeys, and racecar drivers tend to top the All-Interview list. The boxers are a walking, talking paradox. They are mostly gentle souls, who try to rip your face off only when wearing trunks. Outside the ring, they are soft-spoken and have surprisingly weak, dead-fish handshakes. Apparently, they don't want to injure their hands while greeting some overeager fan with a viselike grip. I think it is the managers and promoters who make boxers crazy; they don't start out that way. (One little story sums up boxing promoters for me. Someone I knew was fairly new at the promoting game and he was dealing with a big-name promoter. Part of the deal for his boxer was that he got two free seats for the boxing card that night. Fair enough, except the boxer was given one seat in section 106 and another in section 437. From then on, the new promoter remembered that when he got free tickets he had to write into the contract "two consecutively numbered seats.")

The best team-sport athletes to deal with are hockey players. This surprises many people who see hockey players as toothless goons, many of whom come from foreign countries, speaking very little English. Frank Deford explained it best, though. He wrote that all hockey players want to do is skate around and then go out for a beer, *eh*? I don't recall hockey players ever hiding in the trainer's room after a tough loss or lashing out at reporters for columns they've written. And hockey is still the only sport where they organize handshakes after a bitter playoff series. A little camaraderie, *eh*?

Next down the team-sport good-guy ladder are football players. I particularly enjoy interviewing offensive linemen. Nobody ever talks to these guys—in fact, the only time they're ever mentioned is when the referee calls out their numbers when they get a holding penalty. Consequently, they're a pretty good lot, and a rather simple lot, too. One lineman told me his entire reason to live was to "pull left, pull right, or go straight ahead." Now there's a rather uncomplicated soul. Star football players, however, fall another rung down the ladder. They can be grouped together with basketball players. These athletes have been interviewed since they were in diapers, so the novelty has kind of worn off. As a result, more often than not when they get approached for interviews, they glaze over.

On the bottom of the ladder are the baseball players. I've never really figured it out. But after the zillionth time of getting turned down for an interview with the words, "I'm busy," I've sort of shied away from asking. What does their busyness actually include? In no particular order: batting practice, more hitting in the cage, more hitting off the batting tee, reviewing video, lifting weights, adjusting their jocks, hiding in the trainer's room, rubbing on eye-black, and still more hitting: the buffet spread. Pitchers are different, and maybe they deserve to creep a step up the ladder—perhaps because they don't have as much hitting to do. There are some really quotable pitchers out there. I loved Bill "Spaceman" Lee of the Red Sox. One time I called him in his hotel room and he explained to me that he had pitched poorly that day because of the six-packs he had downed before the game. He was kidding, but he was quotable. Another good-guy interview is Al Leiter, the former Mets pitcher. I like the way he breaks things down. Reporters always like to deal in all the controversy swirling around the club-house. In recent years there was no shortage of rotten stuff to talk about when it came to the Mets. But Leiter handled it coolly and intelligently. "That's all a bunch of garbage," he'd say. The only thing that counts for him: the sixty feet six inches between the pitcher's mound and home plate. Zoning in on that, and tuning everything else out. When he described it, he really drew you into his world. Leiter is sure to become an announcer upon retiring from baseball.

●   ●   ●

My least favorite interviews fall into two categories: the coaching deathwatch and any interview following the first game of a playoff series. It's tough to interview a coach who everyone knows will soon be fired. But you still have to ask the questions, and the poor coaches still have to answer them. In 1989, Joe Walton was coaching the Jets when the team brought in Dick Steinberg as general manager. The Jets were in the midst of a 4–12 season, and it was clear to everyone that Steinberg's first move would be to fire Walton. I, of course, had to ask Walton his reaction to Steinberg's hiring. I'll never forget the look in his eye. If eyes could sigh, that was the look. He knew, I knew, he knew that I knew, and I knew that he knew that I knew. I asked, he answered, and I've hated that moment ever since. I also despise the first-game postgame interview. "It's only one game," I'm sure to hear. "We haven't won anything yet." Yuck.

Enough of the leasts. Here's another favorite: my favorite quote. I interviewed Reggie Jackson in the Yankees' locker room after a game in 1979. It was at the height of the Reggie–Billy Martin–George Steinbrenner nonsense. Each of these egomaniacs was vying for the biggest headline. So I asked Reggie about his latest dustup with Martin. Reggie began his answer as follows: "It's a royal pain in the *tuchas*." There it was—the first and only time that I heard Yiddish spoken in the clubhouse. And from Reggie Jackson, no less.

The runner-up: this gem from Bernie Williams. Williams had hit the game-winning, three-run home run to lead the Yankees to victory over the Anaheim Angels in a 2002 playoff game. After the game, in a press conference, he was asked about the moment. Williams said, "It hasn't really sunk in yet. I figure when I go to bed tonight I'll probably have a great moment." When the laughing died down in the press room, Williams added, "Not that great of a moment."

My funniest interview subjects were Jayson Williams and Rodney Dangerfield. I've already written at length about Williams, but Dangerfield? In 1986, the Mets invited Rodney to throw out the first pitch at Shea Stadium. He wasn't invited for Opening Day, but rather for the second game of the season. Opening Day was always a sellout, but few fans showed up for Game Two of the season. This invitation was typical because, of course, the late Rodney Dangerfield got "no respect." Rodney wore a Mets uniform, which was funny in itself, and I interviewed him in the dugout. Rodney said something like, "I get no respect. They gave me the locker next to the mops." It may not be fair to include a professional comic in a list of funniest sports interview subjects. To that objection, though, I remind you that Dangerfield starred in one of the greatest sports movies of all time, *Caddyshack*. Enough said.

23

WE INTERRUPT THIS BROADCAST

Sportscasting is my profession, but I think I recognize the proper place of sports in society. Sports is a diversion—a terrific diversion, yes, but still just a diversion. As much as I get immersed in the drama and the excitement of a pennant race or a locker room soap opera, I try to keep things in perspective. Every so often, when I get caught up in the fun and games and the goofy bloopers, the real world has a way of jolting me back to reality. There are the major events: 9/11, the shuttle explosion. Other times it's personal: Darryl Strawberry being diagnosed with cancer, or Ken Caminiti, the former National League MVP, dying at the age of forty-one of a drug overdose. And sometimes it is very personal: like the 1983 Big East basketball game I called while my father-in-law was dying of cancer. These are all moments when arguing whether a thirty-year-old former Japanese pro should really qualify for Major League Rookie of the Year honors seems ridiculously trivial.

After doing the six P.M. sportscast for WBZ in Boston in the 1970s, I generally would head home for dinner before returning to prepare for the eleven o'clock news. I lived about twenty minutes from the station. The night of August 8, 1974, was no different. Except this was no ordinary night. At nine P.M., President Richard Nixon addressed the nation from Washington and became the first sitting president to quit. My wife and I sat in stunned silence as we watched his speech. There had been some riveting moments in our lifetime, including the assassination of Nixon's opponent in the 1960 election, John F. Kennedy. This moment ranked right up there. I turned to Jill and said, "I guess I won't be needed on the late newscast." So I called into work and my news director told me that indeed I had been cut—but not entirely. Instead of my normal four minutes, I'd be given two. I couldn't believe it. What could I possibly talk about—even for two minutes—that would have any significance whatsoever? The Red Sox had a game and there was a golf tournament in the area. I felt dumb reporting the results. But that's exactly what I did for the first of my two minutes. I spent the remaining time saying the following:

Finally, I feel I should say a couple of things tonight. I have no delusion about what place sports has in our society. There is just no way that 5–3 and 1 under par are more important than one of the single biggest stories in our life. For many people, sports is just mumble-jumble jock trivia. For many others, it is an honest release from our daily problems. I'm in the second category, or I wouldn't do for a living what I do. But on the day that the President of the United States resigns, I honestly don't consider the Red Sox score and the PGA very important stories. Only one real story happened today and it's interesting that both of the principal men involved are intense sports fans. Both played varsity sports. And if it weren't for Mr. Nixon's love of the Washington Redskins, the TV blackout rule would still exist to-

day. Mr. Ford has said that the first thing he does every morning is read the sports page. Thousands of us do. But not every day. And today is one of those days. That's sports.

The news director who thought two minutes should be spent reporting sports scores that night never said anything to me about my commentary. He went on to become a major news executive at NBC.

On January 28, 1986, the space shuttle *Challenger* exploded soon after takeoff. One of the seven crew members aboard was the first civilian in space, schoolteacher Christa McAuliffe. She was from New Hampshire. The moment it happened I was driving a rental car in the Boston area. I was there to broadcast a Big East basketball game on ESPN. Like everyone else, a lump came to my throat. This was one of those moments that will be forever etched in my memory. Normally, we would begin a basketball broadcast with upbeat music, flashy pictures, and our best sports-announcer voices. The goal is to make the upcoming game sound like the greatest showdown since David met Goliath. Not that night, though. When the broadcast began, the camera was focused on me. There was no music, no attitude, just me standing on the Boston Garden floor explaining that Christa McAuliffe was from nearby New Hampshire and that the game would go on—with a heavy heart for everyone.

Here's something I'll never understand. When teams win championships, why do the celebrations often turn violent? In 1984, the Detroit Tigers won the World Series. The team's slogan that season was "Bless You Boys." A nun supposedly said it, and it stuck. So how did Tigers fans bless their team after they beat the Padres in five games to win the World

Series? They rioted. It got really ugly. Jill and the boys had come to the game in Detroit, and they were frightened. The next day we learned that somebody had been killed during the riot. When I flew back to New York, the man sitting next to me was a Detroit homicide detective. He told me the death wasn't connected to the baseball "celebration," which made me feel a little better. (As an aside, the guy told me that even though he was a homicide detective, he was going to New York to do voice-overs for a movie. Doesn't everybody? Turns out he played Eddie Murphy's boss in the first *Beverly Hills Cop*.) Six years later, though, when the Detroit Pistons won the NBA championship, eight people were killed in street violence. No one was disclaiming the connection that time.

When the Rangers won the Stanley Cup in 1994, it ended fifty-four years of frustration. How did fans celebrate in big bad New York City? Peacefully. There were no incidents, no arrests. The Vancouver Canucks lost to the Rangers. That night, forty thousand fans rioted in the streets of Vancouver. There was a million dollars' worth of property damage, hundreds of injuries, and a fatality. If the Canucks had won, people said the riots might have been worse. The year before, in Montreal, fans of the Canadiens celebrated that franchise's twenty-fourth Stanley Cup championship by turning over cars, setting fires, breaking windows, and injuring policemen. Damage was in the millions. Los Angeles Lakers and Chicago Bulls fans have also rioted after championship victories, as have Denver's hockey Avalanche and football Broncos fans. The mayhem itself has almost become a sport.

Recently, after the Red Sox finally beat the Yankees in 2004, college kids all over New England partied. They probably would have partied anyway, but the victory gave them an excuse, and some of the parties got out of control. Revelers set fires on the campus of the University of Massachusetts at

Amherst, while in Boston they gathered outside Fenway Park. Boston police tried to restore order and thought they were exercising crowd control. One policeman fired a projectile filled with pepper spray. It hit a young woman, a student at Emerson College, in the eye. She died of her injuries.

It makes no sense. Fans celebrate their team's success, and the end result is tragedy. Some have explained away these incidents by saying that the sporting events just give people an excuse to let off pent-up steam. Others blame the riots on alcohol. Whatever it is, it's sad.

I can't tell you how often race and religion come up in what I do. I'd like to think that I'm color-blind when it comes to reporting sports. But I've found that a significant segment of the population views everything through the filter of race or religion. I remember a letter I received that began, "Every stand you take favors blacks," and ended with some choice anti-Semitic slurs. When I would criticize the troubled Mets and Yankees baseball player Darryl Strawberry, I'd invariably get calls or letters calling me a racist. When I took Strawberry's side on a controversial issue or sympathized with his struggles against addiction or cancer, some viewer would call me a "N—lover."

In Boston, I once said that a player had the right not to salute the American flag. I got a bunch of "Jew" mail that time. Another time, in 1975, I broadcast a Knicks-Celtics game from Madison Square Garden. Before the game, someone sang "America the Beautiful" rather than "The Star-Spangled Banner." I commented on the air how "America the Beautiful" is a great song and so much easier to sing. Maybe "America the Beautiful" should be sung all the time, I suggested. It didn't occur to me who wrote the song. It was Irving Berlin, though, and he just happened to be Jewish. I was sent a postcard. It was unsigned, as such responses generally are when written by bigots. The writers are so resolute in their convictions, but they're ashamed to attach their names to the letters. The writer asserted that "people like you won't be happy until they play 'Hava Nagillah.'" I laughed when I read the card. But it really wasn't funny at all.

In 1993, I agreed to do some broadcasting work for WFAN Radio in New York. I quickly had a change of heart, but it was too late. I had signed a contract and the radio station wanted me to stick to it. The resident morning guru at WFAN is Don Imus. When he got wind of my wanting out of the deal, it was fodder for his patented shtick. One of his characters spoke in a German accent and referred to me as "Lenny the Jew." I'm no theologian, but that struck me as anti-Semitism. I said so on the air, and that touched off a minor firestorm. The program director of WFAN at the time was Jewish, as was the station's general manager. Were they in any way outraged by the insensitivity of Imus's comment? If they were, they certainly didn't let me know it. Imus was their meal ticket. Get the ratings, and you can do pretty much whatever you want. Imus's defense? "It was an Austrian accent." Oh.

❦ ❦ ❦

The night of January 16, 1991, the United States bombed Baghdad for the first time. I sat in the sports office at the TV station fixated on the footage of those green tracer lights blazing through the night sky. On another monitor in the office, though, was the Knicks game at Madison Square Garden. It was like theater of the absurd. (But not quite as theatrical or as absurd as the famous Bronco chase. It was June 1994 and the Knicks were also playing at the Garden. In fact, it was Game

Six of the NBA Finals against Houston. NBC was broadcasting the game and split the screen between Patrick Ewing battling Hakeem Olajuwon and the police following a white Bronco on a California freeway.)

When terrorists attacked the World Trade Center and the Pentagon on September 11, 2001, the baseball season was winding down and the NFL season was just beginning. The big question for some in the sports world: what should be done about the games? Pete Rozelle was the NFL commissioner in 1963 when President Kennedy was shot. It was a Friday. On Sunday the NFL was open for business. None of the games was televised, but they were played nonetheless. Before he died, Rozelle called that decision the worst of his life. In 2001, the geniuses who run Major League Baseball and the National Football League wasted little time making their decisions. No baseball games would be played for six days, and the NFL would take the following Sunday and Monday off, but the seasons would be completed. All missed games would be made up.

With no games to report on, there were no sportscasts for the three days following 9/11. I had plenty of time just to watch the horrible events and to wonder if sports would make any sense once the games were restarted. WNBC asked me to host a live three-hour children's show. Youngsters from age ten through high school discussed their feelings with educators about the attacks and this awful time in our lives. I was honored to be asked to participate. That was on the Saturday after 9/11. But my first sportscast after the attacks was Friday, September 14, at five o'clock in the evening. I delivered the following commentary:

We sports reporters talk in terms of dramatic games, devastating losses, heroes. Words we should delete from our sportscasting vocabulary. And I must admit I'm a bit troubled by the NFL and Major League Baseball only announcing post-

ponements. Baseball will make up the games, adding the missed week at the end of the season, pushing the World Series into November. They cite the sanctity of the 162-game schedule. Some will argue about the pennant races or Barry Bonds's pursuit of McGwire's home run record as a reason to make up the games. And I do think it's nice that the retiring veterans—Cal Ripken in Baltimore and Tony Gwynn in San Diego—will now play their last games at home. But all of that seems so insignificant today. Making up the games, to me, comes off as a way to insure that income from missed games isn't lost. I would rather they not reschedule. To simply make up the games, in my opinion, equates terrorism with a rainout. Let the sports record books show for all time that the games were canceled because America was attacked. Let those blanks in the record forever stand as a tribute to those innocent souls who were taken from us.

It was like whistling in the dark. Many of my coworkers and plenty of viewers said they agreed with me. Obviously, the sports powers that be did not. The games were played. The seasons were prolonged. The World Series lasted into November; the Super Bowl was played on February 3. Everyone made his money. There are times I'm not proud to be a member of the sports community.

And then there are times when doing what I do allows me to honor an individual truly worthy of the word *hero*. One such day was April 23, 2004. Two years earlier, Pat Tillman, the talented safety for the Arizona Cardinals football team, had walked away from the NFL and a $3.6 million contract. He

WE INTERRUPT THIS BROADCAST

joined the army to train as a Ranger. His brother, Kevin, enlisted as well. They wanted to contribute directly to the antiterrorism effort. Pat Tillman was killed chasing al Qaeda and the Taliban in Afghanistan. He was twenty-seven years old. I had never met Pat Tillman, but when I heard the news I felt as if somebody had kicked me in the stomach. The feeling only got worse when it turned out he was killed by "friendly fire." What a wake-up call. A guy throws a winning touchdown pass and we call him a hero. Mickey Mantle hits a homer and I call him *my* hero. If these are heroes, what word do we have for Tillman? How can anyone in sports be a hero when held to the standard of Pat Tillman? That day, the Arizona Diamondbacks baseball team had a game. There was a moment of silence in Tillman's honor. The players and fans bowed their heads. The American flag waved. The stadium was actually silent; it was stunning. I showed that moment during my sportscast. It gave me goose bumps. Then I said:

> *I think it's safe to call Pat Tillman the "anti-athlete" of 2004, or at least the vision we have of pro athletes. The ones who draw attention to themselves. Not Pat Tillman. When he left the Arizona Cardinals he turned his back on a multimillion-dollar contract. What did he say about it? Nothing. He wasn't in it for the publicity. And now the twenty-seven-year-old Army Ranger pays the ultimate price for his country in Afghanistan. There is little we can say other than "Thank you."*

The next day was the NFL draft. Whatever slight interest I might have had in that meat market had evaporated.

243

24

SPANNING THE REST
OF THE WORLD

MAY 1993, FALLSBURGH, NEW YORK. Sherry Skramstead owned a trotter named Son of Account. When the racehorse turned thirteen, she had him bar mitzvahed! She draped a prayer shawl around his neck, put a prayer cap on his head, and had her son read a few lines out of a prayer book. After the ceremony, they ate cake and played Jewish music. I asked a rabbi if there was something sacrilegious about this. He said not at all, that there is nothing in the liturgy that suggests animals can't have such a celebration. But the rabbi didn't leave it at that. He added: "It must have been one helluva bris!"

AUGUST 2000, FRONTIER STADIUM, ROCHESTER, NEW YORK. Zippy Chippy was not the zippiest chippy at the racetrack. In fact, to this point, he could boast a sterling career record of 0 and 86. His eighty-seventh race was a forty-yard dash against Jose Herrera, a speedy outfielder for the Rochester Red Wings. Herrera won. The following season, Zippy sought his revenge against Red Wing Darnell McDonald in Man v. Beast II. The race promoters extended the race to fifty yards to give Zippy an edge. McDonald led for the first forty, but then Zippy pulled away. He won by a length—I don't know whose length.

OCTOBER 2003, TAMPA. A coffin race was staged. One guy sat in an open coffin while two teammates pushed the coffin down the course. I didn't see the finish, but I'm told the race ended in a "dead heat."

VALENTINE'S DAY 1996, PEPSI COLISEUM, INDIANAPOLIS. Indianapolis Ice players wore pink jerseys with big hearts on their backs and sleeves. The Ice played the Kansas City Blades. It was a rare Central Hockey League game without a single fight. Apparently love does conquer all!

VALENTINE'S DAY 1998, CORESTATES SPECTRUM, PHILADELPHIA. At halftime of the 76ers game, there was a mass wedding. Boxing referee and judge Mills Lane officiated. "Life sentence, no parole," said Lane. "Let's get it on!" A touching matrimonial thought.

DECEMBER 1995, CHICAGO STADIUM. Former Chicago Bull Bob Love married Rachel Dixon during halftime of a Bulls game. They said their vows, kissed, and walked off, arm in arm. Before leaving the court, though, Love took a ball in his left hand and tossed it into the basket—a quick score before the honeymoon!

25

CAST OF CHARACTERS

JULY 1990, TIGER STADIUM, DETROIT. Steve Lyons hit a slow roller to the first baseman. He slid headfirst into the bag, safely. He stood up, called time, and absentmindedly dropped his pants to shake the dirt out. Lyons claimed that when he ran back to the dugout, a bunch of women in the stands waved dollar bills at him!

Fans always ask me, "What kind of people are these sports stars?" The truth is they're just people . . . people with extraordinary athletic gifts. And lucky for some of them, the gifts pay big dividends. If your gift is hitting home runs off major-league pitchers and you stay healthy, then you're set for life. If your gift is winning at shuffleboard, it might help you score some older babes at the retirement home, but that's about it.

Who's the most unforgettable? The funniest? The weirdest? I get asked that all the time. I guess I could fill books with portraits of the famous and infamous stars that I've come in contact with. But for now, here are just a few more snapshots of some of the guys who have made the last forty years of my life so interesting. Sometimes they made me laugh, sometimes they made me think, sometimes they made me furious, and sometimes they just made me say, "Oy." But they always kept things interesting.

WILT CHAMBERLAIN

In the 1960s, the Boston Celtics were basketball's kings and Wilt Chamberlain was the "enemy." Wilt the Stilt was kind of a mythic figure. All sorts of college and pro rules were changed because of him. The lane was widened to make it harder for Chamberlain to hang around the offensive end waiting for a pass. The foul shooting rule was changed. Chamberlain would leap from the foul line and put the ball in the basket before hitting the floor. Pretty cool. The rules makers didn't think so. So because of Wilt, free-throw shooters have to stay behind the foul line until they release the ball. (The change definitely hurt his free-throw shooting. He was awful shooting foul shots under the new rule.) The offensive goaltending rule was instituted because of him. How many athletes can claim to have had the rules of the game changed to offset their dominance?

When Wilt played for the Philadelphia Warriors, he once scored one hundred points in a game against the Knicks in Hershey, Pennsylvania. The date was March 2, 1962. I remember my brother telling me of the feat the next morning. *Wow,* I thought. That made a big impression. The absence of film or video of the game makes it seem more important; it's left to the imagination. (That's what my dad always told me about radio. He preferred it to TV. Even after the radio drama was basically dead, I'd catch him listening on a Sunday night to replays of the old *Lone Ranger* series. "Hi-Yo Silver!" certainly seemed more dramatic on radio than TV.) A footnote to the hundred-point game: The poor soul who tried to defend against Chamberlain that night was Knicks center Darrell Imhoff. The following night, the Knicks and Warriors squared off again, this time at Madison Square Garden. When Imhoff left the game, he received a standing ovation. He had held Wilt to a measly fifty-four points.

When I was announcing Celtics games in Boston in the 1970s, there was much talk of who was the greater player: Wilt Chamberlain or Bill Russell. Red Auerbach loved to boast how Russell was better. Sure, Wilt scored all those points, but after all he was a "hundred feet tall." Russell, though, was Mr. Defense. He blocked shots and was the "smarter player." And look at all the rings Russell had compared with Chamberlain. If Auerbach could pick one player, he said he'd pick Russell over Chamberlain every time. After listening to this rhetoric for five years, I'm sure my view was skewed. Russell was the great warrior; Wilt, the big loser.

Wilt, of course, took umbrage at that assessment. He told me it wasn't fair, that it was based on team accomplishments. And anyway, his team beat every other team before losing to the Celtics. "How does that make me a loser?" he would ask. He also said that his personal winning percentage was about the same as that of the Celtics. And he may be right. In his early years, Boston always had the better record, but from 1966 through 1972 Wilt's teams were superior in the win-loss column. Finally, Chamberlain would point out that Elgin Baylor never won an NBA championship, but still many people considered him the best forward in the game. No one thought of Baylor as a loser.

It was often said that Chamberlain wasn't a good guy. I don't know where that came from. Perhaps people were afraid to approach such a huge human being so they transposed that fear into their feelings about him. I, for one, never thought he was a bad guy. Russell, on the other hand, was tough to deal with. When Russell was named coach of the Seattle Supersonics in 1974, I wanted to interview him when he returned to the Boston Garden the first time. I called him in his hotel room in New York, where the Supersonics had played their previous game. I introduced myself and asked if he would sit for an interview.

"No." Not loud, not angry, just "no." So I said, "Okay, can I just ask you now on the phone how you feel about coming back?" "No," he said. Then silence. That was it. I don't even think I said good-bye, I just timidly hung up the phone. When I told this story to Auerbach, he just chuckled and said, "That's Russ."

The first time I met Chamberlain was at Disney World in the early 1980s. I had gone down to tape a *SportsWorld* episode for NBC. It was a game featuring Meadowlark Lemon and the Bucketeers. Lemon was a longtime Harlem Globetrotter and this was some kind of Globetrotters rip-off. Chamberlain was the guest player for the Bucketeers. The game was played on an outdoor court in Kissimmee, Florida. It poured, and the game, scheduled for Sunday, was rained out. We taped the following day, despite ridiculously windy conditions. (I never heard of the Bucketeers after that game.) I brought along my two young sons, Michael and Daniel, because the combination of Disney World, Wilt Chamberlain, and television was just too much of a lure. We all went on a boat ride the night before the rainout. Wilt was there: all seven feet of him. The man *was* a giant! I've been around a couple of others, including Kareem Abdul-Jabbar and Manute Bol. Bol is just ridiculous—seven feet seven inches. I had to stand on my tiptoes and hold up the microphone high over my head to interview him. Kareem and Bol are beanpoles, but Wilt was massive, incredibly well-built even long after his playing days were through.

The bad guy–loser rhetoric had made an impression on me, so I timidly approached Chamberlain with my two kids. He was incredible, though, just as he was every other time I talked with him: warm, gregarious, funny, interesting, caring—all the things you never heard about the guy. My six-year-old son, Daniel, asked him how he drove a car. Wilt joked that he didn't really fit in any cars, so he sits with the driver's side door open and pushes along the ground with his foot, as though he's riding a scooter. He seemed to enjoy the hell out of life, even when he was speaking with some dorky sportscaster and his two kids. Wilt agreed to pose for a picture with my sons. The picture came out great; you see my two sons and every bit of Wilt *except his head,* which was cut out of the picture.

I interviewed Chamberlain several times after that, including one time after his book, *A View from Above,* came out in 1991. In the book, he famously claimed that he had slept with twenty thousand women. The braggadocio was ridiculous. I got the feeling that Wilt knew it, too. But he wrote it and his editors left it in to sell some books. I'm sure it worked. It's a good thing the editors of this book didn't ask about my romantic history. It starts off with an all-boys' high school that didn't have a senior prom and kind of goes downhill from there.

⚾   ⚾   ⚾

I was getting ready to do a newscast in Atlanta before a Mets-Braves playoff game in October of 1999. My producer back in New York told me through my earpiece that Wilt had died of heart failure at the age of sixty-three. It turns out he had suffered from heart problems for years, but the public didn't know it. A lump came to my throat. It was humbling to think that somebody so big, so seemingly healthy, so much larger than life could be dead. At that moment on the air, I wished I could summon up that Cosell ability to deliver the perfect eulogy. Instead I said something heartfelt, my personal feelings about the loss of a legend. But thinking of Wilt brought a smile to my face. I loved reading all his obits, especially the ones that described him as a gentle giant, that told stories of how, if he had wanted to, he could have easily injured his defenders, broken their hands or wrists when he went up for a dunk. But he'd ease up, he wouldn't do it. Chamberlain genuinely felt that nobody loved a big man. The Boston Celtics certainly didn't. But I did. In many ways, his death got to me more than The Mick's.

PETE ROSE

Charlie Hustle is the perfect nickname for Pete Rose. I remember booing him at the Polo Grounds in the early days of the Mets. The nerve of the guy: walking on four pitches and then running to first. What a hot dog! Of course, that's the fan's attitude. Once I became a sportscaster, I couldn't really be a fan anymore. If I don't like a player personally, I can't let that affect how I broadcast. Dave Kingman may have been a lout to female reporters, but my job was to talk about his mammoth home runs. That's what counts in the box score. But, of course, it's human nature to root for the guys who go out of their way to be friendly to the media. At the 1974 World Series, Steve Garvey said to me, "Wait right here. I'll talk to you after I take batting practice." And he actually came back. He even said, "Nice sports coat." It's hard not to like the guy after that. Another example: Before Super Bowl XXI, Giants quarterback Phil Simms promised he'd do a one-on-one interview, and he kept his promise. (During the interview Simms said, "We're gonna be aggressive" during the game. Dummy that I was, I didn't know "aggressive" was code for "We're going to pass a lot." Simms set a Super Bowl record, completing twenty-two of twenty-five passes, and the Giants beat Denver 39–20. Everyone was surprised, but not Phil. And I shouldn't have been either had I known how to decipher football code-speak.)

In contrast, there was Reggie Smith who played for the Red Sox. After he was traded to the St. Louis Cardinals in 1974, I called him up and asked for his reaction to the deal. He wouldn't talk to me. He said I had "misquoted" him on television the last time I had interviewed him. Let that sink in for a second. Okay, time's up. Smith let us interview him on camera, we aired the interview, and somehow he thinks we misquoted him. I don't think he should speak to *himself* anymore!

Pete Rose was always in constant motion, always had an opinion, and always knew every fact or statistic about himself. (I have a hunch that most players know their own numbers, but they pretend not to.) Rose really didn't seem to care what anybody thought about him. If he ticked you off, tough! One time I went to interview him when he was playing for the Montreal Expos. Pete was living in a hotel apartment in Montreal, and while the camera crew set up in the living room, I walked into the bedroom. Pete was on the phone. He didn't say hello to me, he just said, "What do you think of the Celtics?" I like the Celtics. After all, I had announced their games for five years. I always thought they were a classy organization. In fact, one of my fondest memories as a sportscaster was walking across the parquet floor at the Boston Garden. I had been in town about six months. A throaty voice came out of the balcony: "Hey, Len Berman." I was starting to strut, thinking the fans knew my name! The voice continued: "You suck!" I knew then that I had arrived.

Anyway, Rose wasn't really asking my general opinion about one of the greatest franchises in sports history. He wanted to know if I liked their chances that night against the spread. Now, I'm not the guy to turn to for gambling advice. In fact, I'm pretty naive when it comes to sports gambling. After losing my thirteen cents to David Nussbaum when the Yankees lost the 1955 World Series, the only other time I bet on a game was in college. The kid across the hall would drive his car from Syracuse to Cortland, New York, and place his bets. I gave him a check for $25 and bet on the football Giants. They won, and I was ecstatic—until the kid returned and said, "Bookies don't take checks."

I didn't think too much about the fact that Rose was bet-
ting on the Celtics game at the time. Of course, that changed
in 1989 when Rose was banned from baseball for gambling.
The official banishment didn't definitively state that he bet on
baseball, but baseball commissioner Bart Giamatti told reporters that Rose had. For fifteen years, thereafter, Rose denied
it. It's part of that "running to first base" mentality of his. He
did things decisively and with flair. Ball four: I'm running to
first. They say I did something, I say I didn't. Done. So now
comes the question about whether Rose belongs in the Baseball
Hall of Fame.

First, my philosophy on the Hall of Fame. To me, the Hall
of Fame means Cobb and Ruth and maybe a few others. So
when somebody asks me if Joe Schmo belongs, it's an easy call.
If there is even a question, the answer is no. Only no-brainers
belong in Cooperstown. Of course, that doesn't happen. Each
of the major sports Halls of Fame need inductees every year or
they can't have a ceremony. But I think the Halls should be reserved for the all-time greats. Today, far too often, the inductees are the very, very goods. I was struck by what Mickey
Mantle once said about Rose. This was before Rose was
banned. (Mantle himself was once banned from the game. His
crime: public relations work for a casino. Seems pretty tame in
comparison.) Mantle said, "I don't think Pete Rose is that great
of a player. . . . Rose played twenty-five years. If I coulda
played twenty-five years I'd have three thousand hits. . . . And
in twenty-five years, how many RBIs did he have? Twenty-
five?" (Rose actually played twenty-four seasons and drove in
over thirteen hundred runs.) Mantle allowed how he would
"pay to see Rose play," but he concluded that Rose is "not one
of the superstars." That goes to the core of one anti–Hall of
Fame argument. Some guys just accumulate stats based on their
longevity. Is staying power equal to greatness?

Nonetheless, I think it's absurd that Pete Rose is not in the Hall of Fame. He's the all-time hit leader, for goodness' sake. He amassed 4,256 regular-season hits, plus 86 more in the postseason. (For some reason, postseason stats don't count toward career numbers.) Rose had 67 more hits than Ty Cobb and 485 more than Hank Aaron who is number three all-time. Halls of Fame should honor on-the-field accomplishments and nothing else. Otherwise, where do you draw the line? Gamblers aren't permitted, but wife abusers are? If you're found liable in a civil suit of killing your ex-wife, should you be thrown out of the Hall of Fame?

After fifteen years of denial, Rose wrote a book and pulled a Bob Arum. Arum was the boxing promoter who in the early 1980s told a couple of newspaper reporters: "Yesterday I was lying, today I'm telling the truth." (Arum was reportedly arguing the merits of a couple of boxers and changed his mind from one night to the next.) I have a thing about lying. If a person lies to me, he's lower than dirt. (Okay, not white lies. When a woman asks, "How do you like my dress?" you're allowed to fib. You can't say, "It was nicer when it was drapes.") Lying I hate. (And I hate the word *hate*.) It comes from my dad, the most honest person in the world. Anyway, Rose said that, yes, he bet on baseball but only as the manager of the Reds, and he only bet on his team to win. That's still rotten on several levels. First, it's against the rules of baseball. Second, there's a chance he might have ruined someone's career in the process. Suppose you are the manager of a team. Your starting pitcher is doing pretty well through six innings, but his pitch count is up there and he is starting to tire. Do you leave him in there? Probably so if the guys in the bullpen are real dogs. But what if he blows out his arm? You've got money on the game, so maybe you ride your horse just a little bit longer than you normally would. Finally, the cover-up bugs me. You have to raise an eyebrow when someone lies for fifteen years and then supposedly tells the whole story. What is really true? And what is fiction?

As a television sportscaster, I don't get a vote—only newspaper writers do—but I think Rose killed his chances for the Hall of Fame with his so-called admission. He just doesn't get it. Even if baseball commissioner Bud Selig is willing to reinstate Rose, which is the first step, sportswriters do the voting. All along they've suggested to Rose that if he would just come clean, he'd get into the Hall of Fame. Now Rose thinks he's come clean—in the form of a bestselling book—and the writers won't do it. Why? They didn't like being lied to for so many years and, frankly, they don't believe him now. Even with all the mud and rumors and gossip that writers trade in, truth is still at the core of journalism and Rose has run roughshod over the truth with a Mack truck.

But you know what, having said all that, I still believe strongly that Rose deserves to be in Cooperstown. Let's keep sports as sports. Leave the moral judgments to a higher authority.

DWIGHT GOODEN

I'll never forget the first time I interviewed Dwight Gooden. It was in 1984, and Gooden was the Mets' rookie phenom. Talk about pulling teeth. He couldn't string two words together. It was a painful interview to do and even more painful to watch. But so what if he wasn't comfortable speaking on camera? Gooden had the arm and body of a Hall of Famer. But like his buddy Darryl Strawberry, he threw it away on drugs. Of course it's easy for the fans and media to say trite things like, "What wasted potential!" But it was true. Wouldn't both Gooden and Strawberry be certain Hall of Famers if not for drugs? On top of everything else, what gets me is the illegality of it all. I once said that on the air and a newspaper reporter questioned me about the statement. I had said that in addition to drugs destroying you physically, emotionally, and monetarily, they are illegal. After he wrote his article, I spoke to the reporter and explained my point. "Oh yeah, right," he acknowledged. I mean, how many ways can you screw yourself up? When Gooden entered Smithers Institute for rehab in 1987, it was shocking. He had tested positive for cocaine in spring training. Talk about a fall from grace.

Two months later, Gooden made a comeback at Shea Stadium. People debated what the fans' proper response should be. Some said he should get a standing ovation. Others said, "Boo the guy." I thought polite applause would be appropriate, but not a standing ovation. What exactly would the fans be saluting? "Hooray for the druggie, clean for now!" He won that night. But he fell off the wagon several times after that. More suspensions and more comebacks. And then the Yankees signed him after the 1995 season. His signing was just another of the zillion things that went absolutely perfectly for the Yankees in 1996. On May 14, 1996, Gooden threw a no-hitter against Seattle, and his teammates carried him off the field on their shoulders. It was the final scene from a quintessential made-for-TV movie.

Anyway, despite all the drugs and all the suspensions, I couldn't help but like Gooden, and Strawberry, too. As he matured and became more comfortable with the media, Gooden turned out to be a good interview subject. In 1997, at the Yankees' spring training, Gooden graciously agreed to a live interview. He lived in St. Petersburg, and he had a minor leaguer living with him at the time. We shot some tape in his home and then we went to his mother's house. From her backyard, we did our interview on the news. The minor leaguer had tagged along, and after the news we told him that it was his turn. The kid fancied himself to be a budding singer. So Gooden and I coaxed him to look into the camera lens and give it his best shot. He sang a Latin love song in Spanish—with feeling. Marc Anthony, he was not. Gooden and I could hardly contain ourselves, we were laughing so hard. We knew we'd never air the tape, but Gooden had convinced the kid that talent scouts would be watching back in New York and that this was his best shot at a recording contract. To this day, whenever I see Gooden we both chuckle, though neither of us says a word about the incident. We don't need to.

ARTHUR ASHE

In the history books, he will be remembered as the "first African American man to win the U.S. Open and Wimbledon." That's why history can be so dull at times. Arthur Ashe was so much more than that. It's just not that he broke color barriers, but the way he did it that made him so special. He never called attention to himself. At Wimbledon in 1975, he was a big underdog. At match point, when he beat Jimmy Connors in the final, he simply clenched his fist. That was about as expressive as Ashe got.

The next year, I ran a Tennis Fantasy where viewers could play with pros at the Longwood Cricket Club in Boston. Arthur agreed to be one of the commentators. So did Dan Rowan, of the hit TV comedy show *Rowan & Martin's Laugh-In*. After about five minutes on the air, Arthur turned to me and said, "Let Rowan do the commentary instead. He's much funnier." Of course, Arthur wasn't there for his comedy shtick. We taped another Fantasy with Arthur several years later on

Long Island. There are people who played that day who will remember the Fantasy for the rest of their lives. Arthur had a quiet dignity about himself. When you were around him there was a certain calming effect that seemed to take hold. But he didn't think it was incongruous that in a "gentleman's game" such as tennis, guys like John McEnroe and Connors got so much attention. Arthur thought that they were "good for the game," that they added "pizzazz" that the game so sorely needed. How unfair that he suffered a heart attack at the age of thirty-six and died of AIDS in 1993 at forty-nine. The last time I saw him was in the press box at the U.S. Open a couple of years before his death. He was just standing there, off to the side, pretty much ignored. He was one of the most significant figures in American sports history, yet he was standing there quietly, taking in the action. No posse. No entourage.

IRVING JAFFE

When you think of speed skating, what name comes to mind? Apolo Anton Ohno, perhaps. Ohno won a gold and a silver medal in short-track speed skating at the Salt Lake Games in 2002. Before Ohno there was Dan Jansen, who won the gold at Lillehammer in 1994, after disappointments in the two previous Winter Olympics. And, of course, on the women's side, there was the incomparable Bonnie Blair, who won five golds and a bronze in the 1988, 1992, and 1994 Games. Finally, there was Eric Heiden. He won his five gold medals in just one Olympics, the 1980 Lake Placid Games. No American athlete had ever won five golds in a single Winter Olympics. Heiden did it in style, setting four Olympic records and a world record. To top it off, his sister, Beth, won a bronze medal. Between the two, the Heiden siblings took home half of the U.S. medal stash from Lake Placid. And Eric alone took home fully five-sixths of the American golds from Lake Placid. The sixth medal? It was won by the U.S. ice hockey team. That may explain why Eric Heiden isn't better remembered.

But the truth is, when you're speaking of Lake Placid and speed skating, the story doesn't begin with Heiden. It begins with Irving Jaffe. His name may sound like that of an accountant or an optometrist, but Jaffe could fly. He competed in the 1928 and 1932 Winter Olympics. In 1932, the Games were also at Lake Placid. By today's standards, he would have been a huge star. He won two gold medals in 1932, one each in the 5,000- and 10,000-meter races. Only fourteen golds were handed out at the entire Olympics.

Jaffe, though, wasn't welcomed at the Games. He remembers seeing signs around Lake Placid that read: NO JEWS OR DOGS ALLOWED. He told me he was sick about the signs, but they didn't deter him from competing. Four years later, at the Summer Olympics in Berlin, with Hitler looking on from the stands, Jewish athletes were treated even worse. One of them was one of my mentors, Marty Glickman. Marty was supposed to run a leg of the 400-meter relay race for the United States. At the last minute, though, he was pulled from the race. The U.S. Olympic Committee, headed by Avery Brundage, made up a story about how the German team had hidden some of its best runners to spring a surprise on the unsuspecting field in the relay. The United States would therefore make a switch. Glickman and Sam Stoller were replaced by Jesse Owens and Frank Metcalfe. Owens and Metcalfe were unquestionably faster than Glickman and Stoller—but it was no coincidence that the team's two Jewish athletes were the ones pulled from the relay. With Owens and Metcalfe, the United States won the race easily, but there is little doubt that a team with Glickman and Stoller also would have won by several meters. It was a blatant case of anti-Semitism that prevented Glickman from winning a gold medal. Years later, the U.S. Olympic Committee gave Marty some kind of commendation, and Marty was gracious about it. But in truth, he was robbed of what was rightly his.

In 1980, leading up to the Lake Placid Games, I interviewed Jaffe, hoping he could reclaim some of the glory that was also rightly his. He said that during the Depression he pawned both of his gold medals, never to see them again. I tried to help him track them down. After I did a story on WCBS-TV, I received a call from a lady who said she thought she had them. They were stashed away in a safety deposit box at the Bowery Bank on Forty-second Street, she said. She agreed to open the box while WCBS cameras filmed the moment. I was excited, Jaffe was excited—even the bank's manager was excited. He couldn't wait for her to show up. It seems she hadn't paid the fee on the box for months. When I heard that, my heart sank. Well, you can probably guess the rest. She was a no-show, and Jaffe never got his medals back. He died the following year.

Here's the kicker. When the Winter Olympics returned to Lake Placid in 1980, Irving Jaffe wasn't even invited. For goodness' sake, he had won one-seventh of all the gold medals handed out in 1932 and nobody on the U.S. Olympic Committee cared. I guess nobody thought his was an accomplishment that should be celebrated. Jaffe was hurt, and though he didn't say it, he had to be wondering if Jews and dogs were welcome in Lake Placid in 1980.

CHARLES O. FINLEY

Before there was George Steinbrenner, there was Charles O. Finley. In fact, Finley passed the torch to George in so many ways. Finley owned the Oakland Athletics, and when he didn't want to pay his ballplayers millions, Steinbrenner was only too happy to. Finley had built a dynasty in Oakland. With Reggie Jackson, Catfish Hunter, Rollie Fingers, Vida Blue, Bert Campaneris and Joe Rudi, the A's won three straight World Series titles from 1972 to 1974. But on November 4, 1976, it was all over for Oakland. That day, at the Waldorf Astoria hotel in New York, baseball changed forever. With the first free-agent reentry draft, players were given their freedom. For many of the A's stars, that pretty much meant freedom from Charlie O.

Finley watched from the balcony at the Waldorf. He lost six players that day, including Reggie Jackson, Joe Rudi, and Gene Tenace. He later described the scene as a "den of thieves." All of the baseball owners were "out to cut one another's throats."

The first word many people think of when Finley is mentioned is "cheap." I prefer to think of him as an innovator. Before 1961, baseball uniforms were all "prison gray," as Finley described them, on the road and "egg-shell white" at home. He brought in gold and green. With white shoes! For better or worse, we owe the designated hitter and night World Series games to Finley. He asked, "Why would you want to see a pitcher hit? The average pitcher couldn't hit my grandmother." Everything was about making the game more interesting—and more profitable. He wanted to restore "balance," as he called it, to the game. He remarked that when balls and strikes were introduced in 1881, it was nine balls and four strikes. He wanted three and three. He said in football it's eleven players against eleven. In hockey, it's six on six. Basketball is five on five. But in baseball, it's not only one (batter) against nine (fielders), but the nine get four balls, and the one gets only three! (White Sox announcer Kenny Harrelson had another way of putting it. Harrelson said, "Baseball is the only sport where when you're on offense, the other team has the ball!") Charlie thought changing it to three balls and three strikes would not only create more of a balance between offense and defense, but it would make the game more exciting. Finley also pushed for the adoption of an orange baseball. He thought the batter would see the ball better, and the fans would be able to follow the flight of the ball more easily. The only people who didn't like the idea were pitchers—and the other owners. When they found out Charlie O. would get a royalty of five cents per ball, they quickly scoffed at the idea.

Finley fought with just about everyone. During the 1973 World Series, the A's lost the second game to the Mets when his reserve second baseman, Mike Andrews, made two consecutive errors in the twelfth inning. What did Finley do? He fired Andrews. Right in the middle of the World Series. Baseball commissioner Bowie Kuhn and most of America didn't agree with the move, and Kuhn ordered Andrews reinstated. Finley later said he should have sued Kuhn, and he said he would have won. (By the way, he and the commissioner battled incessantly. Bowie's last name is pronounced "Kyoon," but Finley would always pronounce it "Koon." I think he did it just to irritate him.) Finley claimed he had had a doctor examine Andrews, and the doc said Andrews would risk injury to his shoulder if he continued to play, so that's why he did what he did.

Although it often didn't seem true at the time, I think he was right about most things in baseball. He was wrong about one thing, though. He told me that the stupidity of the owners will lead to just one outcome: bankruptcy. There were twenty-six teams in 1982 when I interviewed him for my *SportsPeople* show on WCBS-TV. He said that "within ten years, they'll be down to twenty." In 1992, there were still twenty-six teams. And some twenty years later—despite talk of contraction—there are thirty teams.

Finley was as colorful and as entertaining and as infuriating as they came in sports. He died in February 1996. Somehow it seems fitting that he didn't witness the rebirth of the Yankees dynasty the following October.

REGGIE JACKSON

Yankee Graig Nettles was once asked what was the best part of playing in New York. "Getting to see Reggie Jackson play every day," he said. And the worst part about playing in New York? "Getting to see Reggie Jackson play every day!" The action was always around Reggie. He saw to that. Everything seemed to stop dead when he came to the plate. No beer was sold in the stadium when Reggie was batting. No one went to the bathroom. Reggie was bigger than life.

When I was just starting out in New York, I was down in Fort Lauderdale for spring training. Reggie turned to me and said, "Len Berman, right?" I was beaming. The great Reggie-Reggie-Reggie of the three home runs in one World Series game had recognized me. Of course, there were times in other years that he pretended he had no idea who I was. But that was Reggie—and I was just another network guy wearing a blue blazer with a logo on it. I once did a feature on slumps for NBC. I wanted to talk with Reggie, who was then playing for the Angels and in a slump. Like many athletes, he was happy to talk when he was doing well, and not so happy otherwise. But he said he'd talk to me after batting practice, so I hung around the Angels' dugout. When batting practice ended, though, Jackson complained to his manager, Gene Mauch, that my producer and I were hanging around the dugout and should be evicted.

A few years later, in 1987, Jackson was playing for the Oakland A's. The star of the team that year was a rookie named Mark McGwire. Big Mac (who was considerably less big then) hit forty-nine homers on his way to winning the Rookie of the

CAST OF CHARACTERS

Year Award. It was a record number of homers for a rookie. NBC sent me out to interview McGwire for the *Game of the Week* pregame show. This was before ESPN and satellite TV began broadcasting what seems to be a hundred games per night. The *Game of the Week* was still a big deal. Players were excited for national exposure, and they not only watched the game but they were also cooperative when it came to doing interviews. So McGwire and I sat on directors' chairs along the third-base line for the interview. Right in the middle of our discussion, he was pied. You've seen it a million times. Baseball players load up a pie tin, or even just a towel, with shaving cream and throw it into the mug of the person being interviewed. When Soupy Sales used to take a pie in the face, it was funny. The first time you saw a baseball player get it, it was also funny. But about the thousandth time: not funny. (It's kind of like The Wave. The first time the fans did it, it was kind of cute. The zillionth time? Sit down already!) Who was it that creamed McGwire, disrupting our national TV interview? None other than Mr. October, Reggie Jackson. Jackson was finishing up his career with the A's and batting all of .220 that season. But there he was to glom the spotlight away from the kid who truly deserved it. I thought it was terrible.

Another year, at spring training, I made the mistake of telling Reggie that I had covered the Red Sox and that nobody worked harder in the spring than the old grizzled veteran Carl Yastrzemski. The Red Sox always had the reputation of being a country club. But Yaz was different. He would bust it every day of spring training. Reggie responded: "Nobody works harder here than me." And he then proceeded to try to prove it. For the rest of that day, he would look around to make sure I was watching and then do his version of busting it. (It reminded me of when I was in the Reserves and the sergeant said, "Drop and give me twenty." I would count out loud as I did the push-

265

ups, but when he wasn't looking, I'd keep counting loudly but just lie on my stomach resting.) At one point, Reggie went up to Bucky Dent in the batting cage and started giving him personal instruction. Bucky didn't care for that. It was all part of Reggie's show. When the workout ended, Reggie trotted across the infield, waving at me with a huge smile as if to say, "Look at me! I'm running!" What a showman. But hey, that was Reggie!

PURNAL GOLDY

Remember Purnal Goldy? Okay, you're not alone. But I was at Yankee Stadium when he made his major-league debut. It was June 1962 and I was sitting in the upper deck when the Yankees' "Voice of God," public address announcer Bob Sheppard, announced that Goldy was pinch running for the Detroit Tigers and that he was making his major-league debut. For some reason, this made a big impression on me. It's probably because his name struck me and my friend as being funny. I didn't meet a lot of Purnals growing up in Queens. And though I knew plenty of Goldmans and Goldbergs, I can't say I knew any Goldys. Put the names together and you've got something unforgettable. (Not quite as unforgettable as the name of a kid I went to summer camp with. His last name was Liss, and his parents—honest to God—named him Richard! Can you imagine being a young boy at summer camp with the name Dick Liss?)

I have no remembrance of what Goldy did once he got to first base. Goldy does, though. I spoke to him in 2004. Over forty years later, he fondly remembered his first game in the Bigs. He said he was "so nervous his legs could barely function" and that he must have looked ghostly white. (In fact, he said, he could *still* feel his legs shaking.) Moose Skowron was the Yankee's first baseman. Moose turned to him and said, "You'll be okay, kid. Second base is down there." Goldy never made it to second. The next Tiger's batter hit into a double play; Goldy got about six steps off first and that was it.

Goldy was brought up from the minor leagues because Al Kaline was injured—so Purnal Goldy replaced the great Al Kaline, "but not very well," as he said to me. He wasn't needed once Kaline returned. His major-league career lasted exactly twenty-nine games. He calls it his "meteoric disappearance." I asked him if they took the ball out of play and gave it to him when he got his first major-league hit. He laughed and said, "No, they didn't do things like that." But he did hit two homers in a game against Don Schwall of Boston on the television game of the week. (Those were two of his three career homers.) He also has a baseball card to prove he was a major leaguer. His son-in-law buys them whenever he comes across one so that Goldy's grandkids can each have a Purnal Goldy card of his own.

As for his name, he said that others found it unique as well. He would receive letters from small newspapers that assumed he was black and wanted background information. I told him the name Purnal Goldy didn't sound like that of a ballplayer. He said, "I didn't look like one either." His major-league debut, by the way, was the only time he ever played in Yankee Stadium. And I was there to see it!

26

CRITICAL CONDITION

SEPTEMBER 1990, TINKER FIELD, ORLANDO. Sportswriter Jerry Green wrote that if the Orlando Sun Rays minor-league baseball team sold out the stadium for a game he would "eat his words." They did...and he did. He sat at a table in front of the fans and was served his column, covered in tomato sauce. He then proceeded to eat the entire plateful of newspaper!

Tommy Lasorda once said, "Opinions are like assholes. Everyone's got one." I don't know if Lasorda was the first to utter those words, but he has certainly made the quote his own. One of my favorite sports stories involves Lasorda. It was 1983 and the once-vaunted Dodgers infield had turned over. For years, Steve Garvey had manned first, Davey Lopes was at second, Bill Russell at short, and Ron Cey at third base. The Dodgers had won the World Series just two seasons before. But like all good teams, at some point this one started to disintegrate, and in 1983 they were really kicking the ball around. Let's just say there wasn't a Gold Glover in the mix. Russell was still at short, but now journeyman Greg Brock was at first, Steve Sax at second, and Pedro Guerrero at third. Guerrero was a converted left fielder—and the conversion was far from smooth. As the story goes, a frustrated Lasorda was ranting and raving in a team meeting. He asked Guerrero a simple situational baseball question: "Bases loaded, nobody out. You're playing third. What are you thinking?" Guerrero's response: "Please God, don't let them hit the ball to me!" Now Lasorda hit the roof. He yelled at Guerrero to cut it out and tell him what he's really thinking. "Okay, okay," Guerrero said, "Please don't hit it to Sax, either!"

That's one of the funniest "inside baseball" stories I've ever heard. Was it true? I couldn't tell you. But some of these things get repeated often enough that they may as well be gospel. It's the same thing with newspapers. So many people think that if something is in the paper, It's Gotta Be True. That's why Chris Berman and I will forever be brothers—after all, the *Los Angeles Times* said so. It's just the way it works. I have a little game I like to play whenever I speak to a group. I ask the audience, "Who here has had anything written about them? School paper, trade publication, *New York Times,* bathroom wall? Anywhere." Lots of hands go up. Next I say, "Keep your hands up if every fact was correct and every quote was exactly in the context you delivered it." Invariably, every hand goes down. The point is that journalism isn't an exact science. When people say, "It was in the *New York Times,*" we shouldn't treat the information as if it had been written on a stone tablet and passed down from Mount Sinai. I don't mean to pick on the *Times;* it's every news organization, WNBC included. (One night on *Live at Five,* we had a news story that came off the wires: scientists had discovered a new solar system. That part we got right. But then we announced on the air that this new discovery was just twelve hundred miles from earth. I was sitting next to anchorman Dean Shepherd, getting ready to do my sports, and thought, "Wow, there's a new solar system in Toledo." I started laughing, and someone did a little checking. The newswriter at WNBC had left out one little word when writing his story for the newscast. It was supposed to be something like twelve hundred kazillion miles from earth!) News stories are written and reported by people. What you read, hear, and see is no more than some guy's version of things. Yet that's the stuff that becomes history years from now.

One guy once wrote an article about me, though, where every quote and fact was absolutely perfect. His name is Robert McG. Thomas Jr., and, yes, he wrote for The *New York Times*. Before the interview, he apologized to me. He said that sports and television were not his regular beats. I asked him what he generally covered? Thomas was an obituary writer. Figures. If you write obituaries, you *have* to get all the facts right. You don't want some dead guy's relative calling and giving you the what for!

*   *   *

When Mel Allen was calling Yankees games, I don't remember picking up the paper and reading detailed analyses of the job he was doing. "Gee, in Tuesday's game in Cleveland, Mel shouted 'Going . . . going,' but it turned out to be a foul ball! C'mon, Mel, get your head in the game!" Newspaper or magazine criticism of sports broadcasters just didn't exist back then.

The first time I was ever aware of a sportswriter critiquing television sports was after the 1969 World Series. The Mets had pulled off their miracle against the Baltimore Orioles. The following week a column appeared in *Sports Illustrated* called "TV Talk." It was written by Wilfrid Sheed, the noted novelist and essayist. Sheed's column was about NBC's postseason baseball coverage. The subheadline was a tip-off of things to come: THE WORLD SERIES BEGINS, AND ALREADY ONE YEARNS FOR THE SOUNDS OF SILENCE. He proceeded to barbecue the various announcers who had worked that year, using words such as *banal* and *ill at ease* to describe the jobs they had done. He concluded his column by writing, "Whether baseball commentators are really less articulate than other people or just pretending is a question that probably can't be settled by a short series."

I was at Syracuse at the time, and I was stunned. I had never read anything like this column. The following week, two letters to the editor appeared in *Sports Illustrated*. One was from the president of ABC Sports, Roone Arledge. And the other was from some college radio announcer in upstate New York (*me!*). Roone wrote that with this column, "instead of any kind of enlightened criticism, we apparently are going to be fed a weekly serving of sarcasm, carping and nitpicking." He asserted that cherrypicking isolated, meaningless sentences out of fifteen hours of World Series broadcast is not only "unenlightening, but *unfair.*"

Here's what the college kid wrote: "That *S.I.* carefully dissects TV sportscasting while TV does not criticize the press is an unfortunate paradox of our free-press system." Clever, huh? Let's get ready to rumble! I went on to say that while sportswriters have erasers when they work, live sportscasters don't. I had another line that the editors cut out. I wrote, "When Mr. Sheed got through watching the World Series (and critiquing the announcers), I hope he knows who won." So there was my little sarcasm coming out. It may not have been the sharpest response, but to this day I'm honored to have shared a page with the great Roone Arledge. That's as close as I ever got to him.

⬤　⬤　⬤

One of the most sarcastic critics is a fellow named Norman Chad who has written for a wide variety of publications. About thirty years after Sheed's column, Chad penned a back-page article for *Sports Illustrated* in which he wrote something like, "Outside of Al Michaels and Vin Scully, all sportscasters are game-show wannabes." A cute line, perhaps, but not at all fair. Turns out that in his formative years Chad had given stand-up comedy a shot. At the time, the back-page column was titled "My Turn." So I stepped up and took "My Turn." I wrote that Chad's "stand-up routine" had completely missed the mark, that it was unfair to great play-by-play men like Dick Enberg. I finished my piece by writing: "Here's a bit of comedy for you, Mr. Chad. Outside of Mike Lupica and Dave Anderson, all sportswriters are obituary-writer wannabes. Stop it, you're killing me!" It was no surprise that *Sports Illustrated* didn't publish my submission. In fact, the magazine never acknowledged having received it. I do have a hunch, though, that they forwarded it to Chad.

This sarcasm and carping, as Roone put it, is the stock-in-trade of the TV sports critic. While serious, thoughtful criticism is fine, to nitpick from a body of work is ridiculous. One time on a newscast, I showed a boxer getting his lights punched out. As he wobbled around the ring, I made fun of his not knowing where he was. A writer criticized me for doing that. He pointed out that the boxer could have been hurt. The critic was right, and I haven't done it since.

I've had my lights punched out by critics a few times since then, though. A few years after he wrote his *SI* column, Chad did a "slice and dice" review of my work on a boxing broadcast. This time, I decided to write him directly. I wrote that I could understand that he wasn't wild about my boxing play-by-play—he wasn't the only one. But then I proceeded to point out some of the things I had done well during the telecast. I know it's ridiculous. Why in the world should I have to go through a telecast and pick out moments to defend myself? The whole idea of a televised boxing match is entertainment, and yet here I was picking the broadcast apart as if it was some eighteenth-century English novel. So I wrote Chad this letter, and much to my surprise he wrote back. He said he had gone through his notes and that yes, indeed, he had jotted down the things I had done well. They were duly noted, scribbled in his reporter's notebook, just not written about in his column. What got me was how articulate and intelligent Chad's letter was. It was a thoughtful appraisal of the job I had done: good and bad. I thought, *Hey, this letter would make a great column!* Knock off the sarcasm and write something intelligent. So I wrote to Chad again—promising it was my last letter (I figured he didn't want me as a pen pal)—and I told him just that. He was a good writer and should try doing it straight. I never heard from him again.

Chad wasn't the only critic to find fault with my blow-by-blow announcing. Let's just say I got raked over the coals. I should have known things would get a bit rocky for me ringside the night of April 19, 1991. I was at the Convention Center in Atlantic City for the first fight card I ever called live. The featured fight pitted Evander Holyfield against George Foreman for the heavyweight championship. Nothing like starting out small and working your way up. The undercard to the Big Fight included a couple of lightweights named Lupe Suarez, who wore pink hot pants, and Jorge Paez. Paez was promoted as "The Clown Prince of Boxing." His hair was cut in a checkerboard pattern, and he would strut and dance around the ring. Macho stuff like that. In the third round, Suarez and Paez butted heads. Blood from a cut above Suarez's right eye sprayed everywhere, and the fight ended in a rare technical draw. The blood flew so far that some splattered on my tuxedo shirt. This was right at the height of the AIDS scare in boxing. The referees and handlers wore rubber gloves. I thought I should have been issued a rubber suit.

I called boxing for the next couple of years. The truth is that in television you're never as good as you think you are, and you're never as bad, either. Well, some writers apparently thought I was that bad. I wondered if some of the criticism was because the bouts I was announcing were part of a new, monthly pay-per-view experiment. This didn't sit well with a lot of boxing writers; they didn't think people should be charged on a monthly basis. Occasional big fights, fine. But every month? They worried that this might be the harbinger of things to come. Every fight on pay-per-view? Every sports event? So I think there was a natural resistance to our efforts to begin with.

In addition, the boxing writers saw me as an outsider. The writers who cover the various sports are like a special fraternity, protective of their turf and of their sport. I wasn't a member. Some of them absolutely killed me in print. One review in a major sports publication gave me credit for "one of the worst jobs of blow-by-blow announcing in the history of heavy-weight championship fights." Just one of the worst? I couldn't be *the* worst? *I never win anything!* Anyway, a couple of months later another boxing publication came out, and under a differ-ent writer's byline were the exact words of the earlier sterling review. Word for word. Apparently in the "boxing club," bad announcing is a crime. Plagiarism is not. I know, this all sounds like excuses. Maybe I *was* a terrible boxing announcer. But I'm not quite ready to concede the point—after all, the first rule of boxing is Defend Thyself.

I may not have been the best, but I didn't receive universally bad reviews. Many of the fights were staged in Trump casinos and I'd run into The Donald every now and again. He would say, "Hey, you're doing a great job." He is some smoothie, that Donald. No wonder people like him. Come to think of it, though, Trump has said the same thing to me since my boxing announcing career ended, so maybe he didn't even know I was calling bouts. Anyway, I'm sure he had nothing to do with it— at least I never had his signature "You're fired" directed at me—but after a few years I wasn't doing boxing anymore.

⬤   ⬤   ⬤

When *USA Today* first began publishing in the early 1980s, the paper had the first regular national column dealing with radio and television. Rudy Martzke wrote the column, and he still writes it today. I can't tell you how many broadcasters and executives have made decisions based on what Martzke writes. The following happens all the time. An announcer will broadcast a game and a network executive will say to a colleague, "So-and-so called a pretty good game." And then the other exec will counter, "Yeah, but I didn't see anything in Martzke."

An NBC Sports executive named Michael Weisman had this take on the critics. He said that for the most part TV sports critics are not journalists, at least not in the strictest sense of the word. They're columnists. Their job is to write interesting columns to get people to buy the paper. Fairness and objectivity, unlike in other parts of the newspaper, may not come into play. Where a newspaper writer covering an issue at city hall is supposed to report both sides of an issue, these guys aren't. Columns can be part fact, part opinion, and part entertainment. It doesn't mean I have to like it.

(The truth is, nobody likes to be criticized. On air or off. Try it. Next time you're on the bus, walk up to someone and say, "Sir, you're dressed a little slovenly today, and you might try not to drool on the guy sitting next to you." What are the odds that the guy will answer, "Why, thank you, kind sir; I appreciate your constructive criticism. Thanks to you I'm going to try to improve my appearance, not to mention my lot in life." More likely it'll be, "Go fuck yourself.")

The newspaper columnists aren't the only critics I've had to look out for over the years. Quite a few viewers and even some coaches and athletes—à la Bobby Orr and Bep Guidolin—have gotten into the act as well. Chuck Fairbanks, the coach of the New England Patriots from 1973 to 1978, was the first sports figure to call me and complain about something I said on the air. When I think about Coach Fairbanks, I think of my worst moment in broadcasting. The Pats had an exciting kick returner named Mack Herron. And then one day during the 1975 season, he was gone. Fairbanks fired him. Just like that. Turns out there was a party the night before and things apparently happened that shouldn't have. To this day, I don't know the whole story, but people who were at the party said there were drugs involved. Fairbanks read a one-line statement to the press. That night, he was coming to the WBZ studio to tape the station's Patriots pregame show. I got a call from the team's PR man. "If you mention Mack Herron, Fairbanks will get up and walk out of the studio," I was told. When Fairbanks arrived for the interview, I begged him to make a comment. "Just say what you said in the prepared statement." He refused. So I had to go on the air and interview him without mentioning the day's big news. I can honestly say that that broadcast made me feel like a whore.

It wasn't the Mack Herron incident, though, that inspired Fairbanks to give me a piece of his mind. During the 1978 season, a couple of Patriots players held out for more money. When the guys, two excellent linemen named John Hannah and Leon

Gray, finally signed, I said something on my sportscast about how "now the Patriots won't have any more excuses." Boom! I got a phone call at home from Chuck Fairbanks. When I called him back, he said, "I don't make excuses." "I didn't say you did," I responded. "I said the *Patriots* wouldn't have any excuses." To this Fairbanks replied: "I *am* the Patriots."

Jets football coach Walt Michaels once called me as well. He coached the team from 1977 to 1982. I had criticized the Jets for taking a penalty instead of yardage during some middle-of-the-season game in 1979. Michaels called to point out that the whistle was blown before the play, so he had no choice but to take the penalty. (Some penalties, such as false starts, are dead ball fouls. Everything stops.) I found it odd that he would take the time to call me. I was just a weekend sportscaster then. Did an NFL coach really care what I had to say?

Another time, I criticized the Mets during a sportscast. The Mets were trailing by a number of runs, and one of their base runners got thrown out stealing. I asked on the air why they would be running when they were down by four or five runs. Months later, as I walked into the clubhouse at Shea Stadium, Joe Torre, who then managed the Mets, motioned for me to come into his office. He asked me if I remembered what I had said a few months earlier. "Well, it was a full count, and we were trying to stay out of the double play," he explained. "We weren't stealing." Torre didn't say it belligerently. Rather, he came across like a teacher. I appreciated his approach. And I learned my lesson. I now always check the count before commenting on the appropriateness of an "attempted steal."

Some of the feedback I get from viewers is helpful. Some of it is informative. And some of it is just plain nasty. I try to answer every letter, card, or e-mail message, but it's not easy. In June 1975, I received a letter from a woman that began: "Mr. Berman, I think you are the biggest jerk." I was glad that she underlined "jerk." I might have missed the point otherwise. She was apparently upset that I wasn't in attendance when the Southbridge High Pioneerettes won the state softball title. (I'm not making that up.) The writer ended her letter by declaring, "I hope you drop dead or get runned [*sic*] out of Massachusetts for ever!!!" Again, I'm glad that she added the extra two exclamation points. Hers was one of the letters I didn't answer; had she provided a return address, though, I think I would have. At the very least, I felt sorry that she had been runned out of English class when they were being learned that grammar stuff!!!

Here are some excerpts from a few other happy and not-so-happy viewers. Keep those comments coming.

After a Celtics-Knicks game I received a mailgram. This was 1974. (Do they still have mailgrams today?) It began:

> *Your play-by-play commentary was an atrocity. Satch's commentary was discriminating to my six-week-old dog.*

(Tom "Satch" Sanders had filled in for Bob Cousy that night.) The sentiment actually went downhill from there. I answered this one, and the writer followed up with a telegram. (Do they still have those?) He wrote:

> *Dear Len,*
> *I would like to apologize for my words in my first mailgram. They were the words of a poor loser.*

I almost felt bad for the guy. A simple response had walked this guy off the ledge.

I have also received more than my share of letters from bigots. For some reason, I held on to this one, which was written in 1976:

> *Every stand you take favors blacks. Take yourself on a tour of Mattapan or even your native Queens and see how all your black buddies have __ruined__ former Jewish areas.*

This letter was unsigned and ended with a bunch of expletives.

In October 2004, during the Yankees–Red Sox playoff series and then during the World Series, I took great joy in tweaking my friends in New England, even if they had the last laugh. After Game Two of the World Series, with Boston up two games to none over St. Louis, I showed the infamous Bill Buckner play. After all, it was the eighteenth anniversary of the error. I also made the point that the Red Sox had won the first two games of that World Series before flaming out. I ended my commentary with, "This is a public service announcement, to keep Red Sox fans humble."

Well, it obviously didn't keep Red Sox fans happy. I received the following e-mail:

> *I guess you thought it was funny. It wasn't. It was cheap. It was mean. It was gratuitous. You should apologize to everyone who is rooting for Boston to savor some joy in October.*

Actually, I thought I *should* apologize to this guy. So here goes: I'm sorry you don't have a sense of humor. My condolences.

I don't want to give you the impression that all my "fan" mail is nasty or unsigned. Thank goodness for letters such as the following, which was sent to me while I was still working in Boston:

> *I was a faithful viewer of yours for three years before moving to Florida. I want to tell you how much I miss hearing your commentary. All of the sports reporters here (in Tallahassee) report the sports news . . . no zest, enthusiasm or creativity. . . . I regret that I won't be hearing editorials on the commercialism of sport, pro athletes' inflated egos, and the like. But I do appreciate what you are trying to do for sports, people, and Boston.*

I also appreciate when viewers send me their own commentaries, such as this one from an elderly woman:

> *Somebody should have a long talk with the World Series players about the constant spitting while the camera is on them. Also some of them chewing gum during the Star Spangled Banner. . . . A person with any class at all wouldn't spit in front of just one other person, but these characters spit for thousands of people to see. The only thing that turns me off worse is all those mustaches. They look like what they are—a breeding place for germs.*

And I like it when viewers take the time to fill me in on a bit of history as well. I once received a newspaper article from a man who was obviously concerned about free agency in baseball.

> *Oscar Walker says he is sorry that he signed so early with the Buffalos, as he has had several flattering of-*

fers since. This is but one of the many instances of folly exhibited by professional players in not remaining with clubs in which they are sure of their pay and are well treated because some other club offers them one or two hundred dollars more salary for a season. . . . The rolling professional, like the stone, gathers no moss.

This article was written in 1879 and published in a newspaper called the *Buffalo Commercial Advertiser.*

Sometimes viewers send me grooming hints. My favorite letter of this type came from a man in the Bronx. He wrote:

You seem to be wearing a very unflattering, cheap-looking hairpiece. Back in 1952 and 1956 both presidential candidates Eisenhower and Stevenson were bald. Nobody seemed to mind. So my advice is to discard that rug and let your pate shine through. You'll be in wonderful company: Julius Caesar, Tom Landry and Bing Crosby just to name a few.

I thought this guy was wasting his time writing to me. My hair is real, but that's not the point. This guy should pen *The History of Baldness.*

As much as I enjoyed the shiny pate letter, though, it isn't my all-time favorite personal attack. That letter arrived soon after I landed my job at WBZ in Boston. A writer from Dorchester, Massachusetts, wrote to the station's general manager.

I understand you held a contest for this position and Mr. Berman was the winner. Heaven help the loser. . . . I have nothing against this man personally, as a matter of fact if I wanted a boy of my own I would like to have him just like Mr. Berman until the boy reached the age of 10 years and then I would take him out and drown him.

Sweet, I thought. This guy even signed his letter. I knew then that by choosing to be on television I was going to reach all sorts of people—whether I wanted to or not.

27

COMMISH FOR A DAY

THANKSGIVING DAY, 1999, PONTIAC, MICHIGAN. The game between the Detroit Lions and the Pittsburgh Steelers goes overtime. Referee Phil Luckett marches to the center of the field for the coin toss to decide who gets the ball first. Steelers captain Jerome Bettis calls tails. The coin lands on tails. But Pittsburgh loses the toss. Luckett mistakenly thought Bettis yelled heads. So Detroit "wins the toss" in error. They take the kickoff and proceed to win the game with a 42-yard field goal. The Steelers never touched the ball in overtime even though they really won the toss in the first place.

It was one thing for my elementary school to invite me back as a Principal for a Day, but it's not like they really let me do anything. I mean, how much fun would it have been if I got to call for recess—at eight A.M? No one has invited me to be Commissioner of Sports for a Day—not yet anyway—but that's not stopping me from putting forth my candidacy. If I could rule the sports world for twenty-four hours, here is what I'd do.

8:00 A.M.: Over breakfast, I'd straighten out the seasons. The late, great Betty Furness—actress cum spokesmodel cum consumer affairs director cum reporter—once said to me, "It seems like there are two seasons nowadays: baseball and Christmas." Winter sports should be played in winter. Summer games in summer. Have you ever been to an NBA Finals game in Phoenix in June? It's a thousand degrees in the shade. This is a winter sport? A half century ago, the Syracuse Nationals won the NBA title in mid-April, not late June. The 1955 Brooklyn

Dodgers? Game Seven was October 4! Today, the World Series stretches into late October or even early November.

9:00 A.M.: I'd begin the workday by sorting out the postseasons. Playoffs would be for winners. Pure and simple: if you don't have a winning record, go home. The "worst" playoff team in NBA history was the 1967–68 Chicago Bulls. They qualified for the playoffs with a regular-season record of 29–53. The Bulls actually won one game against the Lakers, but they were out in five. Of course my rule might affect the bottom lines of the NBA and NHL, but here's the thing. As commish, I'm going to work for everyone involved—the players, owners, and fans—not just the team owners paying my salary. The leagues may think they need to wring every dollar out of the sports consumer, but I don't.

10:00 A.M.: While I'm on the subject of dollars and sense, I'd next fix the economics of the games. My solution? Revenue sharing. Give Kansas City teams the same chance to win the pennant that New York teams have. Their fans deserve it. Teams must take the handouts and spend it on players. The owners can't just pocket the money. But if this means the mayor of KC is going to bet New York's mayor over the outcome of the series, I'd take all the money back. That's right. I would outlaw the dopey bets of politicians. No more slabs of baby back ribs against pizza pie bets. The first politician who makes one of these wagers after I'm named commish gets impeached.

11:00 A.M.: Put-upon fans would get another break as well. I would make a few good seats available in every section of every stadium for every game at reasonable family prices. A lottery would determine who gets the tickets. After the games, every player would have to take a few minutes to sign autographs. And no little kid would get run over.

12:00 P.M.: During the games, I'd ban organ bleating while the ball is in play, and electronic sound effects and scoreboards urging fans to get louder LOUDER LOUDER! I'd implode any scoreboard that reads, I CAN'T HEAR YOU!!!!! Fans know when to cheer.

1:00 P.M.: Over lunch, I would institute a twenty-second pitch clock in baseball. A pitcher takes the ball, touches the resin bag, blows on his hand, stares in for the sign, checks the runner at first, then steps off the rubber. Throw the ball already! Twenty seconds, that would be the rule. And fans could do the count-down: 5-4-3-2-1-PITCH! For his part, the batter can't step out of the batter's box unless he has an appendicitis attack.

2:00 P.M.: A corollary to the appendicitis rule. Faking would be outlawed in sports. In soccer, players lie on the ground as if they're dead. Then when the other team is penalized, the player magically pops up: *It's a miracle, Lord, I'm cured!* In basketball? No moaning, groaning, or flopping. These guys are nine feet tall and weigh six hundred pounds. If a feather touches them going up for a rebound, though, they let out a bloodcurdling screech and go flying into the fifth row in an attempt to draw a foul.

3:00 P.M.: Drug testing in sports? Easy. I'd institute year-round random testing in all sports. Mine would be a zero-tolerance regime. You cheat? You're a goner.

4:00 P.M.: Boxing is still run like the Wild West. I'd start cleaning up this mess by getting rid of all the confusing weight classes—there'd be no more bantam superflys weltering around. The alphabets—WBC, WBA, IBF—would be history as well. I would bring all of boxing under one roof. One champ. Three divisions. Light, middle, and heavy. With liberty and justice for all! I also like the idea of a Super Sunday of Boxing during which one lightweight champ, one middleweight champ, and one heavyweight champ would be crowned. One day, once a year. If I've got a little extra time this hour, I'd also get rid of the staged weigh-in. What's the point of this ritual? Sometimes, the boxers are weighed two or three days before their fight. So a guy makes weight, then eats his face off for the next two days. Promoters and trainers have also been known to put their feet on the scale at the same time as their fighters if the guy needs to go up a weight class, or to hold the boxer up under his arms to make him lighter if he is in danger of being judged too heavy for a weight class.

5:00 P.M.: Hockey? Don't even get me started. I'm going to need a couple of hours here. First, the sport is simply too clogged up. I'd begin by eliminating eight teams. And then I'd enlarge the rinks and the size of the goals. Something has to be done to improve this small-rink, big-players, low-scoring game. And get rid of all of that goalie equipment. What do they have strapped to their legs, mattresses? I often think about Blackhawks goaltender Tony Esposito. His wife once sewed some mesh material between the legs of Tony's uniform pants so that when he spread his legs he would have a better chance to stop the puck. One game, Tony's brother Phil won a face-off and got the puck to Bobby Orr at the point. Orr took the slap shot and it rifled right between Tony's legs. It should have been through for a goal. Instead, the puck came flying out and almost hit Phil in the head. Phil skated back to the bench thinking his brother was wearing a rubber jock! Phil swears that he didn't squeal on his brother, but after ten or twelve games the NHL got wise to what was going on and put a stop to it. It's time for the league to wise up again. The athletes are gifted skaters. Give them room to showcase their talents and open up the game. And get rid of the tie game! If a hockey game is tied at the end of an overtime period, there should be a shoot-out, as there is in soccer. Give five guys on each team a shot on alternate breakaways. It would be exciting, and far more satisfying.

6:00 P.M.: I know that for a lot of people, the fights are what makes hockey great. But I hate fighting in hockey. That should come as no surprise to anyone who has watched my sportscasts over the years. The fans say, "Great game. Rangers won and there were *two* fights!" Then I go on the air and pompously decry violence in sports. (But then, of course, I show the replay, play it again in super slow motion, tsk-tsk the fighters, and show the fight one last time.) Years ago, I showed footage of a big hockey fight during which the cameras zoomed in on the faces in the crowd. The fans had huge smiles. Two meatheads were beating the tar out of each other—in the name of sport—and the fans reveled in it.

Only in hockey could a guy who spent half the season in the penalty box be a sought-after free agent. His stats read seventy-five games, one goal, four thousand penalty minutes. But the teams think, *Gotta get a goon!* How proud their moms must be. "My son the goon was just signed by Montreal!" (Apparently it's not just the men's game, though. A friend saw a woman wearing a hockey T-shirt the other day. It read DADDY'S LITTLE GOON.) But that's the way it goes. Philadelphia has a goon, so Boston needs one to even out the balance of power. Of course it's bound to go too far. That's always the case. In February 2004, Vancouver's Todd Bertuzzi—not a goon, but a skilled hockey player—went after center Steve Moore of Colorado. This was retaliation for something that had happened weeks before in a game between the Canucks and the Avalanche. Bertuzzi didn't just skate by and whack Moore. He stalked him! He grabbed onto his jersey and then sucker punched and fell on top of him. Moore crumbled to the ice, fracturing three vertebrae and stretching the nerves in his neck. It is not clear whether he will ever play again.

This time I wasn't alone in decrying the violence. Everyone in the media went nuts, as well as a good portion of the public. Police authorities in Vancouver even investigated the incident. But here's the thing: in hockey if you assault somebody, you get a suspension. Do the same thing on the street, and you get five to ten. Normally, I don't think the police should poke their noses into the game. Hockey is, after all, a contact sport. But I felt differently about the Bertuzzi incident. Bertuzzi didn't have a reflexive reaction to something that had happened. What he did to Moore was clearly premeditated. There's no place for that in sport. If hockey can't police itself, maybe the police should. What was Bertuzzi's punishment? He was suspended. In 2004, he missed the remaining thirteen games of the season plus the playoffs. His financial loss totaled approximately $500,000—a lot of money, but not so much when you take into account Bertuzzi's four-year deal was worth a reported $28 million. And I thought he caught a big break when a plea bargain saved him from serving any jail time. The league also fined the Canucks $250,000, saying that the team should take some responsibility for what happened. Sounds noble. But then, based on the same theory, shouldn't the NHL have fined itself?

Hockey is the only team sport where you can get away with fighting. The NHL even has its ridiculous third-man-in rule. The idea is that boys will be boys, but we've got to draw the line somewhere. So the first person to join a fight already in progress—that is, the third man in—is automatically ejected. That's where they draw the line in hockey. So to the people who run hockey, and to many of the players, fighting is just part of the game. I think hockey would be just as popular without the fights, though. Look at playoff hockey or Olympic hockey. Skating, passing, scoring. There are rarely fights, and the game is great to watch. Phil Esposito has an interesting take on this. He said none of this happened in the NHL before players started wearing helmets and face guards. The extra layers of protection emboldened them. In the old days, Espo said players would never lift their sticks to hit an opponent. If they accidentally touched somebody high with their sticks, they would apologize. So is that the answer? Should we let the inmates run the asylum?

This will happen again. Before Bertuzzi, it was Boston's Marty McSorley whacking his stick across the head of Vancouver's Donald Brashear. McSorley, too, faced a criminal trial and was suspended by the NHL. (He was convicted of assault with a weapon but received a conditional discharge. He served no jail time. His one-year suspension effectively ended his seventeen-year career.) That wasn't the end of it, and unless things change, we'll be having this conversation again a few years from now.

7:00 P.M.: Fixing football's overtime would be next on my list. If the game goes to OT, both teams should have to touch the ball. It's ridiculous that a team can win a coin toss and then march downfield to kick a winning field goal. One day, the Super Bowl will be decided by a coin toss.

8:00 P.M.: It's dinnertime, but I've only got one day, so I'm not taking a break. Nor should the NFL. I'd do away with the extra off week before the Super Bowl. After their teams win the AFC and NFC championships, fans are all revved up. So what does the NFL do? It gives everyone a two-week cooling-off period. I would penalize the league for delay of game!

9:00 P.M.: The instant replay in the NFL is a whole other problem. The idea is to correct *obvious* mistakes, so let's leave it at that. If it takes the referees longer than thirty seconds to figure out the call, then it's not obvious. The endless reviews bring the game to a standstill. Players—and the fans—are left to freeze for minutes on end, while some weeny ref stares at a television monitor. Play on!

10:00 P.M.: I would allow all kinds of end-zone celebrations, so long as the dances, raps, and autograph signings stop short of taunting an opponent. If players want to make complete fools of themselves, they should be permitted. I would, however, ban those NBA introduction production numbers. The in-the-dark laser show worked for Michael Jordan and the Bulls, but enough already.

11:00 P.M.: In golf and tennis, I'd say let 'em cheer. A baseball batter faces flashbulbs and fifty thousand screaming fans, yelling all sorts of things about his mother. But golfers and tennis players? If there's one tiny camera click, Tiger or McEnroe (who once complained about the noise of a courtside refrigerator) throws a hissy fit. Bring on the noise. You want quiet? Go to church.

12:00 P.M.: While I'm visiting the country clubs, I'd outlaw green, red, pastel, and multicolored golf pants—and any outfit designed by Serena Williams. I'd round out the hour by taking care of the uniforms in basketball. Basketball players will be forced to make a choice. Either they return to the short-shorts of the 1980s—women love them—or they start wearing dresses. The current crop of "shorts" nearly reaches their sneaks.

1:00 A.M.: In the last three minutes of basketball games, all time-outs will be only twenty seconds. When the final minute or two of an NBA or NCAA game lasts half an hour, it is ridiculous.

2:00 A.M.: At this time, I'd throw out collegiate sports polls—except in football. What's the point in basketball? There's a playoff at the end of the season, so who cares if East Cupcake is ranked twenty-third on February 12. In football, I can understand it. There isn't a playoff, and I'm not in favor of one. I love it at the end of the season when two or more teams claim, "We're number one!" Why have a playoff and spoil all the fun? And while I'm sorting out this mess, I'd insist that NCAA tournament basketball games be played on actual college campuses. There's nothing like the ivy-covered, higher-education feeling of the New Jersey Turnpike running through the Meadowlands of East Rutherford.

3:00 A.M.: I'd wait until all the corporate CEOs are tucked away for this one. Corporate naming of stadiums, bowl games, pregame and postgame shows, and the rest has got to go. Need a reason? How about "Enron Field" in Houston? I might tolerate it more if there was some creativity involved, something like the Tidy Bowl in Flushing. Same goes for ballpark advertising, although I kind of like the Gap ads that read simply "Gap" on the outfield walls in baseball stadiums. They are, of course, situated in the gap. But that's about it. Thankfully a revolt by purists forced Major League Baseball to rethink its decision to sell *Spider-Man* ads on the bases in 2004. But what's next? The Mounds Bar pitcher's mound? Home plate, brought to you by Home Depot? MapQuest ads lining the base paths? Or will it be racehorses decked out like NASCAR cars? Oh, and beer commercials! They may be the lifeblood of the sports broadcast, but here's my new rule: no more dopey commercials featuring men salivating over scantily clad women. It may be impossible, but I'll challenge Madison Avenue to come up with a way to sell beer that has no sexual innuendo, no male idiocy, and no flatulent animals.

4:00 A.M.: I'd better take care of this before the hunters awake and head out. Either hunting is not a sport, or we arm the animals and make it a fair fight.

5:00 A.M.: At this hour, I'd turn my attention to the rule books. The dopiest rule in baseball? A relief pitcher comes in with a four-run lead in the top of the ninth. He gives up a grand slam homer. Now the game is tied. His team comes to bat in the bottom of the ninth and the leadoff batter hits a homer to win the game. The relief pitcher did nothing but *screw up*. So what happens? He gets the win! Here's another. A pitcher is working on a perfect game and there's a foul pop-up that his third baseman drops. It's ruled an error. The pitcher then proceeds to strike out that batter and then nobody reaches base. Twenty-seven batters up, twenty-seven down. A perfect game, right? Wrong. The error on the meaningless foul ball has spoiled the bid. No hits, no runs, no base runners, but no perfecto! Dumb, dumber, dumberer.

5:30 A.M.: Take cover, stat freaks. At the end of the 2004 NBA regular season, Bob Sura of the Atlanta Hawks became the first player in seven years to record three straight triple-doubles. Or so he thought. He had at least ten points, assists, and rebounds in each of three games. Going into the final seconds of the third game against the Nets, though, he only had nine rebounds. With moments to go, he had an uncontested layup. He missed the shot on purpose and got the rebound as time ran out. His tenth rebound was bogus, and the following day the NBA disallowed it. The league ruled that since Sura wasn't really trying to score, it wasn't a field goal attempt and so there was no rebound. That's true. But now are we going to base stats on intent? A quarterback who purposely throws a ball out of bounds to stop the clock or so that he won't be tackled is still charged with an incomplete pass. How about a foul shooter who misses on purpose at the end of the game so his team can get the rebound? Is that not a foul shot? In Sura's case, he shot the ball, he got the rebound. Sure it was bogus, but he did it. Saying he didn't is equally bogus. That's why while I'm commish I'll also throw out all of the stat books.

Actually, there was one manipulated stat I liked. In 1998, University of Connecticut basketball player Nykesha Sales ruptured her Achilles tendon two points shy of setting the school scoring record. So the U-Conn and Villanova coaches concocted a little deal. Sales went onto the court, scored an uncontested layup, got the record, and left the game. I thought it was pretty cool. But what a firestorm of controversy. "Not fair," people cried. "An insult to the integrity of the game!" "What about the girl whose record she broke?" It went on for days. I thought it was a nice thing. That's the problem with stats. You can read them any way you want. Throw 'em all out! It would reduce the clutter on the screen and the verbiage coming out of the mouths of sportscasters (not to mention fans who don't know the name of their own senator, but know who leads the league in intentional walks).

6:00 A.M.: I'd have plenty of new rules for the television guys, and with my term running short I'd have to work quickly. When college basketball games end, the director would not be allowed to show the two coaches walking up the court slowly to shake hands. At the end of a dramatic game, the players and fans jump around like crazy, but on screen we see an excruciatingly boring shot of the coaches. I'd rather see the excitement and emotion of the players out on the court. That's why I'm watching this game! Same goes for tennis. After an amazing match, I want to see the exhausted winner drop to his knees, not a cutaway to the guy's mom hugging his girlfriend.

6:15 A.M.: Does every TV replay have to come whooshing onto the screen with a sound effect? Not in my production.

6:30 A.M.: Those scoreboards and game clocks on the screen with commercial logos the size of Buicks. Gotta go as well. You can hardly make out the action. I like to see the score and time, but let's keep it discreet. On the radio, though, I'd create a type of score and time box. Every three minutes, I'd have the audio dip and a voice would state the time, score, and teams playing the game. That's for those times when my radio announcer friends are telling those hilarious stories about what happened to their luggage on the last road trip and forget to mention what's going on during the game they're supposed to be describing.

6:45 A.M.: I've already mentioned that I'd like there to be a separate audio channel that just has crowd noise, with no announcers. Well, as commish, I'd also set up a third audio channel. This one would have announcers, but it would be a cliché-free zone. On this channel, baseball players would never "go yard." They'd hit home runs. No jargon, just simple English that even nonfans can understand.

7:00 A.M.: I'd save my final hour for the postgame shows. There would be no more tossing pies in the face of the star of the game while he's being interviewed. And, finally, athletes will not be allowed to thank God. Don't get me wrong. I have nothing against God, I just feel that God has better things to do than to make sure that Harry Halfback runs for the winning touchdown. For that matter, with all the problems of the world, I also don't think God's sitting up there plotting his annual ten plagues against the L.A. Clippers.

I know this is all the very definition of sports fantasy, but it's my fantasy, and I'm sticking to it. And along the way, I hope nobody gets hurt.

ACKNOWLEDGMENTS

To Burton Rocks who first had the confounding notion that I should write a book. To Tony Seidl who offered his encouragement and sage advice. To my aptly named agent, Lisa Queen, who took the ball, ran with it, and hopefully scored. To my editor, Henry Ferris, who actually thought this was a good idea. (I hope he's right.) To Stephen Levey who somehow whipped this material into some semblance of order. To Jay Horwitz of the Mets, for his help with the cover photo. To all of the WNBC producers over the years from Carmine Cincotta to Lauren Spencer who diligently scoured the earth in search of "Spanning the World" video. And last but not least to the entire Berman family. None of the Berman clan has to read this book. For better or worse, they've all lived it! (And that way I get to save a bundle by not having to buy all of them individual copies.)

INDEX

INDEX

INDEX

INDEX

INDEX

INDEX

INDEX

INDEX

INDEX

INDEX